Drupal

Creating Blogs, Forums, Portals, and Community Websites

How to set up, configure, and customize this powerful PHP/MySQL-based Open Source CMS

David Mercer

PUBLISHING

BIRMINGHAM - MUMBAI

Drupal

Creating Blogs, Forums, Portals, and Community Websites

First published: May 2006

Production Reference: 1040506

Published by Packt Publishing Ltd.
32 Lincoln Road
Olton
Birmingham, B27 6PA, UK.

ISBN 1-904811-80-9

www.packtpub.com

Cover Design by www.visionwt.com

Credits

Author
David Mercer

Reviewers
Jason Flatt
Kobus Myburgh

Technical Editors
Niranjan Jahagirdar
Maria Menezes

Editorial Manager
Dipali Chittar

Development Editor
Louay Fatoohi

Indexer
Mithil Kulkarni

Proofreader
Chris Smith

Production Coordinator
Manjiri Nadkarni

Cover Designer
Helen Wood

About the Author

David Mercer was born in August 1976 in Harare, Zimbabwe. Having always had a strong interest in science, David came into regular contact with computers at university where he minored in computer science.

A programmer and professional writer who has been writing both code and books for about seven years, he has worked on a number of well known titles, in various capacities, on a wide variety of topics. This has afforded him a singularly unique oversight into the world of programming and technology as it relates to furthering the goals of business.

David finds that the challenges arising from the dichotomous relationship between the science (and art) of software programming and the art (and science) of writing is what keeps his interest in producing books piqued. He intends to continue to write professionally in the future.

David balances his time between programming, reviewing, writing, and furthering his studies in Applied Mathematics. When he isn't working (which isn't that often) he enjoys playing guitar and getting involved in outdoor activities ranging from touch rugby and golf to water skiing and snowboarding.

Visit www.contechst.com for an overview of articles, books, and other projects by David.

A big thanks to the team at Packt for giving me the opportunity to work on this book. Thanks to the excellent contributions made by the reviewers as well as my family and friends who have supported and encouraged me over the last six months or so.
"Ad astra per aspera."

About the Reviewers

Jason Flatt is a computer solutions provider, specializing in Linux systems and Drupal websites, living in his hometown of Las Vegas, NV with his wife and five sons. Jason can be contacted at drupal@oadaeh.net.

Kobus Myburgh is an IT consultant, working at a large university in South Africa, focusing on IT innovations particularly useful to the students of the university, as well as keeping the student IT facilities in mint condition, including software, hardware, as well as network and internet connectivity.

Kobus obtained his Honors B. Sc. degree in IT at the same university and is also a part-time lecturer, currently teaching third-year students about Expert Systems, with a strong focus on this sub-section of Artificial Intelligence.

He also has extensive knowledge and experience in web design and development, particularly in PHP, HTML, and CSS, and has been involved with the Drupal project since its inception in 2001.

Table of Contents

Preface

The Internet is arguably one of the most profound achievements in human history. It has become so pervasive in our lives that we hardly even notice it—except when it happens to be unavailable! It's one of those things that make you sit back and wonder how people got along without it in the *old days*. Without the ability to surf the Internet to order groceries, do our banking, book flights and make travel arrangements, meet friends, meet partners, download music and videos, study, run businesses, trade shares, run campaigns, express views, share ideas, learn about other people... where would we be?

Fundamentally, in a world of so many people, where the sheer vastness of our societies is a hindrance to communication, the Internet has stepped up to the plate and brought everyone that little bit closer together. Utilizing a stunning array of technologies, spread out over the entire globe, the Internet has simply dropped the barriers of time and geographical distance to turn the entire world into a local community center.

Lately, the all-encompassing focus of commerce on the Internet has begun to shift slightly. Millions upon millions of people are waking up to the possibility of sharing their lives and experiences with others through the medium of weblogs (blogs for short). Others simply want an online presence to show off their work, art, or music. Still others have important causes and need the Internet to disseminate information or provide a meeting point for like-minded people. Whatever the demands, the Internet has to find a way to efficiently meet these needs or face being superseded by something else in the future.

What the Internet needs is something that makes it easy for people to do whatever it is they want without having to pour intellectual resources into understanding the technologies on which the Internet is based. What the Internet has got is precisely this—Drupal!

Drupal is what you need to use to build anything from a static homepage, to a fully-fledged, customizable, and interactive website in several languages, with tens of thousands of users all over the world. Assuming you fall somewhere between these two extremes, this book is what you need to guide you on your way.

This book will help cut down your learning time by providing precisely the information you need when you need it. It will help to reduce the trial and error associated with learning any new technology and provide you with a methodical and efficient learning process so that you become a knowledgeable and competent website creator and administrator.

What This Book Covers

Chapter 1 introduces you to the world of Drupal and looks at where Drupal comes from, where it's going, and what it can offer you. Because it is important to understand the nature of the tasks that lie ahead, it also discusses how to plan and build your website, taking a sneak preview of the book's demo website in the process. Finally, we scrutinize the Drupal community and learn how to make the most of Drupal as an organized, living entity and not just a piece of software.

Chapter 2 deals with how to get everything you need up and running on a development machine and also briefly looks at how all the requisite technologies gel together to produce your working Drupal site. Once everything is up and running, and after looking over some of the more common installation problems, the chapter presents a short tour of Drupal in order to give you an idea of what to expect.

Chapter 3 looks at the most general settings that all Drupal administrators need to contend with. Everything from determining your site's name to dealing with the cache or file system settings gets treated here before we look at more focused and complex issues in the chapters to come.

Chapter 4 sees us adding functionality to the newly created site. The focus of this chapter is really on modules and how they can be added and enabled, and also how to obtain modules that are not part of the standard distribution. This chapter ends off with a discussion on how to control blocks.

Chapter 5 concerns itself with the topic of access control. Drupal has a sophisticated role-based access control system, which is fundamentally important for controlling how users access your site. This chapter will give you the information you need to implement whatever access controls you require.

Chapter 6 gets to the heart of the matter by beginning the book's coverage on content. Working with content, what content types are available, administering content, and even a discourse on some of the more common content-related modules serve as a basis for moving to more advanced content-related matters that follow in the next chapter.

Chapter 7 gives you the edge when it comes to creating engaging and dynamic content. While this chapter doesn't require you to be an expert in HTML, PHP, and CSS, it does introduce you to the basics and shows how, with a little knowledge, extremely powerful and professional content can be created. That's only half the story, because later on it looks at categorization and how this particular feature of Drupal sets it apart from everything else out there.

Chapter 8 gives you a run down of how attractive interfaces are created in Drupal through the use of themes. As well as discussing briefly some of the considerations that must be taken into account when planning your website, it ends off by looking at how to make important modifications to your chosen theme.

Chapter 9 really adds the icing on the cake by looking at a host of more advanced topics. From creating flexible content types and generating revenue from ads, all the way through to building dynamic content using AJAX, you will find something to enhance your website and add that something special.

Chapter 10 takes a pragmatic look at the types of tasks you will need to be proficient in so as to successfully run and maintain a Drupal site. Whether it's setting up cron jobs or making backups of your database, everything you need to do throughout the course of running your newly created website will be covered here.

Appendix A deals with the all-important topic of deployment. Because all major work should be done on a copy of your website on a development machine, this appendix presents a sound process for taking the finished product and making it available for public consumption on your host site.

Conventions

In this book, you will find a number of styles of text that distinguish between different kinds of information. Here are some examples of these styles, and an explanation of their meaning.

There are three styles for code. Code words in text are shown as follows: "We can include other contexts through the use of the `include` directive."

A block of code will be set as follows:

```php
<?php
if (module_exist("adsense"))
{
  print adsense_display("468x60", 2);
}
?>
```

When we wish to draw your attention to a particular part of a code block, the relevant lines or items will be made bold:

```php
<?php
if (module_exist("adsense"))
{
  print adsense_display("468x60", 2);
}
?>
```

Any command-line input and output is written as follows:

```
$ mysql -uroot -p drupal < C:\apache2triad\htdocs\drupal\modules\
  taxonomy_block\taxonomy_block.mysql
```

New terms and **important words** are introduced in a bold-type font. Words that you see on the screen, in menus or dialog boxes for example, appear in our text like this: "clicking the Next button moves you to the next screen".

> Warnings or important notes appear in a box like this.

Tips and tricks appear like this.

Reader Feedback

Feedback from our readers is always welcome. Let us know what you think about this book, what you liked or may have disliked. Reader feedback is important for us to develop titles that you really get the most out of.

To send us general feedback, simply drop an email to feedback@packtpub.com, making sure to mention the book title in the subject of your message.

If there is a book that you need and would like to see us publish, please send us a note in the SUGGEST A TITLE form on www.packtpub.com or email suggest@packtpub.com.

If there is a topic that you have expertise in and you are interested in either writing or contributing to a book, see our author guide on www.packtpub.com/authors.

Customer Support

Now that you are the proud owner of a Packt book, we have a number of things to help you to get the most from your purchase.

Downloading the Code for the Book

Visit http://www.packtpub.com/support, and select this book from the list of titles to download any example code or extra resources for this book. The files available for download will then be displayed.

> The downloadable files contain instructions on how to use them.

Errata

Although we have taken every care to ensure the accuracy of our contents, mistakes do happen. If you find a mistake in one of our books—maybe a mistake in text or code—we would be grateful if you would report this to us. By doing this you can save other readers from frustration, and help to improve subsequent versions of this book. If you find any errata, report them by visiting http://www.packtpub.com/support, selecting your book, clicking on the Submit Errata link, and entering the details of your errata. Once your errata have been verified, your submission will be accepted and the errata added to the list of existing errata. The existing errata can be viewed by selecting your title from http://www.packtpub.com/support.

Questions

You can contact us at questions@packtpub.com if you are having a problem with some aspect of the book, and we will do our best to address it.

1
Introduction to Drupal

Up until quite recently, the most important thing a newcomer to the Web could do in order to prepare for building a website was to buy a book on how to learn programming in any one of the major web-centric languages like PHP or Perl. Then, the not inconsiderable task of learning the niceties of the chosen language to a respectable degree would consume a fair chunk of time and patience. Once our hapless newcomer had sufficient mastery of the fundamentals, applying that knowledge to program efficiently and reliably, with the tenacity to stick with a job until the site was developed could arguably be described as a Herculean accomplishment.

This state of affairs is, and quite rightly should be, entirely unacceptable to someone like yourself! It's like forcing lawyers to learn the intricacies of architecture, construction, and masonry simply because they require a courtroom in which to work. It should be quite apparent that separating the technical task of *developing the software* for a website from the *function* of that website is a very sensible thing to do, the main reason being that it allows people to focus on what they are good at without them having to devote time and energy to becoming good software developers too.

It's not surprising then, that in recent years the open-source community has been hard at work pulling the programming world out of the software dark ages by providing us with flexible frameworks for building web-based enterprises. These frameworks untie website creators from the intellectual burden of learning software development ideas and concepts, allowing them instead to focus more on goal-/business-oriented configuration and customization tasks.

Drupal is one such result of the software-development evolution and this book seeks to provide you with the fundamental information needed in order to use it effectively to meet your requirements. Because this book focuses more on beginner-level aspects of administering Drupal, you will be pleased to know that there will be little to no coding involved—you're not required to learn how to develop your own Drupal modules, for example. That's not to say your introduction will be elementary; on the contrary, this book will teach you in such a way that you are able to apply your knowledge to tackle problems beyond the scope of this material with confidence.

Before we begin actually building anything that resembles a website, I'm sure you have plenty of questions about the how, what, where, and why of Drupal. Consequently, this chapter will not only provide a backdrop for the rest of the book, but will also serve as an introduction to the technology as a whole, incorporating a discussion on the following:

- Drupal—an overview
- How Drupal came to be
- What Drupal has to offer
- Uses of Drupal
- Building a Drupal site
- The Drupal community
- The Drupal license

One of the bullets above mentions *Building a Drupal Site*—this section incorporates a look at the demo website, which serves as a basis for all our practical examples. This is needed here because, throughout the book, we will systematically build on each chapter's new information to create a fully functional website. Doing things this way will help relate the lessons you learn to the outcome you can expect on the site. This in turn helps foster sound administration, configuration, and customization methodologies that will help you to develop your own Drupal skills.

Let's begin…

Drupal—An Overview

The most concise description for Drupal is that it is an **Open-Source Content Management System**. If you are new to both computing and Drupal, then this probably doesn't clear things up very much. Let's analyze this phrase quickly to gain a better understanding. First of all, the term *open-source* is used to describe *software whose source code is made available, most often subject to certain conditions, for use or modification by users or other developers as they deem fit*. The specific conditions under which Drupal is made available will be scrutinized more closely in the section *The Drupal License* later in this chapter.

Above and beyond that, what open source means for you as someone who intends to make use of Drupal, is that you don't have to pay for this unquestionably valuable software. You also join a large community (also to be discussed later in this chapter) of Drupal users, developers, and administrators who subscribe to the open-source philosophy—in other words, someone out there will probably be willing to spend time helping you out should you get stuck.

If you think about it, that's a pretty good deal for those who are still not convinced about open-source technologies as a whole—not only do we not have develop the entire site ourselves, but we also get to take advantage of the collective wisdom of thousands of other people. *Is there anything else we can say about open source?* Sure for one thing, you can be pretty certain that with an active community like the one associated with Drupal, development advances rapidly and flexibly because any problems can be spotted early and dealt with effectively. This means that you can expect a high level of stability, security, and performance from your website.

So far so good, but what is the Content Management System (CMS) part all about? It is necessary for us to take a closer look at what this means in order to gain a sufficient understanding of what we are getting into. We can define a content management system to be *software that facilitates the creation, organization, manipulation, and removal of information in the form of images, documents, scripts, plain text (or anything else for that matter).* If you have a need to organize and display fairly large amounts of information, especially when it is likely that content will be created or delivered from a variety of different sources, then a content management system is undoubtedly what you need.

That's basically all you have to know. Drupal provides a free platform, along with its attendant community, for satisfying a wide variety of content-management requirements. Precisely, what type of things one can achieve is the subject of the section entitled *What Drupal Has to Offer* later in this chapter. For now though, let's turn back the hands of time and take a look at how we ended up with Drupal as we know it today.

How Drupal Came to Be

As with so many modern success stories, this one started in a dorm room with a couple of students needing to achieve a specific goal. In this case, Dries Buytaert and Hans Snijder of the University of Antwerp wished to share an ADSL modem connection to the Internet. They managed this via the use of a wireless bridge, but soon after, Dries decided to work on a news site, which would, in addition to the simple connection the students already shared, allow them to share news and other information.

Over time the site grew and changed as Dries expanded the application and experimented with new things. However, it was only some time later in 2001, when it was decided to release the code to the public in the hope that this would encourage development from other people, that Drupal became open-source software. It's clear that releasing the source to the public was the right choice, because today Drupal has a well organized, thriving community of people ranging from approved contributors, forums, a security team, and a global presence, to plenty of users who make invaluable contributions on a regular basis through bug reports and suggestions.

In five short years, Dries and others have taken a small inter-dorm-room application and turned it into a technology that is contributing to the way in which the global society communicates through the Web. This is embodied in their brief mission statement, which reads:

> *By building on relevant standards and open-source technologies, Drupal supports and enhances the potential of the Internet as a medium where diverse and geographically separated individuals and groups can collectively produce, discuss, and share information and ideas. With a central interest in and focus on communities and collaboration, Drupal's flexibility allows the collaborative production of online information systems and communities.*

Ultimately, where Drupal is going and how it came to be are also driven by the philosophies that guide those responsible for developing this technology. As you will see throughout the course of this book, it is fair to say that the Drupal community has so far succeeded in meeting its lofty targets.

What Drupal Has to Offer

From your perspective, as of now, the subject of this section is the most important topic we need to cover. As users of technology and software, we should never be lax in what we demand from the technologies that serve us. It is fitting, therefore, at this stage to discuss what we expect from Drupal in order to ensure that it will satisfy our needs.

There are three different aspects of Drupal we need to consider when looking at whether it is a *good* technology to use in general. Will it be:

- **Reliable and robust**: *Are there a lot of bugs in the code? Will it affect my site if I have to forever add patches or obtain updates for faulty code?*

- **Efficient**: *Does the code use my server's resources wisely? Am I likely to run into concurrency problems, or speed issues early on?*

- **Flexible**: *If I change my mind about what I want from my site, will I be able to implement those changes without redoing everything from scratch?*

A quick search on Google will confirm that there is an abundance of good reviews on Drupal's performance as well as plenty of write-ups praising its ease of use and flexibility. While Drupal will always be a work in progress, it can be taken for granted that the source code you will use to build your website has been meticulously crafted, and well designed. In fact, the previously listed points are taken so seriously by the developers of Drupal that they are written into their set of principles, which you can read over at `http://drupal.org/node/21945`.

While it won't influence us much for the moment, it is worth noting the following:

> A great advantage of Drupal is that the code itself is very well written, which makes modifying it easy. This means that as you attempt more advanced tasks, the very way in which Drupal is written will lend you an advantage over other platforms.

The next thing we need to consider is *What is Drupal like for us, as the administrators, to use?* Naturally, we want things to be as easy as possible so that we don't spend time bogged down with problems or complicated settings, or worse yet, have to modify the source code to suit our needs on a regular basis. Ideally, we want a system that is:

- **Easy to set up and run**: *Can I start creating my site with the minimum of fuss? Do I have to learn about a whole bunch of other technologies before I am able to use Drupal?*

- **Intuitive to work with**: *Once I have begun finding my way around, will it be easy to learn new things? If I am not a particularly technical person, will I struggle to administer my site?*

- **Flexible and easy to extend**: *I know I can make a basic site, but I really want to create a unique and sophisticated world beater—can it be done with Drupal?*

Once again, these are precisely the attributes that Drupal is known for. The questions that follow each bullet point are examples of the type of question each attribute answers. If you have other questions about Drupal that are not specifically mentioned here then try to relate them to the bullet points. If you still struggle, try looking through the forums or searching on Google for your answer.

Finally, and perhaps in some respects most importantly, you need to consider whether or not Drupal creates a good environment for your site's users. Obviously, a technology that is well designed, and easy to administer would still not be very helpful if, for example, its use is prohibitively complex. The best way to find out what type of environment Drupal can provide is to go ahead and check out the Drupal home page at `http://drupal.org`. You should probably register an account and become active in the community (believe me, it will be of great benefit to you in the long run) anyway. So perhaps, treat your registration process as a quick and easy way to see a bit of the site.

It stands to reason that if you can easily make use of the main site that is developed in Drupal, then you in turn will be able to create an easy-to-use site for your community or weblog (also called a blog).

Uses of Drupal

From a purely theoretical point of view, you are hopefully convinced that utilizing the Drupal source code to help you create a website is an excellent choice. Of course, knowing this doesn't help you discover exactly what can be done with it from a practical point of view. You still need to know what types of sites are commonly created with Drupal. As mentioned earlier, any enterprise that requires a fair amount of working with content is a likely candidate for Drupal.

Due to its extensibility and flexibility, you are really not very limited in what you decide to do with Drupal. The following list shows the most common uses at present and comes from the case studies page (`http://drupal.org/cases`) on the Drupal site:

- **Community Portal Sites** (The term *portal* refers to a site that is supposed to be an Internet user's point of entry on to the Web): If you want a news website where the stories are provided by the audience, Drupal suits your needs well. Incoming stories are automatically voted upon by the audience and the best stories bubble up to the home page. Bad stories and comments are automatically hidden after enough negative votes.

- **Personal Websites**: Drupal is great for the user who just wants a personal website where (s)he can keep a weblog, publish some photos, and maybe keep an organized collection of links.

- **Aficionado Sites**: Drupal flourishes when it powers a portal website where one person shares their expertise and enthusiasm for a topic.

- **Intranet/Corporate Websites**: Companies maintain their internal and external websites in Drupal. Drupal works well here because of its flexible permissions system, and its easy web-based publishing. You no longer have to wait for a webmaster to give word about your latest project.

- **Resource Directories**: If you want a central directory for a given topic, Drupal is the right tool for you. Users can register and suggest new resources while editors can screen their submissions.

- **International Sites**: When you begin using Drupal, you join a large international community of users and developers. Thanks to the localization features within Drupal, there are many Drupal sites implemented in a wide range of languages.

- **Education**: Drupal can be used for creating dynamic learning communities to supplement the face-to-face classroom or as a platform for distance education classes. Academic professional organizations benefit from its interactive features and the ability to provide public content, member-only resources, and member subscription management.

- **Art, Music, and Multimedia**: When it comes to community art sites, Drupal is a great match. No other platform provides the rock-solid foundation that is needed to make multimedia rich websites that allow users to share, distribute, and discuss their work with others. As time goes on, Drupal will only develop stronger support for audio, video, images, and playlist content for use in multimedia applications.

I guess I should make it clear that while you can use Drupal for a great number of things, you should perhaps limit what you use it for to those things that complement its design—like those mentioned in the previous list. If you want to retail a large number of goods from your community website, then you might wish to consider using something like osCommerce that is designed specifically for that purpose even though it is possible to retail products off your Drupal site using a contributed module.

Building a Drupal Site

Unlike building a house, development of a website takes place on a *copy* of the site instead of the real site. This means that while the site is being built, it is not available for the public to view and use on the Internet. With a bit of thought, this should make sense. Any potential community member who comes across your site would probably become frustrated with bits and pieces that don't work, error messages, untidy presentation, or any other thing that could scare people away at the drop of a hat.

Some readers may well be wondering what to do with their domain in the meantime, assuming one has already been purchased. The best solution is to put up what is known as a **placeholder page** that delivers a simple message to the effect that this is the right site, the development is in progress on the working site, and that potential members should visit again in the near future.

If you want to learn how to get a page onto your internet site before going any further, then check out Appendix A on *Deployment*, which outlines the process of moving a fully functional website onto a live web domain. The process for doing the whole site and a single page is more or less the same, but naturally, moving a single page is a lot less complicated.

Planning Your Site

Before we take a look at what the demo website is going to be, it is important that as the creator of a new site you spend some time gathering information on the needs of the community you are attempting to serve. Doing this now will help you in the long run because having a thorough understanding of your site's requirements allows you to develop it with specific goals in mind. This in turn gives you a more focused and coordinated approach to the site's development.

One of the best ways to determine what you will need, is to build a list of tasks that the site must be able to perform (by this I mean a written list, not a mental one). Effectively, after creating a list of the various things you need, the site's administrator (most probably yourself) should have a clear enough idea of the requirements to go ahead and begin working. Unfortunately, it is often hard to predict exactly what is needed by simply sitting down and writing. A good way to start is by looking at similar sites. You should go ahead and take note of everything that is useful and desirable on other sites and add this to your list.

If you get stuck, or run out of ideas, it's helpful to try a little thought exercise as follows. Split yourself into two people:

- The community member who knows what his or her needs are
- The Drupal administrator who needs to find out what to build

Use the administrator persona to question the community member about what has to be done. Approaching the problem from two perspectives often helps mimic real-world situations where software developers try to find out exactly what their clients need by asking probing questions before they start working on a project.

If you can get to a stage where you feel comfortable that you understand at least 80% of what is required from your site, then it is probably more efficient to go ahead and begin creating the site, rather than waste time scraping out more information. As Drupal is so well designed, extensible, and flexible, it is quite easy to modify it at a later stage should you need to.

What type of requirements should I be looking at? you may ask. Here is a list of some of the most important topics you will need to decide on:

- The type of site—forums, polls, or other things
- The way you are going to run the site—stats, logging, or performance issues
- The security, roles, and permissions involved
- The need for integration—syndication, aggregation, or alerts

Apart from your site's functionality you should also start thinking about how you want the site to look. Obviously an attractive and unique interface for users to work with is your ultimate goal in this respect. The use of themes to create a visually appealing site is a fairly important topic that we discuss later in the book in Chapter 8, but please do give some thought to this aspect of your site early on regardless.

Of course, you not only want to design an interface that looks pretty, you also want to make it intuitive and easy to use. This is very important as studies have shown that users will often base their opinion of a site on how easy it is to use and not always on other criteria, which you might think important, such as speed. People often *believe* that a slower running site is faster if they manage to accomplish their tasks on it more easily.

There is a brief specification of the site that will be built throughout the course of this book in the section entitled *The Demo Website* later on in this chapter. By observing similar sites and anticipating the needs of your site's users, you can develop a specification for your own Drupal site. Having a site outline or specification to work towards is very valuable in the world of website development—even if Drupal mitigates the need for writing code ourselves.

Analyzing the Proposed Solution

Once there is a specification to work with, we know *what* we need. It is time to look at *how* to deliver it. Off the top of your head, it may seem that one simply sits down and works through the specification list point by point until everything has been checked off. From one perspective this is absolutely fine and certainly at some stage everything should be ticked off the list. But if we look a little closer, the picture begins to get a bit fuzzy because we really need to go back over all the points listed and find out *what is involved* in getting each one done. Knowing what lies ahead is the best way to handle problems preemptively!

The three main areas of concern that we need to deal with are discussed next.

Feasibility

Having a wish-list is a great way to decide on what you want, but that doesn't mean it is feasible. In order to be feasible, the criteria should not involve an inordinate amount of effort relative to the benefits it will return. For example, if the site specification calls for a feature that requires a hundred hours of brutal, frustrating programming, then it is probably not in your interests to waste time doing it if it is not going to affect your community significantly.

Ultimately, it may be better to look for a cheap and elegant alternative either amongst the plethora of contributions, or from third-party software providers. One of the old programming mantras, *There's more than one way to do it!* holds true here.

Phone a Friend

Look at your requirements very carefully. *Are you sure you can actually provide everything that is required?* If not, spend some time looking over this book and the Drupal site to see if you can learn anything new. If you are absolutely stuck, then get on the forums and lists and ask for help. One of the great things about Drupal is that it is a community-driven project, which roughly translates into: *There are generally people around who are happy to help*. Bear in mind that this is not a one-way relationship, and once you have some experience and knowledge to share, there are always people who are grateful for a helping hand.

Critical versus Desirable Criteria

In order to determine the priority of tasks during your site's development phase, it is a good idea to divide all your requirements into two categories—those that are fundamentally necessary to the success of your website, such as finding a service provider, and those that are not, such as deciding on whether to make your hyperlink color dark blue or light blue.

There are a couple of reasons for this:

- Doing so will help you allocate time and resources to certain tasks while putting others on a backburner.

- You are aware of those features that do not necessarily need to be included at all in the event that time is short.

In both these cases, it is important to know what has to be finished and what can perhaps be left out or left for another day. With all that in mind, let's take a look at what the demo site is, and how it intends to meet the requirements of its community…

The Demo Website

In order to do something fairly distinctive, we will, throughout the course of this book, build a wildlife and conservation community site called *The Contechst Wildlife Community*, or CWC, that will cater to the needs of a wide range of people involved in everything from conservation and rehabilitation to research and policy making. The intention of this site is to become a central meeting point for like-minded people who wish to stimulate discussion and exchange ideas and information, which can be in virtually any form.

Not only is the site going to foster a community feeling by creating regular newsletters and posting information on important events, but it is also going to encourage open debate in its forums. It is hoped that the forums will become a popular meeting place, but this will not in any way be the only facility provided by the site. Regular polls will be taken in order to gather information on various important topics and industry experts will be invited to become bloggers for the site.

Of course, it is only natural that we will need a striking and pleasing look and feel for the site, which will end up like this (actually, there is a lot more to the site, but in the interests of fitting everything on one page it has been simplified a bit):

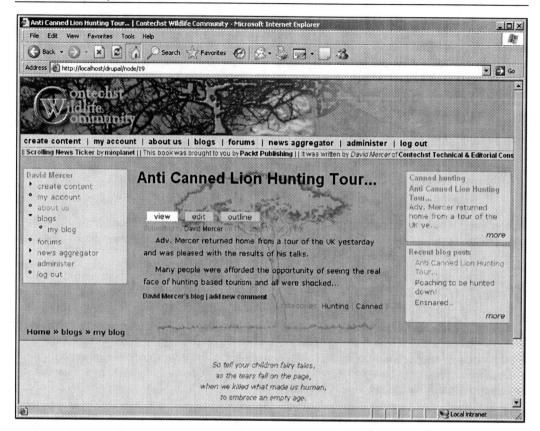

One of the sad facts is that even if this community site is very popular, we will still need to make money out of it just to cover the costs of having someone administer or moderate it. *How can we do this without charging people for membership?* There are two methods open to most sites that have a large associated community: donations and advertising. Accordingly, the CWC will make use of some third-party software and a downloadable module to raise money.

The CWC is designed to show off much of the default behavior of Drupal, and you will see in due course that the following functionality will be enabled from the default distribution:

- **Blogs**: A blog, or weblog, is almost like a journal, maintained by one person only. In the case of the demo site, there will be a bunch of blog writers who post to the site regularly in order to keep the general public informed about their movements and developments in their specific areas of focus.

- **Books**: A book can be created by a wide range of users using pretty much any type of content possible. Polls, pages, weblogs, and others can all be easily added to a book. This is a very interesting feature of Drupal because it allows for the creation of a truly unique online book that can harness the power of web-based dynamic content to give your stories an ultra-modern feel.

- **Comments**: Naturally, in any community, people will feel the urge to comment on topics of interest. Because of this, the Drupal comment functionality allows users to append or attach comments to pretty much any content they like (depending on the permissions set by the administrator). In fact, forums are based on the use of comments, which are added to specific forum topics that have been posted to the site.

- **Forums**: A forum is a medium for discussion and voicing ideas. In the case of the demo site, a variety of different forums will be set up to provide users with an area in which to discuss important subjects and interact. As you will see, you will be able to control the content of forums quite easily if you so desire—in fact, Drupal allows you to examine any and all content that attempts to make its way onto your site.

- **Locale**: This allows you to present your site in a variety of different languages in order to create a truly international site. In fact, Drupal goes one step further by allowing individual users to select their language of preference in order to view it in that language automatically whenever they log on.

- **Polls**: The poll content type allows an administrator (or whoever has sufficient permissions) to create a content type, which contains a question and several options from which poll users can select their preferred answer. This is a useful tool for gathering pretty much any sort of information ranging from what features your users would like to see on your site, to whether or not people believe there is life on other planets.

There are actually quite a few more features that will be utilized in order to make our site fully operational, but we need not go through all of them here as some of them are fairly trivial, and others are explained in detail later on in the book. Trust me, there is plenty more to work on!

From the previous list you can tell that there is already a powerful set of features available to Drupal administrators and we will actually look at how to enable, modify, and use all these features and many more, in due course.

We are not limited to using only those features that come with Drupal by default. Drupal has been designed to make it easy for people other than the developers to enhance it with more functionality. The modular design of Drupal means that creating entirely new functionality is often as simple as copying a few files into your Drupal folders—although, admittedly it can be more complex and we will also look at contributions that require modifications to the database amongst other things.

The CWC will make use of a whole bunch of contributed modules including, but not limited to:

- **Taxonomy Access**: Allows the administrator to maintain exceptionally fine-grained control over who is allowed to do what and on what type of content. As you will see later, there will be certain users whose help is required to moderate the forums but who should not have any other broad-based powers. Using this contribution makes it easy to outline the permissions for any user based on the type of content you want them to work with.

- **Flexinode**: Provides the administrator with the ability to create custom content types. This can be exceptionally useful if there is a specific need that cannot be easily catered for using one of the standard content types like a page or blog.

- **Adsense**: Allows administrators to incorporate advertising from Google. In this way, traffic from your site can be directed to related sites for a small payment. If you have enough traffic moving through your site then these small payments can mount up, providing you with a nice source of revenue.

Not content with simply utilizing various modules to add functionality to the site, we will also get our hands dirty by ensuring we have properly structured the site's content using the taxonomy system provided by Drupal. We will also look at how to add some dynamic additions to the site using third-party scripts and even AJAX.

The Drupal Community

One of the most important resources you will need in the coming days, weeks, months, and years is the Drupal online community. Unlike other open-source projects, which are sometimes criticized for their lack of coherent and in-depth support structures, you will find that Drupal is very well done and fairly easy to learn your way around. There are a host of categories ranging from information, polls, forums, and news to support, which can be found at the home page: `http://drupal.org`.

> It will be assumed in the rest of the book that you have taken some time to familiarize yourself with how the site works.

It is strongly recommended that you regularly make use of `drupal.org` and constantly use different elements and sections in order to become proficient at extracting the information and software you require to run your enterprise—especially since the Drupal site will change from time to time! For precisely this reason, you might also notice that there are small differences between this book and Drupal itself.

All the information contained in the site is well organized and easy to access from the main navigation bar at the top of the page, as shown here:

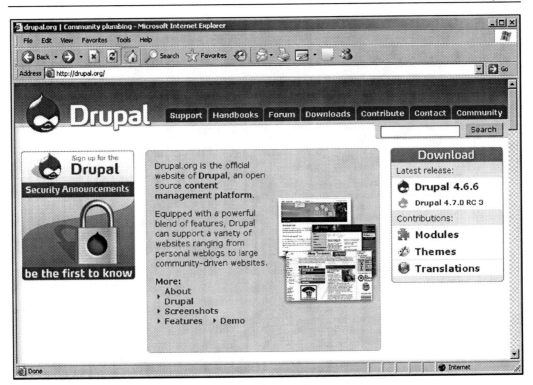

Each and every tab in the navigation bar has a host of its own links and pages although there are some categories that contain inter-related topics. You should note, that when we refer to *community* in this book, we are talking about the entire Drupal community, including all the support structures, developers, users, and so on—not to be confused with the Community tab on the front page that refers more to the different Drupal communities around the world (more on this in a moment).

At any rate, let's go through each and every one quickly to see what they have to offer.

Support

To begin, the Support section can be regarded as a kind of catch-all page, and actually contains a number of links to the various other community pages, many of which can also be opened by using their tabs in the main navigation bar. For example, you can navigate to the Drupal handbook (to be discussed shortly) from the Online documentation section if you need to find out some basic information on Drupal, as shown here:

Support

Online documentation

Take a look at the Drupal handbook if you want to learn more about Drupal or if you need help installing Drupal.

A list of common problems and their solutions can be found in the Troubleshooting FAQ.

Security

Drupal-related security advisories are posted on the security page. If you setup or adminsiter Drupal sites, we strongly advise you to subsribe to the security announcement mailing list by e-mail or RSS. If you identified a security issue, you can contact the security team using the contact form.

Forums and Support

If you are stuck and need help, the forums are the best place to browse and ask for help. Chances are your questions has been asked before so make sure to search the archives first. Please also consult the Tips for posting to the Drupal forums.

Other languages

Looking for support in your own language?

- Drupal Japan (□□□)
- Drupal Hungary (Magyarország)
- Drupal Italia (Italiano)
- Drupal Brazilian Portuguese (Português)
- Drupal Spanish (Español)

Professional services and hosting

If you are looking for a Drupal consultant or Drupal hosting, consult the services page or check the services and hosting forum.

Bug reports

Please help us squish those pesky bugs. First, search the bug list to see if someone has already reported it. If not, submit a bug report.

Feature requests

Until Drupal washes your laundry for you, it is incomplete. You may review outstanding feature requests and new ones too.

Mailing list

If you prefer e-mail, you can subscribe to our support mailing list.

IRC channel

For IRC-based support, join #drupal-support on the FreeNode IRC network (irc.freenode.net). For theme development, join #drupal-themes.

Developer support

We have a handbook, and module developer's forum, a theme designers forum, API reference, and a development mailing list ready to inform and support you.

Drupal.org problems

Briefly, in this section:

- Documentation and help facilities are provided in the Online documentation section, and include help on some common problems as well as installation and general information.
- Links to security advisories and announcements as well as the option to subscribe to the security announcement mailing list or RSS feed are provided under the Security section.
- Links to the forums, in case you need help, are provided under the Forums and Support section, as well as archives and a Tips for posting to the Drupal forums link.
- If you are not an English language speaker, or your community predominantly speaks some other language, then it is worthwhile checking out some of the other language sites under the Other languages section, which includes German, French, Spanish, and Afrikaans.

- Links to a number of professional services related to Drupal, including hosting and consulting, are provided under the Professional services and hosting section.

- Bug reports can be sent in by visiting the Bug reports section. Please be aware that you should always check whether or not a bug has been reported before submitting your own report. Any submission incurs a cost in terms of man-hours because someone has to look over it, and the time wastage can be substantial if everyone keeps reporting the same bug over and over again.

- The Feature requests section gives you the opportunity to look over what other people would like to see incorporated into Drupal as shown here:

Home » projects

issues

- submit
- statistics
- subscribe

Project:	Status:	Category:	Priority:		
<all>	active,fixed,patch	feature requests	<all>	Search	advanced search

Project	Summary	Status	Pri	Category	Last updated	Assigned to
Documentation	a new taxonomy term for snippets new	active	normal	feature	5 min 4 sec	
HTML To Text	Document return value of html2txt_convert() new	active	minor	feature	19 min 57 sec	
Acidfree	pathauto extension new	fixed	minor	feature	3 hours 10 min	

Of course, you can also submit your own requests.

- There is also an interesting option to obtain support over an IRC channel. IRC, or Internet Relay Chat, allows for real-time, typed discussions over the Internet. Joining a group like this is obviously a great advantage in that it immediately gives you access to many other Drupal people.

- There is a support Mailing list section that you can join, a Developer support section, and a forum to raise issues about the actual Drupal website under the Drupal.org problems section. Recently, a new section entitled Books about Drupal has been added too.

If in doubt as to where to go, the Support page is probably where you should start off. More often than not though, you will have a fairly good idea of what you need, and should be able to go straight there.

Handbooks

This section is a great repository of information, catering for a wide variety of different needs. The content is gathered into five main sections as shown here:

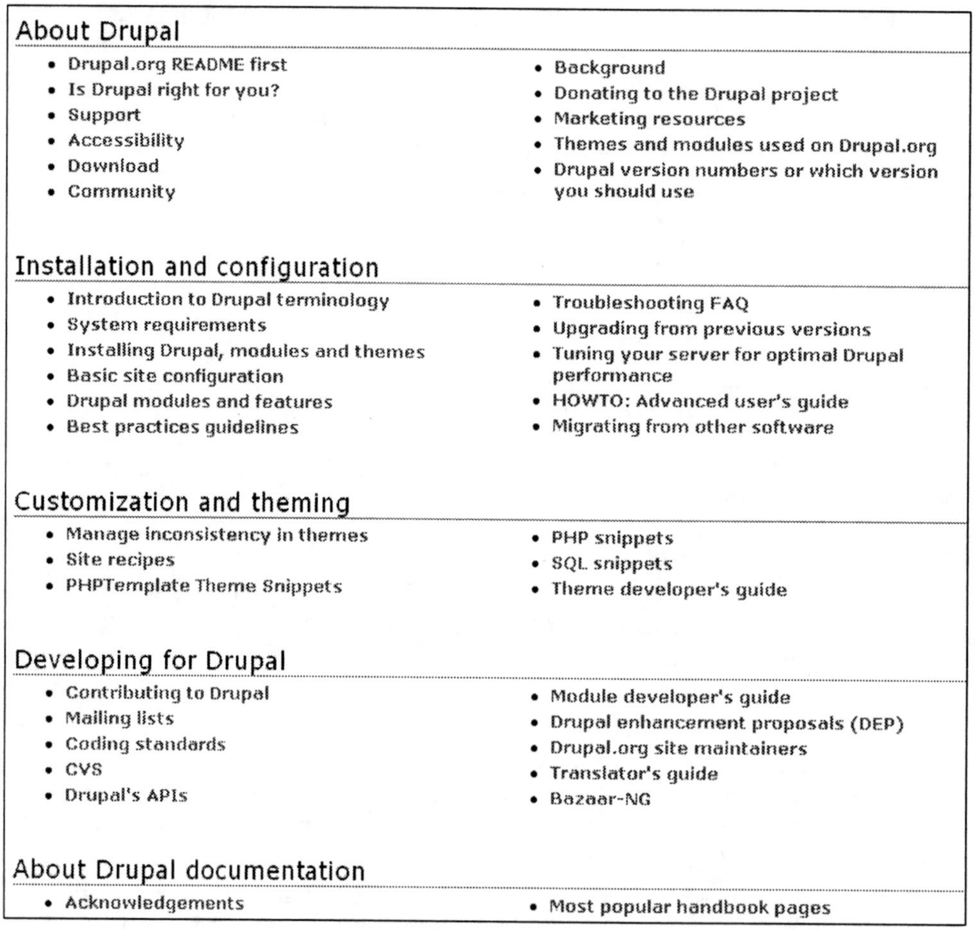

About Drupal

- Drupal.org README first
- Is Drupal right for you?
- Support
- Accessibility
- Download
- Community

- Background
- Donating to the Drupal project
- Marketing resources
- Themes and modules used on Drupal.org
- Drupal version numbers or which version you should use

Installation and configuration

- Introduction to Drupal terminology
- System requirements
- Installing Drupal, modules and themes
- Basic site configuration
- Drupal modules and features
- Best practices guidelines

- Troubleshooting FAQ
- Upgrading from previous versions
- Tuning your server for optimal Drupal performance
- HOWTO: Advanced user's guide
- Migrating from other software

Customization and theming

- Manage inconsistency in themes
- Site recipes
- PHPTemplate Theme Snippets

- PHP snippets
- SQL snippets
- Theme developer's guide

Developing for Drupal

- Contributing to Drupal
- Mailing lists
- Coding standards
- CVS
- Drupal's APIs

- Module developer's guide
- Drupal enhancement proposals (DEP)
- Drupal.org site maintainers
- Translator's guide
- Bazaar-NG

About Drupal documentation

- Acknowledgements

- Most popular handbook pages

Each of these categories contains a series of links to informative pages (that often in turn contain links to other pages) that do a good job of explaining their respective topics. It's worth pointing out that a block appears on the left-hand side of these pages, containing links to related topics under the same category heading in order to help you navigate through the information with ease. The following screenshot shows the Is Drupal right for you? page:

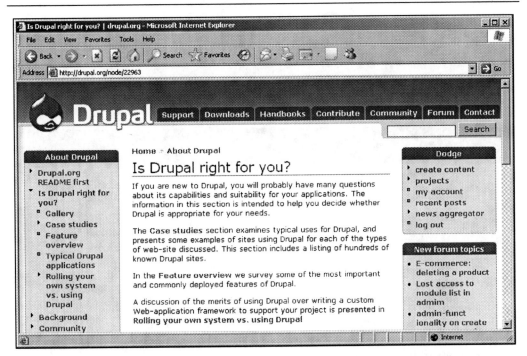

You are urged to look through at least the first section before moving on to the following chapter in order to learn as much about Drupal as possible. It is also a good idea to use these handbooks in tandem with this book so that you can complement the practical advice and experience you gain here with reference-type material presented on the site.

Forum

The forums are probably your single greatest problem-solving resource and information-based asset. Unlike the other types of information on the site (with the exception of the Freenode Drupal IRC), which are largely static, written answers or guides, the forums provide you with an interactive environment in which you can learn and extend your knowledge. Of course, they also provide you with a medium for sharing whatever you have learned as well.

At the time of writing, there were approximately 100,000 support-related posts alone. This should give you a good idea of how widely used these forums are. The following screenshot shows the Forum home page as well as the first few forum categories. From the large number of posts you can tell that this is already a fairly large repository of knowledge and hopefully you will take the time to add to it yourself.

Forums

- Active forum discussions.
- Login to post a new forum topic.

Forum	Topics	Posts	Last post
General Important: no support questions here!			
News and announcements For news and announcements to the Drupal community at large.	402	4779	11 hours 50 min ago by ae2005
General discussion For less technical discussions about the Drupal project. Not for support questions!	2457	13821	29 min 27 sec ago by D3sign3r
Drupal showcase To show your Drupal sites to others.	750	3635	33 min 43 sec ago by marcopolo
Events For events, conferences and other Drupal happenings.	52	385	1 day 8 hours ago by ae2005
Usability feedback For interface guidelines, mockups, and usability feedback.	308	1757	3 hours 39 min ago by coplan

Looking at the entire page, there are three main forum categories—General, Support, and Development—that in turn have a number of subcategories to make navigating the structure fairly easy. You will also notice that there is a block on the right-hand side of the page containing a list of the most recent posts. As well as this, you can also use the search tool, shown at the top right-hand side of the page or at http://drupal.org/search/node, to search for relevant information or users.

Finally, assuming you are a registered (and logged-on) Drupal user, you can also post new topics to the forum using the link given under the page's main heading as shown here:

Home

Forums

- My forum discussions.
- Active forum discussions.
- Post new forum topic.

Before you start posting off hundreds of questions and salutations, please be aware that there is a certain etiquette to using these forums, and it should be followed at all times. Look at the following page before you begin making any posts to the site: http://drupal.org/forum-posting. A quick summary is as follows:

- Make sure you have searched the forums for similar posts already. Use those posts instead of creating redundant information.

- Make your forum post titles informative and meaningful.

- Ensure that you submit a good amount of system-specific information in your support queries—for example, mention the Drupal version you are using along with the database and database version.

- Bear in mind that not everyone using the forum is a native English speaker; so some posts may be construed as rude or abrupt even when that is not the intention.

- Remain polite and reasonable—even if you are frustrated over a particular problem.

- Donate some time to responding to and helping other posters.

- If you would like, enable your contact tab so that people can offer support via email. You can do this by editing your contact information as shown here:

Contact settings

☑ Personal contact form
Allow other users to contact you by e-mail via **your personal contact form**. Note that your e-mail address is not made public and that privileged users such as site administrators are able to contact you even if you choose not to enable this feature.

Some of you may have noticed the link entitled Active forum discussions in the screenshot before last. Clicking on this link brings up a list of the topics that have recent posts, as shown here:

recent posts

	all recent posts	my recent posts		
Type	Post	Author	Replies	Last post
forum topic	Specify upload folder in upload.module new	battra	1 1 new	2 min 21 sec ago
forum topic	Weight for free tagging terms per node? new	doq	3 3 new	4 min 7 sec ago
issue	Multiple links displayed (for each edit) new	coplan	3	4 min 12 sec ago
issue	Opening an empty folder new	sanduhrs	0	4 min 36 sec ago
forum topic	Marketing Offensive new	bertboerland@ww...	15 15 new	5 min 38 sec ago

If you would prefer to view the discussions that you personally have contributed to, then click the My forum discussions link instead.

Downloads

We will be visiting this section again in the following chapter when we begin to set up everything in preparation for the development of your site. However, there are a few interesting points to note before we get there. The first is that you need to be quite careful about the Drupal version, or indeed modules and themes, you download because each successive version makes changes and improvements on previous versions, but also sometimes messes up compatibility with other features.

For example, you can see that the downloads page provides us with some interesting information on compatibility with PHP from the following screenshot:

As you can see, Drupal 4.5 will not work with PHP 5. Now, this in itself is no great problem because it is quite likely that your hosting services will remain with PHP 4 for some time yet. However, at some stage most service providers will upgrade to PHP 5 support since PHP 5 is a far more sophisticated language than its predecessor. Knowing this, you might immediately say that this doesn't worry us because Drupal 4.6 is available (and so is 4.7).

That's quite right, but if you decide to add a module (by this I mean that at some stage you *will* want to add a module) then viewing the projects page at http://drupal.org/project, or by clicking the Downloads tab gives:

Project types

- Drupal project
- Modules

  The contributed modules are **not** part of any official release and may not work correctly. Only use matching versions of modules with Drupal. Modules released for Drupal 4.5 will not work for Drupal 4.6.

- Theme engines

  The contributed theme engines are **not** part of any official release and may not work correctly. Only use matching versions of theme engines with Drupal. Theme engines released for Drupal 4.5 will not work for Drupal 4.6.

- Themes

  The contributed themes are **not** part of any official release and may not work correctly. Only use matching versions of themes with Drupal. Themes released for Drupal 4.5 will not work for Drupal 4.6.

- Translations

  To install these translations, unzip them and import the .po file through Drupal's administration interface for localization. You will need to turn on locale.module if it's not already enabled. You can check the completeness of translations on the status page.

You can see from the notes presented on this page, if you happen to need a module that was developed for Drupal 4.5, and you are using version 4.6, then you are shortly going to experience no small amount of frustration—this is especially valid at this time because 4.7 is brand new, and hence many modules have yet to be updated.

Problems like this can occur because modules are developed separately from the core, which means that it is up to the individual module developer to keep up to date with any changes coming from the main development team.

Naturally, not everyone will keep the modules up to date in a timely manner because often these developers are not getting paid and are under no obligation to do the work at all. They are simply providing us with the best code they can deliver when they can deliver it, and we should obviously be grateful for that.

In terms of how to use the download pages, it is worth noting that there are three links given at the bottom right of each downloadable item's box. These are Download, Find out more, and Bugs and feature requests. Obviously the first option is pretty self explanatory, but you should always take a look at the Find out more option before downloading anything to ensure that you are getting precisely what you want.

For example, the Find out more page for the Acidfree project contains information on Known limitations, a history of Updates, and plenty of material on Releases, Resources, Support, and Development—all pretty useful if you are not sure what Acidfree does to begin with.

That aside, the point of this section is that you should try to *think carefully* about what you want from your site before you go ahead and begin downloading everything. In the next chapter we will put words into practice and make use of this section to obtain a copy of Drupal.

Contribute

At first glance you might be forgiven for thinking that there is very little you can meaningfully contribute to the Drupal community while you are still learning the software. As this is not entirely true, it is worthwhile seeing what there is available to us:

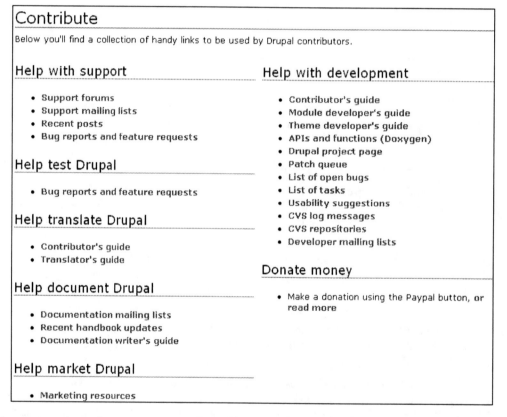

For starters, the easiest way to support Drupal is by making donations—I can all but hear the sighs and groans as you read this, but bear in mind what you are getting is absolutely free. You can also help market Drupal by writing reviews, or incorporating the Druplicon onto your site and so on. There is also always a need for people to help test, translate, support, and document Drupal.

Finally, once you have gained some experience and feel confident enough, you can look towards helping with Drupal development. Whatever you choose to do, you will find that any information or help you require in order to become pro-active within the community is readily available under the Contribute section.

Contact and Community

These two sections are fairly self explanatory so I have lumped them together. The Contact page simply allows you to send an email off to the Drupal team, and you need to remember that no technical support queries will be addressed here—*you must use the support forum for that.* Simply ensure you select the most pertinent category from the drop-down list provided and away you go. An example is shown here:

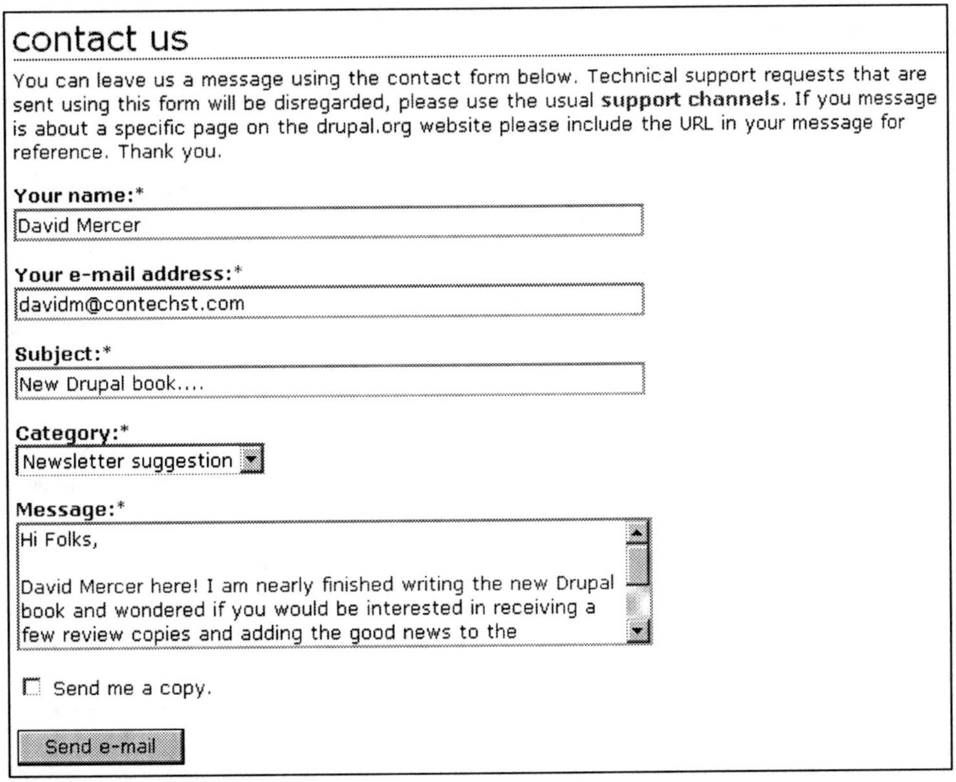

contact us

You can leave us a message using the contact form below. Technical support requests that are sent using this form will be disregarded, please use the usual **support channels**. If you message is about a specific page on the drupal.org website please include the URL in your message for reference. Thank you.

Your name:*

David Mercer

Your e-mail address:*

davidm@contechst.com

Subject:*

New Drupal book....

Category:*

Newsletter suggestion

Message:*

Hi Folks,

David Mercer here! I am nearly finished writing the new Drupal book and wondered if you would be interested in receiving a few review copies and adding the good news to the

☐ Send me a copy.

Send e-mail

That's easy enough to do! Moving on to the Community page, you can see that this gives you access to the various international Drupal communities as well as a few aggregated resources and tag services that you might find interesting to read:

Community

Drupal.org

- Drupal.org forums
- Drupal.org mailing lists
- Drupal events
- Drupal newsletter

Web watch

- Planet Drupal aggregates Drupal-related blog posts of many Drupal developers, users and supporters.
- Drupal talk aggregates lots of Drupal resources, ranging from usenet posts, forum posts, blogs, mailinglists and lots more.

Local communities

- Drupal Japan (□□□)
- Drupal Hungary (Magyarország)
- Drupal Italia (Italiano)
- Drupal Brazilian Portuguese (Português)
- Drupal Spanish (Español)
- Drupal Russia (Русский)
- Drupal Afrikaans (Afrikaans)
- Drupal Germany (Deutsch)
- Drupal French (Français)
- Drupal Belgium (Nederlands)
- Drupal Polish (Polska)
- Drupal Romania (România)
- Drupal Korea (□□□)

Tags

Drupal tags are available in many tagging services, e.g. del.icio.us, Flickr and Technorati.

Incidentally, a tagging service is simply a bunch of pages that have been associated with various keywords. This makes it easy to find content based on a user-defined categorization—doing things this way is also very flexible as you no longer have to pigeon-hole content into predefined categories. You can find more information on tags and tagging at the del.icio.us site: http://del.icio.us/help/tags.

That about wraps it up for our coverage of the Drupal community. You should feel fairly confident that you can use the site efficiently and that you can find help if needs be. Before we continue on to the next chapter, though, there is one more important issue we need to discuss …

The Drupal License

Naturally, you should want to inform yourself of any and all legalities and responsibilities you have when it comes to using software developed by others. To this end, you will find that when you download a copy of Drupal, it will contain a license file for your perusal—it is actually required as part of the license that this copy be included.

If you're like me then you find it challenging to remain awake when faced with the prospect of reading through licenses and other legal documents. So, instead of subjecting you to a verbatim recount of the entire license, I will instead give you the paraphrased version that is intended to provide you with the *essence* of what the license is getting at as it applies to Drupal.

Please bear in mind that what I say here is in no way a legal document. You **must** read the whole license yourself if you wish to follow the letter of the law.

As odd as it may sound, one of the fundamental reasons for using the GNU GPL (General Public License) is to protect and help you—the people who use the software. The GPL is fundamentally different from the licenses of proprietary software, which by and large are designed to protect the rights of the corporate entities that developed and created the software.

Incidentally, the GPL is not tied specifically to Drupal; rather Drupal makes use of the GPL, which is a kind of generic license for distributing open-source software. You can check out the GNU home page for more information on this movement in general: http://www.gnu.org/home.html.

The way things work is that the software is copyrighted and then licensed for everyone to use freely. This might strike you as a little odd at first because *what is the point of copyrighting something if you are simply going to let anyone else make use of it?* The reason for this is that copyrighting and licensing the software gives the developer the power to obligate people who use that software to afford everyone they hand it out to (with or without modifications) the same rights that are vested in the original software.

What this means is that, effectively, anyone who makes use of this software cannot create proprietary software from it. So, if you decide to build upon and improve Drupal yourself in order to sell it on as your own product, then you will be bound by the same terms and will have to release your source code to anyone who asks for it. Remember though, the aim of the GPL is not to take credit for your own work by forcing you to release it under the GPL. If you have developed identifiable programs or code that are wholly your own and are independent from the original source code provided, then the GPL does not necessarily apply to your work.

A summary of some of the main points in the license is as follows:

- You are free to copy the software covered by the GPL as well as distribute these copies however you see fit. The most important thing to do is make sure you don't remove the licensing.

- You can hack around with the source code and create whatever type of derived product you want. Again, you must pass on the same license (as you received it) with the original code, only this time you must make sure you also make it very clear what changes you have made. (This is to protect the original programmers in the event you introduce a virus that destroys the Internet.)

- You mustn't break the terms of the GPL at any stage or you will find your current license to use the software terminated.

- You aren't forced to accept the conditions of the license. (You can tell this from the fact that you don't have to sign anything.) However, if you don't accept the terms of the license, you can't make use of the software.

- If you do decide to redistribute the software yourself, then you can't add restrictions or modify the license in any way. You also aren't required to ensure that the parties you distribute the software to comply with it.

- If you are compelled by a court ruling (or any other legal proceeding) to enforce conditions that do not meet the requirements of the GPL, then you must not distribute the software at all.

- Keep an eye on the version of the license that is distributed with the software. If there is one present then you must use that version or a later one, but not an earlier one.

- There is no warranty on this software, and no one who modifies or distributes the software in terms of the GPL is responsible for anything—especially damages or failure to operate and so on.

At the end of the day, if you are just going to use Drupal to build a website, all you really need to know is that it is both free in terms of price and in terms of who gets access to its source code. The cynics among you may be saying something like: *This all sounds like a bunch of hooey. You can't even provide a warranty or guarantee that the software will work because no one has the money to pay for real development.* Well, you don't need to worry about that. Open-source software is among the best and most reliable in the world exactly because everyone in the world can see the code and improve on it.

The only time you do need to worry about the niceties of the GPL is when you decide to set up a business installing, configuring, and customizing Drupal websites for money, or modifying, and redistributing the original source code.

Summary

This chapter has served as an introduction to the world of Drupal as well as backdrop for the rest of the book. Several important things were discussed here, which will play an important role in the future as you develop your skills and knowledge.

Without a doubt, one of the most important aspects of becoming a successful Drupal administrator is being able to make efficient use of the community. By now you should have registered on the Drupal site and taken at least a cursory glance at much of it. As time goes by, you will hopefully develop relationships with other members and eventually become a great asset for the community at large.

In addition, this chapter took some time to look at the demo website that will be built throughout the rest of the book. This demonstrated that even at a beginner level we are able to create an extremely powerful web-based application that can be used to drive entire communities—all without having to learn any programming at all. That's not to say that there is no work involved—no doubt you found researching and deciding on what your site requires fairly tedious. Remember though that any background work you put in now will pay off later; so it's definitely worth it.

With the introductory material out the way, it is time to get down to business, and the next chapter will see us setting up the development environment as well as obtaining and installing the latest version of Drupal.

2
Setting Up the Development Environment

What on earth is a development environment and why do I need it? It is fairly widely accepted that during the process of building your website, you should not make it available for people to use over the Internet. Making your site *live*, while you are still making changes and breaking and fixing things, means that it is possible for people to find your site, attempt to use it, and form an exceedingly bad opinion of your web development skills. You might, in the worst case, find that you have even inadvertently allowed malicious users to gain access to sensitive information due to improperly implemented security settings, among other things.

Rather than allow the public access to your work in progress, it is far better to set up a PHP-enabled web server on your home or office PC. This server, along with PHP and your database, can then be used to design and build everything just as you want it, before transferring the final product over to the live site. A development environment is precisely that machine, along with its attendant development tools and technologies, where you can build your site. This chapter therefore will ensure that you set yours up correctly and efficiently so that you can begin working on Drupal directly in the chapters that follow.

Specifically, we will discuss the following important topics:

- A brief introduction to the technologies involved
- Obtaining and installing Apache, MySQL, and PHP
- Obtaining and installing Drupal
- Upgrading Drupal
- Troubleshooting common problems
- A short tour of Drupal

Installation and setup for Apache, MySQL, and PHP will only be covered for Windows because we trust that Linux hacks will have everything installed already (or will know how it is done). On the off chance that you don't have everything installed, a quick glance over the instructions given on the software-in-question's site should suffice to get you on your feet. The installation procedure for Drupal is much the same for Windows and Linux; so people using either can follow along with the *Obtaining and Installing Drupal* section.

Before we begin, however, there is one crucial bit of advice to be given:

> Ensure that you have access to a good, preferably lightning fast, Internet connection, as you will be downloading a fair amount of software.

For those users who have already installed various bits of software, you might find it convenient to skip whatever sections you do not need, going over only those that are of interest. As well as providing information on installation, this chapter will also have a troubleshooting section addressing some of the most common errors associated with the setup process for Drupal.

It should also be noted that because Drupal has been developed with flexibility in mind, it is possible to use it off IIS as an alternative web server, as well as utilizing PostgreSQL as an alternative database because support for these are actively being developed. Rather than show how to set each and every one up, we will focus on the most popular combination of Apache, MySQL, and PHP.

The Drupal Environment

I know most of you will be eager to get going at the moment, and might well prefer to dive straight into making modifications to your Drupal site. Before we do so, it will be of real benefit for you to take a few moments to read over this section to gain an appreciation of how everything is put together behind the scenes. Having a basic knowledge of how the various technologies co-operate in order to provide you with a working Drupal site, will help you immeasurably in the long run.

The best thing to do to begin with is take a look at each of the individual underlying technologies we will be using:

- **PHP**: PHP, or PHP Hypertext Preprocessor, is the language in which Drupal is written. Recently it has received a major upgrade and is now more or less a fully functional **Object Oriented Language**, with some very powerful features. PHP is widely used on the Internet for a multitude of different projects and is renowned for its ease of use. The current version of PHP is PHP 5, which is what we will use in this book for our demonstration since the latest version of Drupal is PHP 5 friendly. However, you are welcome to use version 4 because this is what most internet service providers use at present. The good news is that we will not have to delve deeply into programming code in order to build our site—Drupal handles most, if not all, of the complex programming issues.

- **Apache**: This is the web server we will use to serve web pages during the development phase. Apache is the most popular web server on the Internet, with millions of live sites using it every day. In fact, as the Apache website says: *It is more widely used than all the other web servers combined.*

- **MySQL**: This is the database software that we will use to store all the information required to keep the website running. Everything from customer details to product information and a host of other things will be stored in the MySQL database. Keeping with the trend of popularity, MySQL is also the world's most popular bit of database software with over six million active installations worldwide.

Now, since we don't want to waste too much time downloading and installing all the different pieces of software we need individually, we are going to use a package installation, which provides us with everything we need using only one installation. The package we will use for the purposes of this book is called **Apache2Triad**.

Now that we know *what* we are using, it is important to take a quick look at *how* we are going to be using it. The following diagram shows a simplified view of how everything works, with the shaded section denoting the Apache2Triad package containing the Apache web server, PHP interpreter, and MySQL database, with Drupal installed on the system:

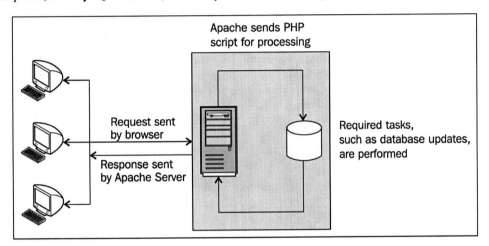

So, whenever a user does anything with your Drupal site (hopefully like contributing meaningfully), here's what happens:

1. The relevant information is bundled off to the server in the form of an HTTP (HyperText Transfer Protocol) request. An HTTP request comes in two forms— either a GET or a POST. For our purposes, it is not important to understand how GET and POST work, as long as you understand that information can be captured from the user and sent to the server for processing using these requests.

2. The server receives the HTTP request and says, *Ah! This is a PHP page that has been requested. I need to send it off for processing by the PHP engine.* The PHP page then gets processed and executed appropriately, and any actions that are required as a result of the user's request are performed.

3. Once that is done, an appropriate response is returned by the server to the user's browser, and the cycle continues.

There are quite a few methods of providing dynamic web content that don't rely on PHP server requests. Instead, processing is done on the client side of the application (in other words, on the web browser). We will take a look at how to enhance your web pages with JavaScript much later on, in Chapter 9, but what you have been shown here is fundamentally how everything works, even if there are exceptions to the rule.

While this section has been a bit of a whirlwind tour of the underlying technologies associated with Drupal, the information contained in here should prove to be invaluable at some stage. For example, knowing how everything fits together will often help you isolate the cause of any problems you encounter, allowing you to resolve them quicker.

Don't worry if this all seems a little daunting at the moment. Bear in mind that Drupal itself handles most, if not all, of the complexity associated with ensuring everything runs smoothly. As you will see, our job becomes one of customization rather than actual software development. With that behind us, let's get on with the installation process.

Obtaining and Installing PHP, Apache, and MySQL

As mentioned in the previous section, we are going to make use of a package installation in order to simplify the task of creating a workable development environment. You will notice that most software installation is really about learning a single process and repeating it for whatever software you need. More often than not, you will:

1. Go to the software producer's site
2. Find the download page
3. Download the software
4. Unpack the software or run the executable file, depending on the method of installation
5. Install the software
6. Configure your installation
7. Test your setup

That sounds easy enough; so head on over to http://apache2triad.net/, which is the homepage for the Apache2Triad project and click the Downloads link in the left-hand box towards the bottom of the screen. (Feel free to browse around to learn more about this useful enterprise.) This will take you to the downloads page on the SourceForge site at:
http://sourceforge.net/project/showfiles.php?group_id=93507.

Select the package you wish to use—for the purposes of this book, release package 1.5.3 was used. At the time of writing, this was the latest stable release, but you should feel free to use a later version, if there is one, as this will not affect how you follow along here. Once you have clicked Download for a package you will be presented with a list of download options. Release package 1.5.3 has only one option as shown here:

Package	Release (date)	Filename	Size (kb)	Downloads	Architecture	Type
⊟ Edge (Apache2.1 PHP5 MySQL5)						
Latest	⊟ 1.5.3 [Notes] (2005-08-31 09:44)					
		apache2triad1.5.3.exe	85933363	21497	i386	.exe (32-bit Windows)
Totals:	1	1	85933363	21497		

This is the package we will download and install. In order to do this, simply click the package name .exe file, which will take you to a list of mirror sites from which you can choose one to provide you with the download. A mirror is simply a server that provides all the same facilities at a different geographical location—this is done to reduce the load on individual servers and provide faster downloads to people all over the globe. Make your choice and click Download to begin.

Depending on your PC's security settings, you may be given the following warning message:

Simply click Run to continue (or Save if you would like to hold on to a copy). At this point, you may want to take a break for a cup of coffee or tea if you have a slow connection as it may take a while.

At some stage during the setup process, the installer will ask you to confirm several settings and you are free to make changes as and when prompted. All the configurable settings have sensible defaults; so you don't really have to bother with this too much. However, you will be asked to enter a password. Please ensure that you use something that is memorable to you and secure. You will need to use 8 characters or more and preferably use some numerical digits as part of the password.

Ensure that you can remember your password as it is needed in order to run the initialization tasks a little later in the setup process.

Once everything has been done, you should receive the following message:

Make sure you save and close whatever important documents you have open before clicking OK. Once your machine has restarted, you will find that you have a whole list of new and exciting options to explore from the Apache2Triad option under All Programs in the Start menu. For example, the following options are made available with the 1.5.3 distribution:

There is quite a lot more than what we really need for our immediate purposes, but just to ensure that everything is going according to plan, click open site root in the Start menu and you should be shown the following web page in your default browser:

This confirms that everything is up and running as expected. Pretty easy so far! One thing to make note of in the previous screenshot is the final link called htdocs. Traditionally in Apache servers, the folder on your file system called htdocs is known as the *root* folder. What this means is that all the web pages and folders for your site must be placed inside htdocs in order for them to be served by Apache. If something is not in htdocs, then it is not possible to browse it!

From this we know that we will have to locate the actual folder called htdocs on the file system in order to know where to put Drupal once we have downloaded it. Assuming you have gone with the default setup, you will find htdocs in the following directory (on Windows machines) along with everything else that was installed and created during setup: c:/apache2triad/.

Before we move on from here, it is worthwhile taking a look at what has been provided as part of the Apache2Triad installation because some of the facilities made available to you could well be most useful as time goes by. You will also find that many hosting packages on live sites offer pretty much the same functionality as you now have on your PC.

Of particular interest and use to us Drupal people is phpMyAdmin, which is a complete database management tool for MySQL. It can make your life a lot easier as you become more advanced and wish to play around with your data. It is entirely likely that you can perform most of the tasks you need by using phpMyAdmin instead of having to learn SQL against the MySQL command-line client.

> If you are struggling to log on to phpMyAdmin or any other part of the site, then try using root as the username and whatever password you set during the setup process.

We now have a platform from which we can begin building the Drupal site. Of course, we still need Drupal.

Obtaining and Installing Drupal

Chapter 1 has already looked over the downloads page on the Drupal site; so there isn't too much to present us with problems at this point. Head on over to http://drupal.org/project/ Drupal+project and click the Drupal version number you wish to download—generally, *the latest stable release* is what you should go for. Click Download to grab the latest copy and save it to your c: drive, or your My Documents folder (or wherever you want).

Now, the Drupal download is different from the Apache2Triad installer in that we will install Drupal ourselves; it doesn't come with its own installer .exe file. Instead we are asked if we would like to Save (or Open) a .tar.gz file. If you find that your PC doesn't recognize .gz files (this is for Windows users), then you need to download a zip program like WinZip (http://www.winzip.com), or preferably an open-source option like 7-zip (http://www.7-zip.org).

Once you are happy that you can open and decompress the downloaded tar.gz file then extract it to the htdocs folder of your Apache installation. If you now take a look, you will see something like this:

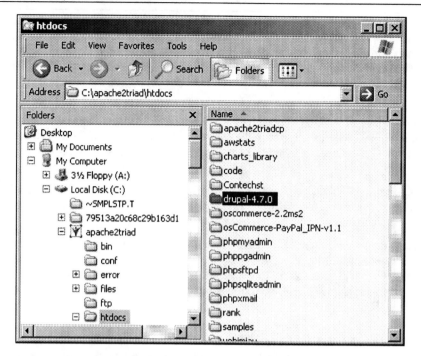

We still need to create a database and populate it with all the necessary tables and structures that Drupal will need in order to function—even though, technically speaking, you could try to browse your Drupal pages because they are now within the htdocs folder. There are a number of ways in which this can be done, but let's stick to the most basic in order to make this section applicable to everyone.

1. Open up a command-line shell. In Windows this can be done by clicking Start, selecting Run and typing in cmd.

2. Type in the following command at the prompt:

   ```
   c:\ mysqladmin -u root -p create drupal
   ```

3. Enter your password when prompted. (This is the one you entered upon setup of Apache2Triad.)

4. Enter the MySQL command-line prompt by using the following command:

   ```
   c:\ mysql -u root -p
   ```

   Once again, enter the same password you have been using until now, when prompted.

5. In order to set a database username and password for Drupal specifically, enter the following command:

   ```
   mysql> GRANT ALL PRIVILEGES ON drupal.* TO nobody@localhost IDENTIFIED BY
   'password';
   ```

6. Remember to substitute values that are relevant to yourself in place of the bolded sections of this command—nobody (your username), and password (your password). After this, you should have a screen that looks something like the following:

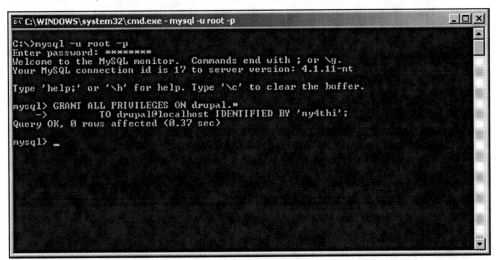

7. Next, type in the following command to ensure these settings take effect immediately:

```
mysql> flush privileges;
```

8. Type quit to exit the MySQL command-line client, and then load the database by typing in:

```
$> mysql -u drupal -p drupal < C:/apache2triad/htdocs/drupal-4.7.0/
database/database.4.1.mysql
```

Remember to enter the correct password you have set for your drupal database user—in this case it is ny4thi as shown in the above screenshot. The bolded sections may change depending on the user you defined in a previous step, and the version of Drupal you have obtained.

At this point all of the database setup for Drupal has been performed and we only have a few configuration tasks to deal with in order to complete the installation process. For those of you who are interested in taking a quick peek at what has happened under the hood during this setup process, open up the MySQL command-line prompt using:

```
$> mysql -udrupal -p drupal
```

Enter your password when prompted, and then type the following at the command line:

```
mysql> show tables;
mysql> select * from <tablename>;
```

The first command will reel off a list of all the tables that are now present in the drupal database. The next command can be used to look at the information in any of the tables given by substituting one of those present for <tablename>. Looking through the results you should be able to see that quite a lot of work has been done to ensure that everything our website needs has been created.

We can now move on to the configuration settings!

Go to your Drupal installation by navigating to `c:\apache2triad\htdocs\`**`drupal-4.7.0\`**`sites\default`—obviously your version number can be different. Open up the `settings.php` file in an editor of your choice and modify the following line that is on or around line 81:

```
$db_url = 'mysql://username:password@localhost/database';
```

For example, the demo site's settings are now:

```
$db_url = 'mysql://drupal:ny4thi@localhost/drupal';
```

because as you know we created a user called `drupal` and gave that user the password `ny4thi`, which allows them access to the `drupal` database that was created using the SQL script provided in the download. The only other setting we need think about at the moment is the base URL that describes the address of your website—it is optional to fill this out; so if you find that there are problems with broken links and so on when you first check out the site, come back to this setting.

Assuming you are not using another server in a network, simply add in the extra folder to the default address and remove the hash (**#**) symbol from the front of the line, as shown here:

```
$base_url = 'http://localhost/drupal-4.7.0';
```

Remember to change the bolded section to the correct Drupal version according to which package you download.

If you have saved your files to some other location, then you will need to make your configuration settings accordingly. Once you are done, save the changes to the file and get ready for the acid test. If everything has gone according to plan, you should be presented with a fresh Drupal website when you navigate to the base URL in your browser, as follows:

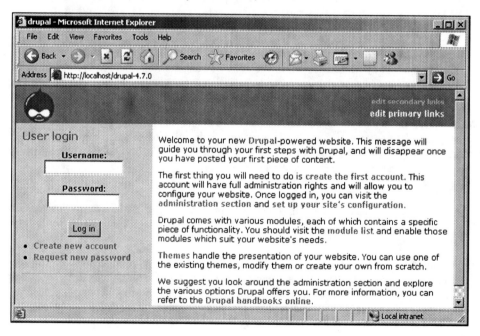

If this is not the screen you get (or something very close to it), then don't worry. There is a troubleshooting section following soon and an entire community, replete with forums to help solve problems. However, if this is what you see, then congratulations, you are now the proud administrator of one default Drupal website. Of course, if you don't feel like typing in drupal-4.7.0 every time you want to access the site, you are free to change the name of this folder.

> Make sure that you make the corresponding change to the $base_url variable in settings.php to reflect any changes to the address otherwise you will end up with a broken site.

Effectively, that is all you need to do in order to install Drupal. Everything else henceforth is configuration and customization. One of the first things we will need to do is set up an administrator's account, and all instructions regarding it are presented on your default web page as shown in the previous screenshot. Before we do take a brief tour of Drupal, setting up the administrator's account in the process, we need to look at a few other issues.

Upgrading Drupal

From time to time it becomes necessary to upgrade your installation of Drupal in order to keep your site up to speed and trouble free. Every now and then, for example, a security issue may be identified and it is important that people upgrade in order to avoid falling prey to malicious hacking. Don't be too alarmed by this. All software, whether proprietary or open source, has weaknesses. Weaknesses are something you are not able to escape. What counts is how they are dealt with once they are found. In the case of Drupal, there is an entire community of people watching for bugs, reporting them, fixing them, and then offering the solutions to all users for free.

So, should it be necessary, it is important you know what to do in order to result in a painless upgrade. As you would expect from Drupal, the process is fairly simple, but before we look at it, I should warn you:

> If you are using a theme other than the default, it is possible that your site may break. It may be best to revert to the default theme before performing an upgrade.

For now, this note should not concern you at all because we have not even talked about themes—it may be handy to remember at a later date though. Let's continue:

1. Make a backup of your current database so that you preserve all the information added by users as well as any configuration changes you have implemented. (Backups are discussed in Chapter 10. Look there quickly if you need to make a backup in the meantime.)

2. Back up the old files, especially those that have important settings like your stylesheet or the configuration file contained in the sites/default/directory. This allows you to re-implement any important settings on the new site.

3. Remove all the old Drupal files from your file system, and assuming you want to run your site from the same location, unpack all the new files into the same folder.

4. Make the necessary changes to the configuration file based on the settings saved in the old one.

5. Log in as the site administrator (this has to be user number 1), then navigate to your Drupal homepage and run the update.php script by accessing it from your browser. For example, the demo site's update page would be http://localhost/drupal-4.7.0/update.php. This will bring up a page of notes as follows:

6. Read through these notes before you click the run the database upgrade script link to ensure that you perform any version-specific tasks that may be required.

7. Click the link to bring up the following page:

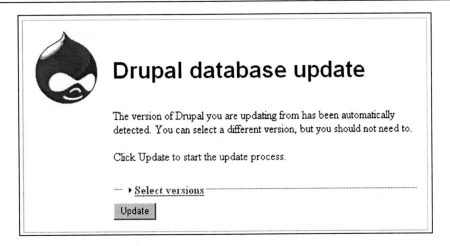

8. Select an update to perform (only if, for some reason, you are not happy with the automatic choice) and then click Update. If everything goes well, you should see a list of updates that were performed, along with the status of those operations; something like this:

Drupal database update

Updates were attempted. If you see no failures below, you may proceed happily to the administration pages. Otherwise, you may need to update your database manually. All errors have been logged.

- main page
- administration pages

The following queries were executed

system module

Update #179

- *No queries*

You are now fully updated and can continue as normal. There is another valuable source of information you should look at, whenever you need to make an upgrade, namely the Drupal site itself: `http://drupal.org/upgrade/`. This page contains useful notes and version-specific issues and instructions that could come in handy.

Troubleshooting Common Problems

In this section, we will take a look at two of the problems most likely to occur during your setup process. We will also take a look at how they manifest themselves and how to solve them quickly. It should be noted that at this early stage there are not many things that can go wrong since the installation routine is fairly well used and most, if not all, of the bugs have been ironed out. This is good news for us because it is likely that any errors are the result of typos or something else quite simple, which should be easy to rectify.

Unfortunately, we can't hope to cover absolutely everything in this section; so we will also outline a brief process that you can use to solve any problem, and not just the ones involved with installation. Having a sound process to follow whenever you encounter problems is immeasurably more valuable that being shown solutions to each and every problem anyway. By the end of this section you should be confident that you can install and upgrade Drupal as well as handle any problems that might arise along the way. So let's begin.

If, instead of the default homepage, you receive a message like this:

then it is likely that you have made a typo in the connection string in the /sites/default/ settings.php file. Recheck this file to ensure that the name and password you supply are correct. If you cannot find the problem, enter your root name and password in the settings.php file to see whether you can log on with that. If that works, then you know that there is a problem with the user and/or their permissions, and not with anything else, so check your GRANT statement in step 5 again, and ensure it matches the settings in the settings.php file.

In the previous screenshot, there was a typo in the username given in the settings.php file that caused Drupal to try to connect to MySQL with the username drupa instead of drupal. Of course, some of you may have gotten past this point only to have been presented with something like this:

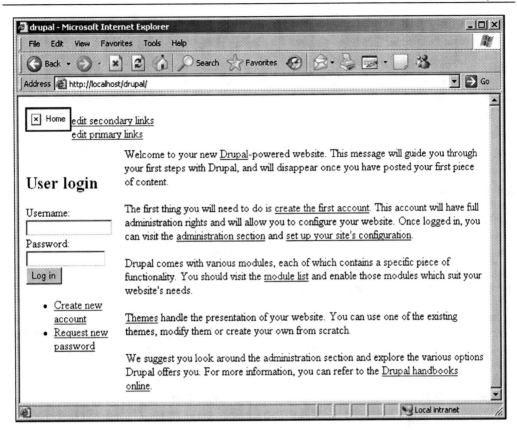

As you can see, we are almost there, but something has definitely gone wrong somewhere along the line as evidenced by the broken link and lack of any formatting and style. The most likely cause of this error is an incorrectly set base URL—this shouldn't be too much of a problem in versions 4.7 and later, as Drupal detects this URL automatically. If, however, you changed the name of the Drupal folder in htdocs to something like drupal instead of the original drupal-4.7.0, then browsing to that address without adjusting the base URL could cause this type of problem.

To solve this, ensure that the address at which you find the page on your browser is the same as that given in the settings.php file minus the trailing slash, as shown here:

```
$base_url = 'http://localhost/drupal-4.7.0';
```

Oh dear, you can see that this is still the old value; so we need to update it to match the address in the previous screenshot as follows:

```
$base_url = 'http://localhost/drupal';
```

Once you have the correct setting in place you will find the site displays itself correctly. *But what if something else has gone wrong?* Well, at this point, the types of problems that can occur are not easily isolated; so it is better that you know *how* to go about solving them. The following list of points highlight the process you should use in order to go about troubleshooting any problems:

1. Scrutinize any error messages you get and attempt to solve the problem yourself.

2. Visit the Drupal forums and search for similar problems.

3. Look through the troubleshooting FAQ at `http://drupal.org/node/199`.

4. View the bug list (`http://drupal.org/project/issues`) to see if your problem is a reported bug.

5. If you can't find bugs, similar posts, or problems, then try posting your queries on the forums and ask someone in the community to give you a hand.

6. To supplement this, get on Google and try using relevant keywords to locate a similar problem, with hopefully a solution presented.

It is highly unlikely you will need to use all six options at this point in time, but at some stage in the future you might find that you require more expertise than is available by searching on the net. If this is ever the case, then don't despair, there are consultants available provided you are willing to part with a fee. For now though, you should be ready to continue with the final few tasks in the setup process, which will be performed in the following section.

A Short Tour of Drupal

Before we move ahead with customization and configuration topics, it is important that we glance over what Drupal actually looks like and ensure it is up and working properly. In order to do this, there are a few PHP settings we need to look at. Once these are taken care of we will have to create the first user who will have control over every aspect of the site. No tour of Drupal would be complete without a discussion of an actual Drupal page, so we will take a look at a sample towards the end of this section once we have finished playing around.

First things first though, let's deal with PHP.

A Couple of Important Settings

I will demonstrate the changes required for the Apache2Triad setup, but if you have gone with anything else (or if you already have everything installed), you might notice slight differences in the way things are laid out. Now, the reason we need to do all this is because we would obviously like any emails that are sent out by Drupal to come from a working email address that we can access, and we need to check that the mail() function, used by Drupal for sending an email, has an SMTP server to work with. As we will end up having to set this somewhere along the line anyway (assuming it's not already set), we may as well do it now.

Open up your php.ini file, which on Windows using Apache2Triad is found in c:\WINDOWS. Search for the lines that read:

```
[mail function]
; For win32 only.
SMTP = localhost
smtp_port = 25

; For win32 only.
sendmail_from = admin@localhost
```

```
; For Unix only.  You may supply arguments as well (default: "sendmail -t -
i").
;sendmail_path =
```

You need to provide PHP with an SMTP server that will work here. If you use Microsoft Outlook on Windows, then you can find which SMTP server you are already using by looking at the servers tab in the Tools | Accounts | Properties menu. As well as this, you will probably want something other than admin@localhost to be set here; so ensure you make these changes accordingly. For the demo site, the following changes were made:

```
[mail function]
; For Win32 only.
SMTP = smtp.dsl.<myserver>.net
smtp_port = 25

; For Win32 only.
sendmail_from = staff@contechst.com

; For Unix only.  You may supply arguments as well (default: "sendmail -t -
i").
;sendmail_path =
```

Obviously, you must have access to a working SMTP server—if you don't have a server to work off, then you can't send emails from your site. This is not a massive problem for the meantime, and certainly, your live site will be able to send mails even if you can't from your development machine.

In order for these settings to take effect you must also remember to restart the Apache server.

You can restart Apache by double-clicking the Apache icon in the process tray (bottom right-hand side of your screen) and selecting Restart in the menu. You can also access the server through the Start menu. Once this is done, you can continue with Drupal as per normal.

Creating an Administrative User

As mentioned on the default Drupal page, you need to click the create the first account link in order to get the ball rolling. This will bring up the registration page, which you can fill in appropriately. Once you click Create new account, Drupal will automatically attempt to send a welcome email (if you receive one, then you know your SMTP setting is working) as well as print out a message as shown here:

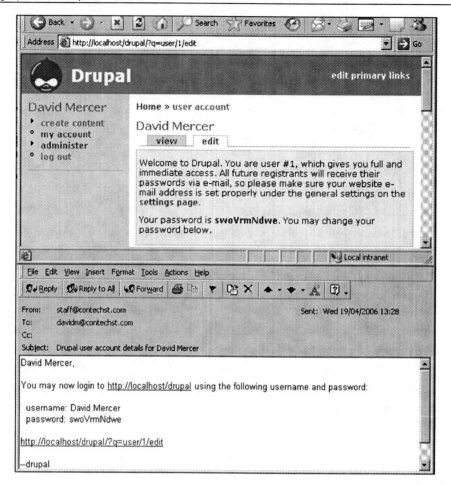

Notice that not only has an email been successfully sent to the address I stipulated in the registration process, but the email comes *from* the address I stipulated in the php.ini file a little earlier.

If you don't have an internet connection, you will still be able to set up your Drupal site but you won't be able to send and receive emails using a third-party STMP server as shown here.

So far so good! The next step is to enter your new password into the website—remember to choose something slightly more memorable than the one that is currently assigned. Once you have done that, simply click Submit at the bottom of the page to continue—you might wish to take a look over some of the other settings that are there and make any quick changes (such as adding a Signature or changing your Time Zone) first.

Using the Administrative Panel

It's time to a have a quick bit of fun before we get to the more serious matter of building our site in the next chapter. Once you are finished with editing your user settings, click the administer link, which is shown in the block on the left-hand side of your page. This will bring up a page like this (with the modules option selected):

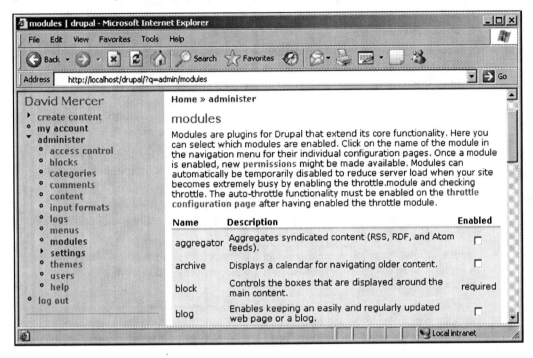

Before we actually play with anything, it is worthwhile listing what each option does, because it can become a bit confusing later on when you get into the thick of things—mainly due to the large number of menu items available, and not because the site is particularly hard to administer. Make special note of the following:

> The sections available under the administer menu item may change depending on the modules you enable, or what contributions you add, or even what permissions users are assigned.

What this means is that you should always ensure you check what new options are available in any given section after you have added and enabled a new module. As you should also be aware that not all users will have the same administer options available to them, you need to check whether they have sufficient powers to complete their intended tasks. We will look at all this in more detail later; so there is no need to get ahead of ourselves at this point.

The following list outlines the core options:

- **access control**: Allows you to set permissions to control what users can do on your site.
- **blocks**: Enabled blocks can be displayed in a variety of places on your site. Blocks can contain all sorts of information such as who's online or the latest forum posts.
- **categories**: Allows administrators to classify and categorize content on the site. Drupal has one of the most sophisticated classification systems in the form of the taxonomy module.
- **comments**: Allows for the administration of comments that are added to the site. Comments are not quite the same as other content types, but are instead *attached* to other content types.
- **content**: Allows for the administration of any and all posts to the site. It provides a variety of filters for cutting down results in order to readily find specific content as well as update options.
- **input formats**: There are a number of different ways in which Drupal can view content from users. This ranges from filtered HTML all the way through to full-blown PHP code.
- **logs**: Enables the recording of a variety of events such as usage information, or warnings, and errors that can then be used during the routine maintenance of a healthy site.
- **menus**: Allows for creation and manipulation of navigational structures. From here it is possible to enable or disable menu items, create new ones, and work with primary links too.
- **modules**: Provide Drupal's functionality (there are many core modules that come with the standard distribution of Drupal, and there are many contributed modules that need to be downloaded and installed) and can be enabled or disabled depending on the requirements of the site.
- **settings**: Provides a convenient page from which to implement the general configuration of the site.
- **themes**: Controls the look and feel of your site. There are a variety of options available by default. Remember that it is also possible to create your own entirely new theme provided you know a bit about PHP, HTML, and CSS.
- **users**: From here you can add, remove, or edit any and all users on your site.
- **help**: Contains links to the Drupal handbook as well as help topics for a variety of modules, followed by a short glossary of important terms.

Let's actually make some modifications to the site to see what we can do. Go ahead and enable the blog module under the modules section of the administer menu item by checking the relevant checkbox under the Enabled heading and click Save configuration. You should notice immediately that there are a few changes to the page that loads up, in the form of blog-related menu items— look for the new my blog link at the top of the menu. Before we see how the actual site is changed, go to blocks (also under administer) and do the same thing there, ensuring you enable a few blocks and select right sidebar under the Placement drop-down list.

Don't worry about what specific changes to make for now. We are simply taking a quick look at how easy it is to do stuff using the administration tool. The following section will look at the effects of some of these changes via a sample Drupal page screenshot.

A Sample Drupal Page

Once you are done making modifications, click create content in the navigation block on the left-hand side and then click blog entry. Once the blog page has been brought up, simply add some content, whatever you want, and click Preview to see how it will turn out, and if you are happy, click Submit. If you now log out, you will be faced with your new default page. Let's take a brief look over it to discuss some of the main features:

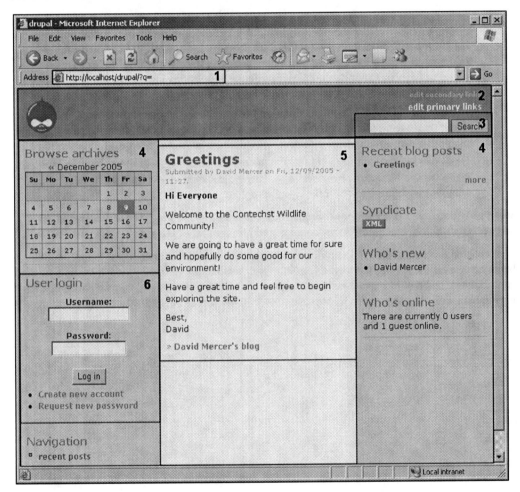

When someone first arrives at your site, as it stands at the moment, they will likely be greeted by something as shown in the previous screenshot. (As you can tell, I have enabled a whole bunch of new modules and set some blocks to display on the right-hand side of the page. As well as this, you can see that I entered a greeting message as my first blog entry, which is dutifully displayed by Drupal on the homepage instead of the initial instructions.) There are several main areas of interest that are highlighted in this screenshot and we should look over them here in order to get a feel for what to expect in the chapters to come:

1. The URL denotes which page is being visited, and can be modified to provide search-engine-friendly formats.

2. The page header contains your site's logo and slogan, among other things. It also provides a link to the homepage and is completely configurable.

3. The search tool allows users to enter search terms in order to locate content within the Drupal site.

4. Left and right sidebars contain blocks, which are effectively containers of information, as well as the navigational links. In this case, pretty much everything has been enabled—which is why there are so many individual blocks down each side of the page. Notice too that we now have blocks on the right-hand side because we set some of them to appear in the right sidebar. Blocks can also appear in other parts of the page, and we will work with these later on anyway.

5. All content in Drupal is contained within nodes such as the one shown here. This doesn't have to be a blog entry—it could be a poll or forum post. Naturally, the method of display is customizable, as we will also see in due course.

6. Users can register and log in to the site to create posts or view content. Permissions and roles can be assigned to users in order to allow them to perform various administrative tasks and so on.

What isn't shown in this screenshot (because the page was just too long) is the footer area. This section can also hold blocks and other content, and like the rest of the site, is fully customizable.

That concludes our short tour of Drupal. In the next chapter, and the chapters that follow, we will begin harnessing the various aspects of Drupal's core functionality (as well as enlist the help of some contributions) and mould it into the site we wish to create. In the meantime, you are encouraged to play around with the site as much as possible in order to get a feel for what you can do.

Summary

In order to provide you with the most efficient method of getting everything done, this chapter covered the installation of PHP, MySQL, and Apache in a package called Apache2Triad. As a result, you now have the foundation from which to build a live site in the coming days and weeks. Having taken the time to set up a working development environment, you can be assured that you have prevented any needless waste of time, and possibly bad publicity, by not working directly on a live site.

Now that you have the facilities provided by Apache, PHP, and MySQL installed on your own machine, you are free to experiment and play with your site as much as you want in order to learn your way around. Of course, installation of the requisite technologies is not the end of the story. We also learned how to obtain and install Drupal itself—hopefully, you found that quite easy!

Following this, we noted that from time to time it is important to upgrade Drupal; so we discussed how to implement an upgrade in order to cover this. No doubt everything went smoothly but you can't always guarantee this, so we took the time to also explore some of the more common problems associated with the installation, and set out a process for solving problems in general.

Finally, we became acquainted with Drupal itself by creating an administrative user and posting some content to the site. We took a bit of time to modify the site quite drastically by enabling a module or two in order to observe the effect it had on the live site. Using this, we then talked about the major elements of an average Drupal page.

If you have gotten this far, then congratulations, you are ready to begin developing your site! Its time to get your hands dirty...

3

Basics I: Site Configuration

The most common trap people fall into when first starting out is that they assume that the *basics* are easy to master, and therefore don't require too much thought. Things are not quite so clean cut in reality because while your site's basic setup is, more often than not, easy to implement, the more subtle problem is knowing *what* you want to implement, and *how* you want to implement it in the first place. Discovering what you need from your site is particularly important for precisely this reason, which is why we discussed it right at the start in Chapter 1.

Does this mean that you should not start working directly on the site unless you know exactly what you want? Not really; like most things, it's a bit of a tradeoff when it comes to starting out with the development of your Drupal website. This is because it is almost impossible to determine exactly what your site will need, and how its functionality should be provided until you have been working with it for some time. Often, you will find yourself modifying the behavior of a site based on feedback from the users.

At any rate, to get the ball rolling, we are going to need to talk about the following Drupal site configuration topics:

- General settings
- Error handling
- Cache and file system settings
- RSS feed settings
- Date settings
- Site maintenance
- String handling

Assuming you have paid close attention to how you want your site to function, and how you visualize it being used, then once your basic settings are complete you should find that the number of changes you have to make down the line are kept to a minimum. Bear in mind though, that changes in Drupal are fairly easy to implement. Don't worry if you have to go back, and change things based on user feedback, or changes to your site in general.

Before We Start

It is sensible to make note of one or two important things before getting our hands dirty. For example, you should make it second nature to check how the changes made to the settings in Drupal affect the site. Learning which setting does what and how it alters the behavior of the site is really the goal of this chapter, and while we won't cover each and every little thing in excruciating detail, you will be shown enough to feel confident about your site's general configuration.

The settings we deal with in this chapter really only affect the site in the broadest sense in that they modify its default behavior—things like what error pages are displayed, or what return email address your site will use. The trickier or more specific settings that apply to a focused area of concern, such as input formats, access rights, or module activation, will be discussed in more detail in the chapters to come.

Having said that, some of the topics we cover here won't apply to you right at this moment. For example, it is unlikely that you will want to work with RSS feeds right off the bat (although you may well want to work with them a little later on). Feel free to skip any sections that are not of immediate value to you, because you can always come back to them when you need to.

Also, some of you might be groaning at the prospect of having to plow through setting after setting in order to get everything just as you want it. Of course, creating a flashy new theme would probably be more exciting, but taking the time to look through and play with all the available settings is an important step towards becoming a competent Drupal administrator. Not only will you learn how to get things done, but also what things *can* in fact be done. Believe me, with software as flexible and powerful as Drupal, there is a surprising amount on offer.

So what are we going to be looking at precisely? If you log in as the administrator, and navigate to administer, and then settings, you should see something like the following page brought up:

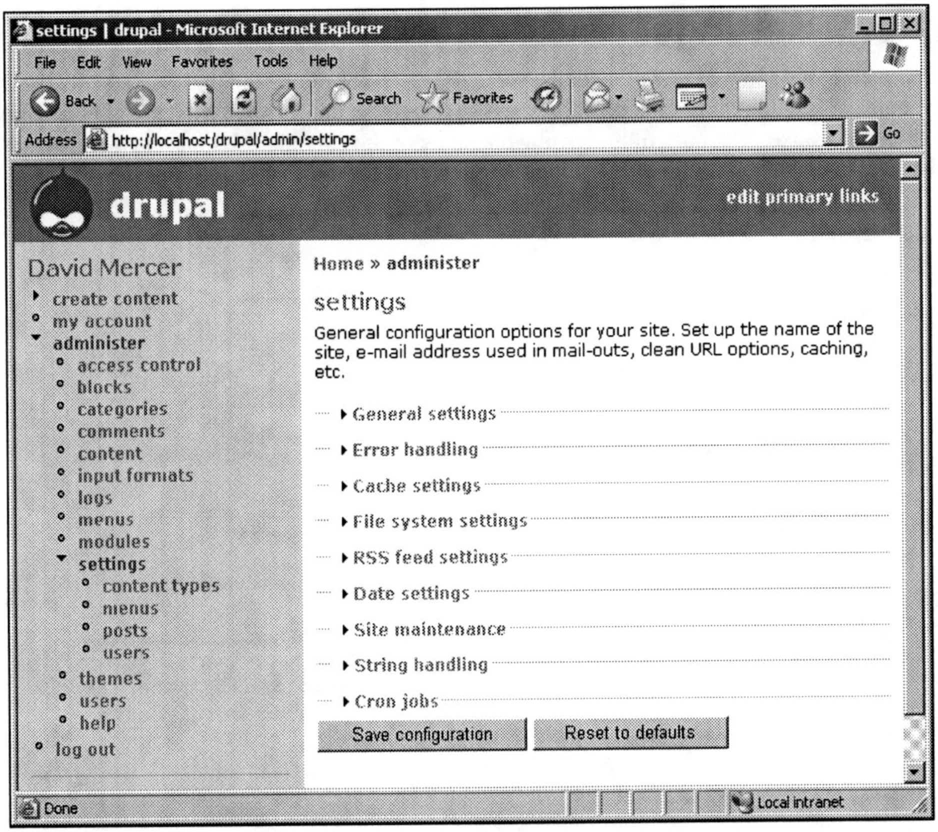

As you can see there are plenty of options to deal with (from the sheer number of links presented on this page), and we will start, throughout this chapter, by working our way down the links provided on the right-hand side of the page. Throughout the course of the book, we will end up covering each and every item under the administer main-menu link.

Some of you may have realized that cron jobs were not mentioned in the introduction as something that is covered in this chapter despite the fact that they are present in the settings page, as shown in the screenshot above. The reason for this is that dealing with cron jobs or scheduled tasks is more of a *site* administration task instead of a specifically Drupal-oriented one. Because of this, everything you need to know about cron jobs is covered in Chapter 10 on *Running Your Website* instead.

Now, it won't always be possible to discuss each setting in order because often Drupal requires us to make settings in several different places in order to effect certain changes. However, this will all seem far less daunting once we have gone through the entire menu, and you are more familiar with how things work.

General Settings

This page contains a mixed bag of settings, some of which are pretty self explanatory while others will require us to think quite carefully about what we need to do. To start with, we are presented with a few text boxes that control things like the name of the site, the mission statement, and so on. For the demo site, the following settings were entered for the first six options:

▼ **General settings**

Name:

| drupal |

The name of this web site.

E-mail address:

| staff@contechst.com |

A valid e-mail address for this website, used by the auto-mailer during registration, new password requests, notifications, etc.

Slogan:

| Live the Wild life! |

The slogan of this website. Some themes display a slogan when available.

Mission:

```
Mission:
To provide a meeting point for concerned citizens of the
world and to focus and galvanize our efforts to bring about
change for the good.
```

Your site's mission statement or focus.

Footer message:

```
So tell your children fairy tales,
as the tears fall on the page,
when we killed what made us human,
to embrace an empty age.
```

This text will be displayed at the bottom of each page. Useful for adding a copyright notice to your pages.

Anonymous user:

| Anonymous |

The name used to indicate anonymous users.

On the face of it, we are pretty much set here. There isn't anything complex about these settings, and it should be fine to move on with the next lot; *or should we check first?* It is important to remember that before we continue it is always wise to use the site to ensure whatever modifications have been made have the desired effect.

After saving the aforementioned changes, the demo site now looks like this:

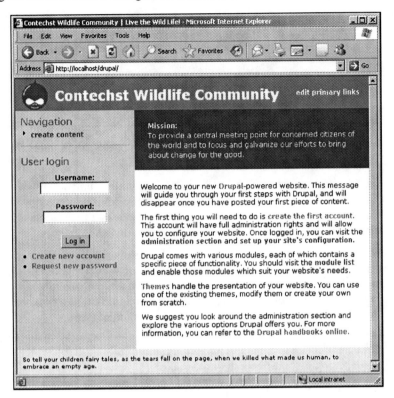

Hmm, this is not ideal! For a start, we seem to be missing our slogan entirely, and the hard hitting poetry we added in the Footer message section isn't being displayed in the format we want it either. *What's going on?* As you can see, things are not always as straightforward as they seem. The reason the slogan is not displayed is because some themes don't display a slogan at all (or simply have the slogan disabled by default), and the reason that the footer has not come out in poetry format is because we haven't told Drupal to format it as such.

Oh dear, it looks like we have already run into problems that, with the information we have at hand, cannot be easily solved. The answer here is to be patient and wait until we have dealt with various other configuration settings and themes in some detail as this will help us to understand how we can modify the actual presentation of the site with a greater level of sophistication.

That's not to say we are entirely without tricks up our sleeve. Bear in mind that Drupal will format HTML (HyperText Markup Language) if you enter it into the text boxes. So, if instead of the original Footer message text, we entered something like this:

```
<p align="center"><i>
So tell your children fairy tales,<br />
as the tears fall on the page,<br />
when we killed what made us human,<br />
to embrace an empty age.
</i></p>
```

The footer message would then appear on the site as follows:

> We suggest you look around the administration section and explore the various options Drupal offers you. For more information, you can refer to the Drupal handbooks online.
>
> *So tell your children fairy tales,*
> *as the tears fall on the page,*
> *when we killed what made us human,*
> *to embrace an empty age.*

This is far more suitable for our purposes since the text is both poetry, and a quote (hence the italics) from a poem called *The Vanishing*.

For some of you, this may present a bit of a problem because you are unfamiliar with HTML. If at this stage you have little to no knowledge of HTML, then you might find it worthwhile teaching yourself a little bit about it before you continue on—if so, jump ahead to the section on *HTML, PHP, and Content Posting* in Chapter 7, for more information on this.

Moving along we see that we also have the option of defining a name for anonymous users. This is fine as it is, but feel free to change this if you have a compelling reason for doing so. The only thing this will do is change the credited name of a posting from Anonymous to whatever you have set (assuming you allow anonymous users to post any content to the site). Let's take a look at the remaining settings in this section before going into an explanation of them:

Anonymous user:

Anonymous

The name used to indicate anonymous users.

Default front page:

node/2

The home page displays content from this relative URL. If you are not using clean URLs, specify the part after "?q=". If unsure, specify "node".

Clean URLs:

○ Disabled

◉ Enabled

This option makes Drupal emit clean URLs (i.e. without ?q= in the URL). You'll need ModRewrite support for this to work. See the .htaccess file in Drupal's top-level directory for more information.

As you can see, we have changed the Default front page to node/2. *But what does changing this setting do?* Well, let's assume that there is a page of content that you would like to be displayed as the default page of your website—before anyone views any of the other content. For example, if you wanted to display some sort of promotional information or an introduction page, you could tell Drupal to display that using this setting. In this case, the second node has been stipulated as the default front page—remember that you have to create the content for this post first, and then determine its ID before you can tell Drupal to use it.

It is probably best that you leave this as is for the moment, until we have discussed how to add content. If you are keen on getting something posted to the site, simply use the create content link at the top of the menu and follow the instructions there. You should be able to get something up and running fairly easily. The important thing about content as it relates to this section, however, is that you need to know the ID of the node you want to specify as the default front page.

This is easy if you bear the following in mind:

> Whenever you edit content, the ID of the node being edited will appear in the URL.

We are not finished yet, because it is possible to specify several options depending on what you require for your front page. In this case, the specific node with identity number 2 has been chosen, but if you prefer your site's blogs to be displayed you could substitute node/2 (in node/ID format) for blog, and a list of the blogs would be shown by default.

A good way to determine exactly how to display the front page you want is to actually browse to the page you want on your site. This could be your blog page, your aggregated news feed (more about feeds later in the book), or whatever. Once you are looking at what you want, take note of the **relative URL path** and simply enter that into the text box provided.

The relative URL path is that part of the page's address that comes after the standard domain, which is shared by the whole site. For example, in this case, setting node/2 works because Drupal maps this relative path to:

```
http://localhost/drupal/node/2
```

The first part of this address, `http://localhost/drupal/` is the **base URL** (recall that you specified this in the previous chapter when configuring Drupal), and everything after that is the relative URL path.

Make sure, however, that everything works properly before moving on. Setting file paths can sometimes be a pain because it is easy to make a mistake and add an erroneous slash here and there—if you're like me, that is.

You can also display content by category by simply entering the correct relative URL path along with the category's ID number—this will require us to learn about how to work with categories before this is of any use, so it is left as an exercise. For the time being the default page of the site now looks like this:

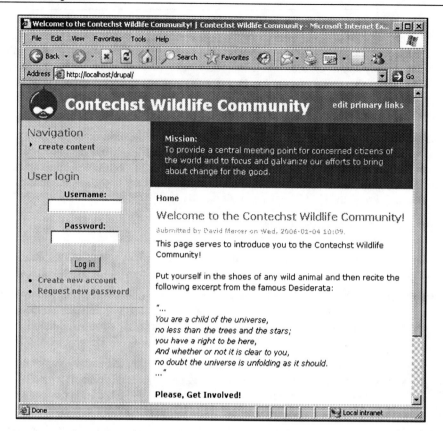

So far so good, *but what did the final setting mean?* Many of you may have noticed that whenever you make a request to Drupal, the URL of the page you are taken to looks something like this:

```
http://localhost/drupal/?q=node/add
```

This is the default form of URLs in Drupal, and it is unfortunate because obviously the ?q= is not very attractive. Worse it may interfere with your site being indexed by search engines. Accordingly, you can remove this from your URLs by enabling the Clean URLs option. In order for this to work you must have the Apache mod_rewrite module enabled (this can be set in the httpd.conf file in your Apache installation). If you have installed Apache2Triad then this should already be the case, but when it comes to deploying your site to your live host you must ensure that they too have it enabled, otherwise you will have to disable Clean URLs.

Error Handling

This section allows you to broadly deal with the problem of errors that may crop up (hopefully not that often). In particular, you may wish to create a couple of customized error pages that will be displayed to your users in the event of a *page not found* or *access denied* problem. Remember that there are already pretty concise pages, which are supplied by default, but should you wish to make any changes, then the process is the same as defining a default page for the site as shown in the previous section. Create the content that will be displayed—an example is shown here for the *page not found* error:

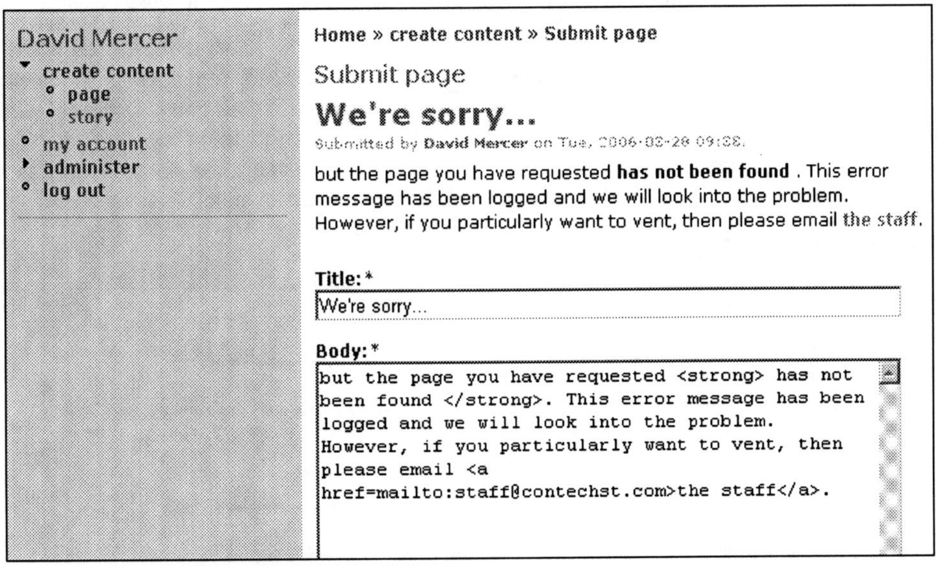

Now, we simply determine the unique ID of this post by clicking Submit, and then looking at the URL displayed in the address bar on the following page—in this case, the ID of the page is 5. Bashing up a similar page for the *access denied* error, and providing Drupal with its ID completes the error page handling. So whenever something goes wrong, the user gets a nice friendly message and the chance to email the staff directly.

Please bear in mind that while we will cover adding, removing, and manipulating content in great detail in Chapters 6 and 7, you might find it useful to know at this stage that you can select the input format whenever you add content by using this drop-down list on the content addition page (useful if you need to do something fairly advanced with your posting):

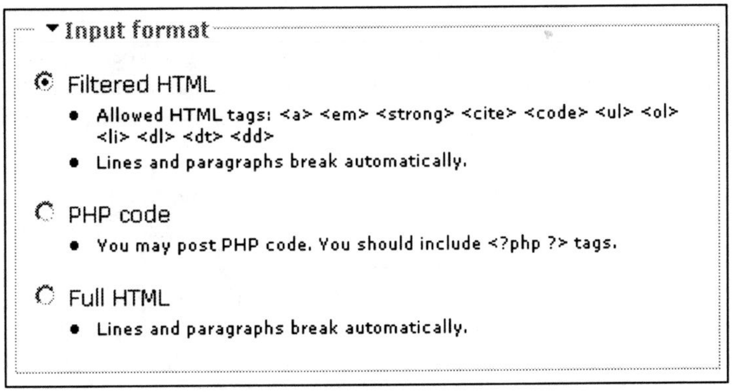

As you can see I have the default option of Filtered HTML that allows me to enter *some HTML code*, and no PHP code. "*Why would they have several options like this*?", you might ask. We will discuss the reasons for this in more detail later on. For now, it is best to stick to Filtered HTML unless you have a specific need to add PHP code, or HTML tags that are otherwise not allowed.

The next option, Error reporting, allows you to decide whether to write errors to the screen as well as to the error log. While you are busy building the site, you will probably find it useful to select Write errors to the log and to the screen, so that you can determine what has gone wrong and when. However, once it is time to go live you should change this to Write errors to the log (seen in the drop-down list), as you don't want everyone to be able to read the system's various errors as this may divulge information to malicious users who might be able to use it in an attack on your site.

The Error handling section now looks something like this:

```
▾ Error handling

Default 403 (access denied) page:
┌─────────────────────────────────────────────┐
│ node/6                                        │
└─────────────────────────────────────────────┘
This page is displayed when the requested document is denied to the current user.
If you are not using clean URLs, specify the part after "?q=". If unsure, specify
nothing.

Default 404 (not found) page:
┌─────────────────────────────────────────────┐
│ node/5                                        │
└─────────────────────────────────────────────┘
This page is displayed when no other content matches the requested document. If
you are not using clean URLs, specify the part after "?q=". If unsure, specify
nothing.

Error reporting:
┌─────────────────────────────────────────────┐
│ Write errors to the log and to the screen ▾  │
└─────────────────────────────────────────────┘
Where Drupal, PHP and SQL errors are logged. On a production server it is
recommended that errors are only written to the error log. On a test server it can be
helpful to write logs to the screen.

Discard log entries older than:
┌───────────┐
│ 1 week ▾  │
└───────────┘
The time log entries should be kept. Older entries will be automatically discarded.
Requires crontab.
```

The final option shown in this screenshot lets you decide how long to keep logged messages. You will probably have to find your way as you go when it comes to making this choice, as it really depends on how busy you are, and how busy the site is. When in doubt, leave it as the default as this is a broadly sensible option.

You will need to use the crontab in order to enforce this setting, and in case mentioning cron jobs at this point has made things as clear as mud, it is important to understand the following:

> Cron jobs (on Windows, these are known as *scheduled tasks*) are simply batches of commands that are run at specific times depending on how often you set them to run. The crontab allows you to stipulate various jobs, and the intervals at which they are to be executed.

As soon as you need to work with the `cron.php` script, which controls all the cron-related tasks on your Drupal site, flip over to the *Cron and Scheduled Tasks* section in Chapter 10.

Once you are happy that you have set your cron jobs appropriately, you can be sure that your automated tasks will be handled by the cron script. That aside, let's take a look and see the new settings from this section in action. For example, I attempted to access a page that did not exist. As expected, the following friendly message appeared:

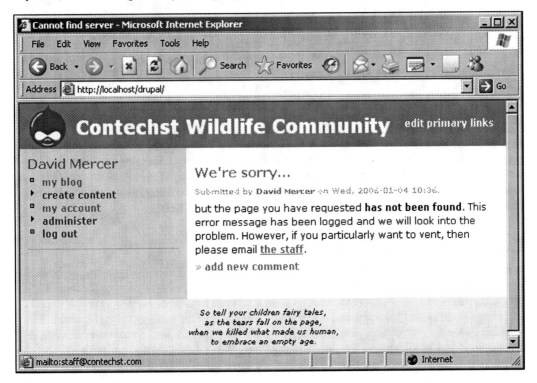

An important point to note is that you should remember to check your logs on a regular basis as part of your overall strategy to ensure that the site continues to run smoothly. Error messages, warnings, and so on, are effectively a window into the operations of the site, and are an indispensable tool.

In order to take a look at your logs, simply click logs under the administer menu item, and you will be presented with a list of *all the events* that have taken place on your site. You can filter these events by selecting an option in the drop-down list under the heading Filter by message type, and then clicking Filter. If you want to look at the details of any error report, simply click the link found under the Message column, and the details of the log report will be displayed, much like this:

Home » administer » logs

details

Type	page not found
Date	Wednesday, January 4, 2006 - 11:07
User	David Mercer
Location	/drupal/
Referrer	
Message	*node/9* not found.
Severity	warning
Hostname	127.0.0.1

That wraps it up for error handling for now. Of course, it is important to realize that this type of error handling does not deal with errors or bugs that may be within the actual source code or file system of your website. In other words, this type of *error handling* is not to be confused with *bugs* within the application, it is simply there to deal with the functioning of the site as it pertains to serving pages. If you come across a bug in your system then you will need to attempt to repair the problem, failing which you can look to the Drupal community for help.

Cache and File System Settings

A cache is a storage place where web pages can be held for quick access by the server, without the need to build them from scratch each time. Obviously, this can speed up a site significantly if it is providing pages that require large data retrievals each time. The problem is that a cached page serves an *old version* of the page, and not the most recent one. This is no problem if you are working with pages which only change once in a while, but if it's important that users are able to see the latest version of a page each time it is requested, then you should not use caching.

So when do we not need caching? For a start, there is no need to use it while you are building your site, because any changes you make while you are setting things up may not display until the cache is flushed—this can lead to no small amount of confusion when you are expecting a change to manifest itself on a page. Accordingly, you should only really enable page caching just before your site is ready to go live in order to test that it works correctly.

The second setting in the Cache settings section, Minimum cache lifetime, determines how long Drupal holds a page in its cache. This is really determined by the nature of your content, and you should be able to work out what is best for your site depending on how quickly the content changes, and how much it is used. If you set the cache to be refreshed every minute, then you can be sure that all content on your site is at most a minute old because the page is refreshed every minute after it is called. A setting of one day means that content might be up to a day old. The longer the cache is held, the better the site's performance, but the more dated the content becomes. Obviously, for registered users or site administrators it is important to be able to view the latest version of each page, so:

Only pages accessed by *anonymous users* are cached!

How you deal with file system settings really depends on what type of content you visualize your site using. It is recommended that you set the Download method to Private straight away, so that you can control file downloads properly from the start. If you know that all files will always be available for anyone to download on your site, then leave it as is.

Assuming you *do* want to make your download method private, then you will need to move the files directory out of the document root so that it is not directly available over the Web. If you do this, you need to enter the *fully-qualified* file path to this folder instead of the *relative* path, because otherwise Drupal will try to find it in the normal place. For example, on the demo site's development machine, the following file path was entered with the Private Download method selected:

```
c:\apache2triad\files
```

As well as this, ensure that the temp directory set is sensible, which in the case of the demo site is c:\apache2triad\temp.

Before we continue though, we should make sure that we can upload a file to the site without any problems. In order to do this, go to the modules section under administer, enable the upload option (found at the bottom of the list of modules), and click Save configuration. Now when you attempt to create content, you are presented with the following File attachments option to go with the actual content:

Once the file has been uploaded, you will see something like the following confirmation message:

67

The new table shown below File attachments in the previous figure has four columns:

- Delete, which gives you the option to delete the attachment from the post
- List, which lists the uploaded file in the attachment
- Description, which is the name of the file
- Size, which is the size of the uploaded file

In this case, the file uploaded is an image and weighs in at 2.45KB. If you are attaching files in order to display them within a page you will need to ensure that they are fairly small. Incidentally, if you do choose to list your attachment, by selecting the List option, then it will appear in the post as shown here:

Attachment	Size
block_back.png	2.45 KB

Users can simply click the link to upload the file. Obviously, if you are attaching the file to your post so that you can display it from within the page, then you probably want to disable the List option. For more information on file attachments head on over to Chapter 7, which deals with *Advanced Content*.

RSS Feed Settings

At some stage in the future you may wish to make use of some of the multitude of RSS feeds available on the Web. When this time comes, you will need to make a few choices about how these will be presented on your website. The options presented in this section allow you to control how many feeds per page you wish to display, and whether you would like to show the title alone, the title plus a teaser, or the entire feed. These options are pretty straightforward and won't affect anything as it stands for the moment.

We will take a closer look at RSS feeds (including a discussion on what they are) when we work with the feed aggregator in Chapter 6.

Date Settings

Everything in this section is fairly straightforward and concerns the date and time values, and formats shown on the site. Select your default time zone according to your local time—for example, the demo site is two hours ahead of GMT.

Following this you can decide whether users should be allowed to set their own time zones according to their location. By default, this is set to Enabled, which is fairly sensible unless you happen to know that the vast majority of your users will be from a fairly small geographic location. For example, if you are running a community site for your local SPCA in Wyoming, then it is unlikely that the site will have members in Kinshasa, and so the Configurable time zones option can be disabled.

Following on from this, there is a set of options pertaining to the format of the date and time displayed on the site, and you should select the ones that agree with the majority of the site's intended users, or alternatively, the site's locality. Nothing too life threatening in there, and you can always make modifications at a later date if a change is necessary.

Site Maintenance

The developers of Drupal should be given a pat on the back for making your life easier than that of most other website administrators by providing you with the site maintenance facility. Before we discuss it though, I should make the following point very clear:

> All major development or changes to your site should be performed on the development machine and thoroughly tested before being implemented or ported to the live site.

There will be times, however, when you simply have to make some changes directly to the live site—even if it is only to implement upgrades that have already been tested out on the development server. If this is the case, then rather than allow users to work on a site under maintenance, you can simply switch the Site status to Off-line, and get on with your work.

You can also add a simple message explaining why the site is currently offline so that when a user attempts to access the site they see something like the following:

Having this facility will make life easy for you in the event that you do have to perform some sort of major work on the site. But be very careful when working on this, because if you log out, then you have just locked yourself out of the site. This is because only user 1 (that is the administrative user) can do anything on the site while it is offline. If you log off and try logging on again, you are no longer the administrative user; you are instead anonymous.

This is not very helpful if you do happen to be the site administrator; so Drupal allows the login page to be accessed as normal. Navigate to `http://localhost/drupal/user`, and you will be able to log in as the administrator and use the site without hindrance. Very important:

> Make certain you do not forget your administrator's password when setting the site's status to Off-line!

Everyone else is locked out until the site's status is returned to Online.

String Handling

At present there is no option for you to consider here, other than educating yourself on the Unicode string handling facilities in place. Drupal makes use of the PHP mbstring extension, which is not enabled by default. Provided you ensure that the live host has this extension enabled, Drupal will faithfully support multi-byte Unicode operations allowing your site to cater to some pretty far out characters in any language you like.

Summary

This chapter has covered a fair amount of ground in terms of setting up the site. We began by looking at some general configuration settings that are important in terms of getting the *nuts and bolts* in working order. Many of these settings will need to be revisited as the site develops, and as you become more adventurous.

However, you have learned some valuable information about where to go, and what's available when you need to deal with the site's overall well-being. From error handling to site maintenance, you should now be able to work with Drupal with some confidence.

It is worthwhile noting that with the standard Drupal configuration, there are also related technologies that are useful to know. In this instance, taking time out to learn a bit of HTML will definitely help to get your content nicely organized, and displayed on the site. Not only will this be of benefit now (and most definitely later on in the development phase), but it is an important tool to have when working with the Web in general.

Of course, if you are feeling up to it, a good understanding of PHP will also help! Take some time to browse over the PHP website at `http://www.php.net` to learn a bit more about the language.

4

Basics II: Adding Functionality

With the general configuration tasks behind us, I am sure you are more than keen to begin working on the layout and functionality for the site. That's not to say we are going to discuss the type of layout that involves themes just yet, because there is plenty of work to be done deciding what goes where before we look at things like fonts, colors, and images. While we aren't working with anything as exciting as new images or flashy graphics, you will find that much of what we cover in this section is a matter of taste, and you can get fairly creative.

So how do we go about building a fully functional website? The answer is to use chunks of free-standing code called modules, which either come as part of the standard Drupal download, or are provided by the good people of the Drupal community. Modules simply sit around waiting till you need them, at which point, Drupal (knowing how to make use of them) calls on all the functionalities provided by the module file(s) in order to fulfill the tasks required of it.

The terms *module* and *functionality*, with respect to Drupal, are synonymous, from the point of view that modules provide functionality. It is possible to add your own functionality directly to your pages too, but that is a slightly different matter, which we will get into later. For now, the discussion of your site's functionality is really a discussion about modules.

Consequently, in this chapter, we are going to take a close look at:

- Adding modules
- Third-party modules
- Configuring modules
- Menus and primary links
- Using modules
- Working with blocks

Be aware that we won't be discussing some of the content-related modules in too much depth, because we will cover the topic of content in great detail on its own, in Chapters 6 and 7. While the focus of this chapter is on getting the basics up and running, we will also look at how to include other modules from the Drupal site in order to demonstrate its power and flexibility. This will also reveal the considerable advantage of having an entire development community at hand to help out.

Adding Modules

It is by enabling certain modules that you will be able to achieve a diverse, and more importantly, functional site. As there are tons of modules available, I can't hope to bore you with the all the ins and outs of every single one. Instead, we will enable and briefly work with each of the ones required for the demo site as these will more than likely be the most popular ones in any case.

If you find that there is a module required by your site, which is not covered here, then don't panic, simply follow the same method of enabling and testing that you will see throughout this chapter, and apply it to the specific module. You will be up and running in no time at all!

Before we begin discussing each individual module, head on over to the modules section under the administer menu item, and decide which you would like to enable initially, based on your site's forecasted needs. Bear in mind that it is very easy to come back at a later stage and add or remove modules—this is part of the beauty and power of a system like Drupal. For the purposes of the demo site, we will need the following modules for the moment (we will need a few more as we continue building the site):

- blog
- forum
- locale
- poll
- search
- upload

Once you have made a selection, click Save configuration, and away you go. Unfortunately, things are not quite as easy as all that, and for at least a few of these modules, we will have to put in some serious thought before we actually implement them on the site. In particular, forum and locale need to be discussed in some depth. Before we do that, let's take a look at what else is available to us, courtesy of the Drupal community.

Third-Party Modules

One of the greatest things about Drupal is that it adheres to the open-source paradigm. This fosters community development, which in turn promotes and increases the diversity of any given project. One of the spin-offs from this is that community members who overcome certain obstacles or create something new and useful can, and often do, take the time to share it with everyone else. This is an exceptionally valuable property of most, if not all, open-source projects.

What this means for us is that we can take a leisurely scroll over a variety of modules that have been made by someone, improved on by someone else, or changed into something else, and pick and choose what we like the most. The converse of this is, of course, that you can make any of your own developments available for everyone else to use when the time comes.

For now, there are certain issues associated with using contributed modules such as the one we are going to incorporate into our site here. It is important to understand that people are providing useful software without enforcing payment. Hopefully, you will take it upon yourself to drop the developers a line every now and then to thank them for any functionality they have spent time and effort on that you may benefit from.

Secondly, because more often then not there is only one developer or a small group of developers, you need to understand that there is no huge budget, with lots of computer geeks tapping away day and night. This means that contributions, like any software, are subject to bugs or errors, and you should always make sure that your site, including the database, are protected by making backups before implementing any changes. (For more information on properly backing up your site, see Chapter 10.) This is in line with best practices when it comes to dealing with software—if something breaks your code, then it is your responsibility, and not the contributor's.

With those two rather serious points out of the way, let's begin.

Downloading Modules

The Drupal website houses a list of contributions that are available for you to add under the Modules tab of the Downloads page (`http://drupal.org/project/modules`). At the top of the Modules page there is a selection of Drupal versions from which you can choose the appropriate one, and then browse the modules by name, category, or date, as shown here:

As we saw in Chapter 1, obtaining the correct version is very important because you cannot assume that a module developed for the 4.6.x family will work with the latest 4.7.x family. In fact, it is probably a bigger issue now than it will be in a year or so, since Drupal has only just reached the 4.7.x family. Unfortunately, the upgrading of contributions is not necessarily done at the same time as the core development; so it may be that there are some modules you can only implement in older versions of Drupal—hopefully by the time you read this, most modules, if not all, will have been made compatible with 4.7.x.

For the purpose of the demo site, one contribution that we will need fairly soon is **Taxonomy Access Control**, which can be found under the Categories section, assuming you are searching by category. Navigate there, click Download, and save the zipped file to your machine. You might find it more expedient to create a directory, say `drupal_downloads`, to save these files to. Of course, once the module is installed you no longer need the zip file. It may be useful to maintain a copy just in case, but if you are certain you won't need it again, remove it once everything is up and running.

That's all there is to downloading modules. Before we move on, it's a good idea to take a look over the list of all modules available to see what you can actually achieve with Drupal. For example, *did you know that you can use Drupal as an e-commerce website, complete with products or services and a shopping cart?* You can implement all types of payment facilities such as PayPal, or credit cards and pretty much anything else that a fully-fledged online store would need—or will be able to once the **E-Commerce** module has been upgraded to work with 4.7.

Learning just what you can easily achieve with Drupal modules now can really cut down the amount of time you spend developing or looking for solutions to problems later on.

Installing Modules

Each module download can be different depending on how it needs to alter the system in order to function. The best way to learn about how to install modules is simply to go ahead and do it. Since we have already downloaded one, let's continue on and install it.

Open up the .gz file that you saved on your machine (refer to the previous section). Depending on the module in question you will have anywhere from one file to tens of files. As many will have license information in them, ensure that you take the time to read over these before you go ahead and use them. Apart from that, the first thing you need to do is open up the readme file as this will, more than likely, have some detailed information on what you can expect from the module, and how it functions.

Assuming you are happy you have the right module for the job, the next file to open up is the install file, usually something like INSTALL.txt. This will give you a list of instructions to follow in order to set things up properly. More often than not, this involves making some sort of adjustment to your database as well as adding the relevant .module file to your modules folder under the Drupal home directory.

Sometimes the developer of the module will add notes to guide your usage of the contribution. For example, in the case of the Taxonomy Access Control module, we are advised not to use it in conjunction with other access-related modules such as **OG** or **node_privacy_by_role**. That doesn't mean you can not—just that you should ensure you know exactly what you are doing before going against *suggestions* like the one provided with this module.

Another bit of advice that might save you a lot of trouble at some stage in the future is to *make a backup of your database*, or any important files, before making use of a module. The reason being is that Drupal is moving to a more user-friendly, plug-n-play type of setup where all that you need to do extract the module file to the modules folder and away you go. The module itself takes care of any changes required to be made to the database automatically. This makes it easier to install it because you no longer have to issue commands like:

```
$ mysql -u<username> -p drupal
<C:\apache2triad\htdocs\drupal\modules\taxonomy_access\taxonomy_access.mysql>
```

in order to get things working. Of course, not all modules work like this, so use the command shown here to execute whatever scripts are necessary for any other modules you install. Remember to change the username, as well as the file path, to reflect the specifics of your system and the module being installed.

With some contributions performing their own database modifications automatically, it is now easier to install a module, but it is also easier to *shoot yourself in the foot*. This is because the changes take place behind the scenes without you having direct control over them. Admittedly, these changes, more often than not, are fairly harmless, but you never know.

To get things moving, we simply extract the contents of the download to the modules folder. Once that is done, there is now a folder called taxonomy_access in the modules directory.

It is good practice to maintain separate folders for each additional contributed module in the `modules` folder. Doing this allows you to keep track of which module files have been added, and which are the core files.

That's pretty much all there is to do behind the scenes, but we still need to ensure that we can make use of this module from the administrator's point of view.

Log in to your site as the administrator and head on over to the modules section under the administer menu item. Scroll down the list of available modules and you should come across your new taxonomy_access module, like so:

taxonomy	Enables the categorization of content.	☑
taxonomy_access	Allows users to specify how each category can be used by various roles.	☑

Enable the module and click Save configuration. That's it, all done!

Naturally, we still need to test out the module and put it to work. It is used in the following chapter however, so we won't discuss it any further here. You should be confident that you can now select, download, and install any module you like. Let's move on and look at how to configure the standard modules that we enabled earlier.

Configuring Modules

Obviously, the nature of the setup for each module can differ wildly from the next. This is because modules can provide pretty much any type of functionality you can imagine, ranging from a simple poll, to a search engine, or whatever. Accordingly, there are a host of different settings associated with each one.

You should also bear in mind that because of the inherent broadness of function associated with modules, the configuration and use of each one can also vary greatly. What this means is that it can be quite confusing at first to find out where to go in order to change settings or simply make use of them.

We will begin with forum and locale, followed by the others, since these two are slightly more complex.

Forum

Before we begin looking at forums, you should ensure that you have enabled both the comment and taxonomy modules since these are required in order for the forum module to function (This will probably be done automatically). Once these are all enabled, you can go along to the forums link under the administer menu item to begin working with it. You will be presented with the following page, which will straight away raise some interesting questions:

```
Home » administer

forums

 list      add container       add forum       configure

This is a list of existing containers and forums that you can
edit. Containers hold forums and, in turn, forums hold
threaded discussions. Both containers and forums can be
placed inside other containers and forums. By planning the
structure of your containers and forums well, you make it
easier for users to find a topic area of interest to them.

                                                  [more help...]

Name                       Operations

There are no existing containers or forums. You may add some
on the add container or add forum pages.
```

"How do I go about organizing my forum(s)?" is probably what you are asking right now. The answer to this really depends on how broad the scope of the discussion topics are going to be, how many people will be using the forums, and the nature of the topics up for discussion. What you are aiming for is an intuitive, logical, easy-to-use structure that will facilitate and encourage discussion by allowing users to easily find information—as opposed to frustrating them with a poor structure that effectively hides topics.

Let's take a look at how to go about organizing the demo site's forum. *Where do we begin?* A good idea is to draw out your structure beforehand so that you can see how everything relates, and make changes before you begin creating or deleting forums. For example, it may seem logical to split up forums depending on location, so that people in the US go straight to the North American forums, and people in Africa go straight to the African forums.

Unfortunately, this has several drawbacks because you would end up with a lot of repeated topics for each continent (since wildlife issues are the same the world over). Even worse, if you were living in the States and were concerned about canned hunting in South Africa, where would you go to discuss this, Africa or North America? It seems that partitioning your forums based on location, in this instance, is probably not a good idea. *So what criteria do we use to categorize our forum content?*

The best way to do it is by issue. People want to discuss issues or topics, and so they naturally look for content based on these criteria. When looked at in this light, the meaning of the add containers tab becomes clear, because now we can organize forum topics based on their common issues.

For example, one of the major areas of concern for wildlife today is the topic of conservation. This in turn has many facets, all of which would no doubt be of interest to the demo site's target audience. The environment is also an issue that should be discussed, and everyone is interested in research these days. These all seem like viable containers because they logically encapsulate the bulk of what people using this site will discuss.

Moving ahead on this line of thought, each of the potential containers has distinct sub-categories that users would intuitively understand as topics for debate—we'll see the actual structure I came up with in a moment. Once you have a nice structure jotted down on paper, it is time to actually implement the forums on the site. Let's set about this by creating the containers first. Click add container to bring up a page that allows you to specify the name of the container, a brief description, the parent, and a weight.

Since you should have already decided on a structure, it is easy to see which container or forum has which parent. The top-level container or forum should obviously leave the parent as <root>. You can set the weight of the container or forum if you would like them to be presented in an order other than alphabetical—the smaller the weight; the closer to the top of the pile it will appear.

Keep adding containers and forums, along with helpful descriptions until you have completed the entire structure. The following screenshot shows how the demo site ended up (There are, no doubt, more topics that could be added or changed, but this suffices for the moment):

Name	Operations
Conservation	edit container
-- Commercial Fishing	edit forum
-- Commercial Hunting	edit forum
-- Initiatives	edit forum
-- Legislation	edit forum
Environment	edit container
-- Human Population Management	edit forum
-- Legislation	edit forum
-- Pollution	edit forum
Research	edit container
-- Enironmental Impact	edit forum
-- Global Warming	edit forum

There are a few things to note here. First of all, there is some overlap in terms of how categories mesh on a conceptual level. For example, Global Warming should logically appear under Environmental Impact, so *why does it have its own forum?* The answer is that you need to think about which issues are likely to be most important. As global warming is a huge issue, it warrants a promotion to its own forum.

Secondly, I have only added a single parent layer of containers, with forums appearing under this. It is possible to add containers within containers and so on, but in the interests of making it easy to find topics, you should try keeping a flat structure instead of creating a deep navigation structure wherever possible. This is because it is easier for people to search a list than to navigate a deep hierarchy.

Finally, there are some configuration options, which you should take a look over before finishing. Most of the defaults are pretty sensible, but you may wish to click the configure tab, and decide on such things as how many posts you want to consider *hot*, or whether to order your posts by date or activity. Once you are done, click Save configuration and your forum is more or less ready to go.

Let's continue with setting up the other modules before we take a look at how to use one of them. In reality you should play around with each and every module, and ensure that it is working to your satisfaction, even though we don't have the space to do so here.

Locale

With locale enabled, you can now click the localization link under administer in order to take a look at what's on offer. Doing so will bring up the following page:

Home » administer

localization

| manage languages | manage strings |

list | add language | import | export

Drupal provides support for the translation of its interface text into different languages. This page provides an overview of the installed languages. You can add a language on the **add language page**, or directly by **importing a translation**. If multiple languages are enabled, registered users will be able to set their preferred language. The site default will be used for anonymous visitors and for users without their own settings.

Drupal interface translations may be added or extended by several courses: by **importing** an existing translation, by **translating everything** from scratch, or by a combination of these approaches.

[more help...]

Code	English name	Enabled	Default	Translated	Operations
en	English	☑	⦿	n/a	

Save configuration

Since there are many European agencies and organizations that deal with conservation and environmental issues, we would like to add, for example, Italian to our website. In order to do this, we simply click add language, select the relevant language from the drop-down language list, and click the Add language button below.

The next step is to actually import the language onto the site so that the translation can be done. In order to achieve this, go and find the relevant language file from the Drupal Translations page at http://drupal.org/project/translations. Search around until you find the relevant file, and then download and unzip the file to your file system. Once that is done, click the import tab and then browse to the .po file from your Drupal page—you should have something like this (depending on the language being imported):

Language file:

C:\Documents and Settings\David Mercer\Desktop\it\it.po   Browse...

A gettext Portable Object (.po) file.

Import into:

| Italian | ▼ |

Choose the language you want to add strings into. If you choose a language which is not yet set up, then it will be added.

Mode:

◉ Strings in the uploaded file replace existing ones, new ones are added

○ Existing strings are kept, only new strings are added

Import

Once you are happy that you have the right language .po file and that you are importing it into the correct language, click Import. From the previous screenshot you can tell that, sensibly enough, we are importing the it.po file (the Italian language file) into the Italian language on our site. Since this is a new import we don't need to worry about replacing any strings in the Mode section. If you were modifying your language translations, then you might consider leaving what you have intact, and only adding new strings by selecting the second option.

When that is done, check the Enabled checkbox on the page that is brought up and click Save configuration. You now have a new language enabled on your site. You can repeat this process for whichever languages are available for download and are required by your users.

The next thing we should discuss briefly is how to manage strings. You might find that an imported language translation doesn't translate everything as you'd like, in which case you need to do it manually. Click the manage strings tab and you will see a search page that you can use to locate the string(s) you would like to change. There is also a list of options to control your search. Once you have found what you are looking for, you can simply edit it accordingly.

Bear in mind that it is possible to create a custom language file, and build up the list of translations for that by using the string management tool under the manage strings tab and manually entering translations—although, this is rather tedious work.

If you get a set of translations fairly complete, or make improvements to a language file, then the community, in general, would certainly appreciate it if you used the export link to share your translation files with everyone. Once you have exported the file in .po format by selecting the language to export and clicking the Export button, you can then set about getting it up on the Drupal site (take a look under the Contribute tab on the Drupal site for more information).

Comments

Since this module is needed by default, along with the forum module, we may as well discuss it here briefly. A comment, as the name implies, allows users to remark about content they find on the site—simple as that. How to figure out who can comment and on what, is the subject of Chapter 5 on *Users, Roles, and Permissions*.

You can find comments under the administer menu item, and clicking this brings up a list of all the comments on your site. The following screenshot shows a typical comments page once a few comments have been added to a particular post:

From this you can see that we have a comprehensive interface for working with comments. There are a few Update options available, and these allow us to delete or unpublish comments. If you never wanted to see a comment again on your site, then Delete the selected comments is the way to go. If you only want to prevent the comment from being displayed, without being removed entirely, then Unpublish the selected comments is the correct update option to use.

Assuming you have decided to unpublish a comment for some reason or other, you will have to look for it under the approval queue tab instead of the main page. The approval queue allows you to search through and edit posts that have landed up here for whatever reason—it may be that you have unpublished them, or it may be that you have decided to force all comments into the approval queue for moderation. However comments land up here, you will find that there are two update options available again, this time you can either delete the comment or publish it.

Clicking on the configure tab, you will find two important categories associated with comments, namely Viewing options and Posting settings. Browse through the available options and make any changes you would like. For example, in the Viewing options section, the Default display mode was changed to Threaded list – collapsed in order to bunch related comments together without displaying the body for each comment. The Default display order was also changed to Date – oldest first so that comments can be viewed as a conversation from the top of the page downwards.

Using these settings, comments on a page now look something like this:

Welcome to the CWC

view   edit

Submitted by **David Mercer** on Tue, 2006-03-28 09:23.

This is an intro to the CWC

» **add new comment**

First comment by David Mercer
     reply to first comment by David Mercer
Second comment by David Mercer

As you can see, earlier comments appear towards the top of the pile, with replies to those comments posted underneath and indented. Of course, this may not be to you liking, and these comments might just as easily been displayed like this:

Welcome to the CWC

view   edit

Submitted by **David Mercer** on Tue, 2006-03-28 09:23.

This is an intro to the CWC

» **add new comment**

Comment viewing options

| Flat list - expanded ▼ | Date - newest first ▼ | 50 comments per page ▼ |

[Save settings]

Select your preferred way to display the comments and click "Save settings" to activate your changes.

Second comment
Submitted by **David Mercer** on Fri, 2006-03-31 07:46.

This is a new comment, and not a reply to the first comment.

⌐ delete | edit | **reply**

reply to first comment
Submitted by **David Mercer** on Fri, 2006-03-31 07:46.

This is a reply to the first comment, so it should be in the same thread.

⌐ delete | edit | **reply**

First comment
Submitted by **David Mercer** on Fri, 2006-03-31 07:45.

This is the body of the first comment...

» delete | edit | **reply**

It shouldn't be too hard to work out what changes were made in order to get the comments looking like this (especially since they are shown in the previous screenshot), so it is left as an exercise for you to do. How you decide to display comments is really up to you, and any decisions made should take into account how comments are used on the site.

The Posting settings section provides a few options on how users actually create their comments. Once again, you should really take into account the type of site you are working on. For example, it might seem sensible to force users to preview their comments, but if you find that you have a bunch of regular community users who post very frequently, then it is going to become tedious for them to continue checking their posts every time.

Assuming you are going to allow anonymous users to post comments, you must decide whether they are to leave contact information with their posts. From the point of view of keeping up the standard of posts to your site, it is probably a good idea to have postings from anonymous viewers sent to the approval queue so that you don't become a victim of spam attacks or cheap advertising. This can be done in the access control section under administer by selecting only the post comments option in the comment module section for anonymous users, as shown here:

| post comments | ☑ | ☑ |
| post comments without approval | ☐ | ☑ |

As with anything, this is a trade-off because you are really giving yourself a lot of work by insisting that all comments from anonymous users are moderated. You might find that in the long run it is better to insist that people who wish to become active community members are registered.

Content Types

Some of you might be frowning at the moment, because *aren't comments content types?* Well, yes, they are, but their configuration is slightly different from the others, so they have been separated out. The three content type modules, which we enabled in the previous section, have similar configuration settings to contend with, so it makes sense to cover them altogether here. If you navigate back to the settings section under administer and then click content types, you will be shown a list of all the available types, like this, depending on what you have enabled:

Home » administer » settings

content types

Type	Operations
blog entry	configure
forum topic	configure
page	configure
poll	configure
story	configure

Clicking configure brings up the relevant configuration page, and since they are all the same we will only look at one in detail here. For interest's sake, we will open up the poll configuration page.

The options on this configuration page are broken up into two sections: the first allowing you to enter some explanatory text and select the minimum number of words required to make the content type valid; the second section, Workflow, is shown here:

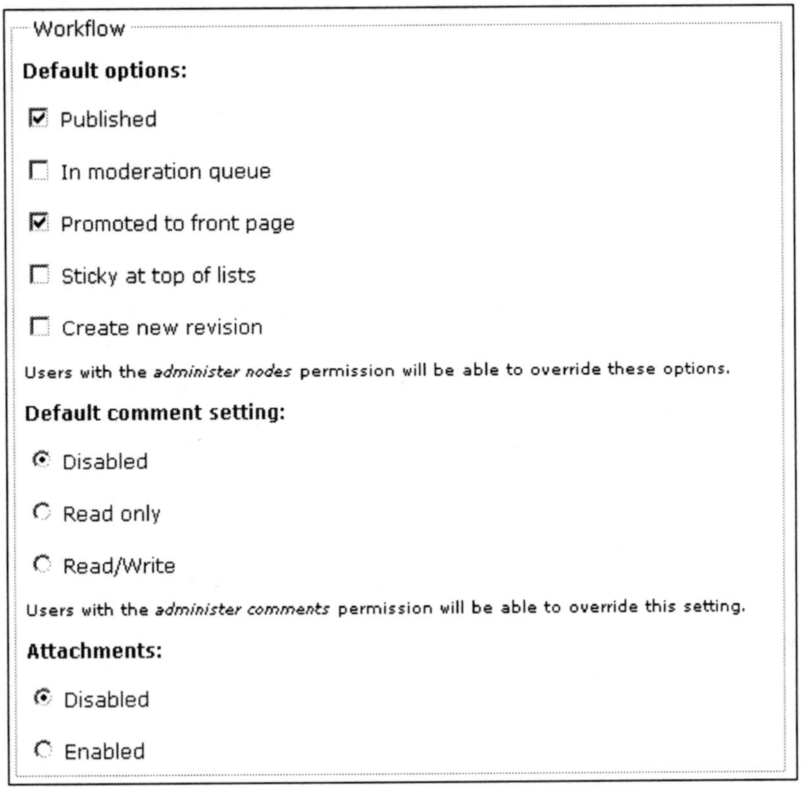

```
Workflow
Default options:
☑ Published
☐ In moderation queue
☑ Promoted to front page
☐ Sticky at top of lists
☐ Create new revision
Users with the administer nodes permission will be able to override these options.
Default comment setting:
⦿ Disabled
○ Read only
○ Read/Write
Users with the administer comments permission will be able to override this setting.
Attachments:
⦿ Disabled
○ Enabled
```

As you can see, comments, as well as attachments, have been disabled because we don't really want feedback on the poll posting itself and we aren't bothered about attaching files to polls—they should simply be straightforward *Q&A* tools. You will need to make choices like this for each and every one of the content types based on how you want the content to be utilized.

You can also decide whether certain content postings should remain at the top of lists as well as deal with a couple of slightly more complex options like Create new revision or In moderation queue— these will be discussed later on in Chapter 6 on *Basic Content*. For now, you might find it better to leave these settings as they and come back to them later once you have all the necessary information.

Search

This is an interesting module to configure because there are some subtle underlying issues, which you should take into consideration when adjusting the settings. For a start, the indexing process that is used to build the search in the database relies on cron (discussed in Chapter 10). You will need to ensure that you have this operating correctly on your live site if you are going to implement a search feature. For more information on cron jobs and the cron.php script provided with Drupal, you can also visit system in the help section under the administer menu item.

It is possible to re-index your site manually by clicking on the Re-index site button at the top of the search page, under the settings menu item. This will cause Drupal to go over the site's content and update its index so that any new content that you specifically wish to be included in any searches will be.

Most of the other settings in this section relate to the performance of the system. For example, as the number of items you choose to index per cron run will also affect the speed of the cron job, you might have to make this setting a little lower if you are running into time-out problems. As well as this, indexing shorter words adds load to your system, because it has to index that many more words in the content.

Finally, it is possible to decide on how to weigh the site search based on three criteria, namely Keyword relevance, Recently posted, and Number of comments. You need to work out which criterion is more important, and which one can be safely downgraded in importance. In the case of the demo site, the following settings were used:

Content ranking

The following numbers control which properties the content search should favor when ordering the results. Higher numbers mean more influence. Zero means the property is ignored.

Factor	Weight
Keyword relevance	5
Recently posted	3
Number of comments	2

The reason for the weightings given here is because we really want searches to hinge on whether there is a strong correlation between the search terms and the content. Effectively, we are saying that just because a posting is new, doesn't make it more worthwhile, and just because a piece of content has been commented on extensively, doesn't make it more relevant. Depending on your criteria, you may choose something completely different—the bottom line is to ensure that the search results are as relevant as possible to the site's users.

Upload

Assuming you are going to allow file uploads to the site, then there are a few settings that are of interest. Click the upload option under settings in administer to bring up the configuration page for uploads. Here you will be able to determine the Maximum resolution for uploaded images, as well as whether to List files by default.

Depending on which version of Drupal you have, it may also be possible to decide what types of files are to be allowed onto the site. Remember that some files can contain harmful or malicious code like spyware, viruses, or Trojans. You probably don't want to run the risk of spreading them around by allowing .exe or other executable files to be made available. Further, you need to think about how much disk space there is available. The last thing you want to do is allow people to upload entire movie files that can take up gigabytes of space at a time; so ensure that the Maximum file size and Total file size per user are kept down to a reasonable limit.

Menus and Primary Links

Before we continue with something new, it is very important to take a look at the site and see whether the changes made so far have the desired effect. Remember: it is of paramount importance that new modifications are always tested out like this. *How do we go about testing out the new modules?* The best way is really to try to use them on the site; so navigate to the homepage and take a look at the site as it stands. At present we have something like this (provided you are logged in as the administrator):

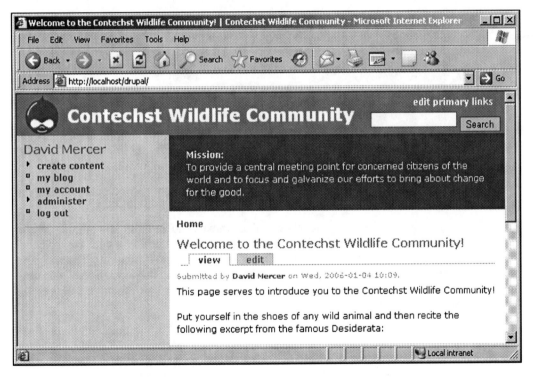

This is certainly not what we would hope for. For a start, there is no immediate way to navigate over to the forums, or even look at a poll. We have enabled these modules and even configured them; *so why aren't they showing up on the site?* The answer lies in the fact that we haven't yet edited our menus or configured the primary links.

You will probably have noticed the primary links link in the top-right corner of your screen already. Go ahead and click it to get the ball rolling. The following screenshot shows a part of the list that is pulled up on the new page:

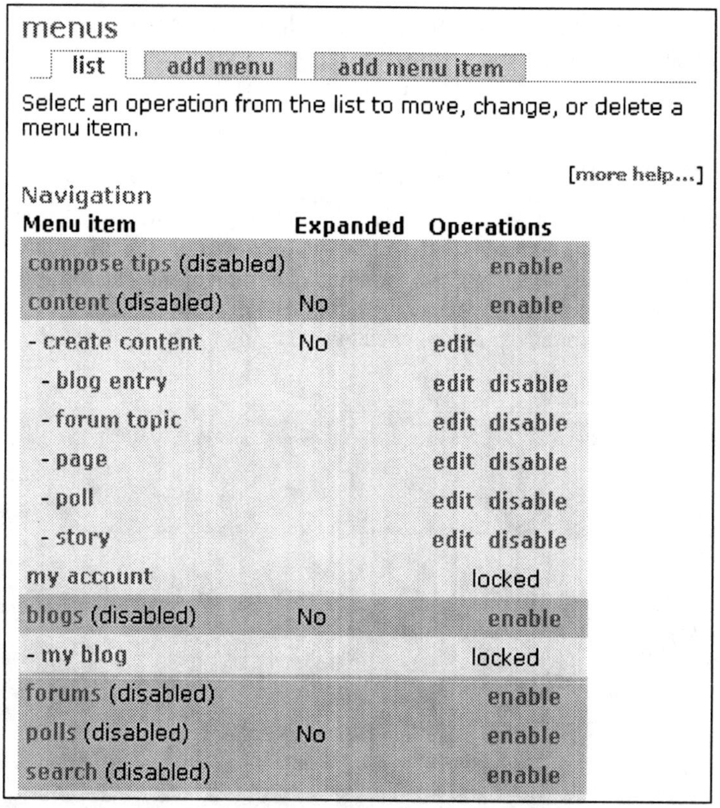

menus

| list | add menu | add menu item |

Select an operation from the list to move, change, or delete a menu item.

[more help...]

Navigation

Menu item	Expanded	Operations
compose tips (disabled)		enable
content (disabled)	No	enable
- create content	No	edit
- blog entry		edit disable
- forum topic		edit disable
- page		edit disable
- poll		edit disable
- story		edit disable
my account		locked
blogs (disabled)	No	enable
- my blog		locked
forums (disabled)		enable
polls (disabled)	No	enable
search (disabled)		enable

The highlighted sections in the screenshot above tell us which menu items are disabled. By default all the new modules that we have enabled, such as forums, blogs, and search are not available in the Menu item list. Let's rectify this by enabling forums (or all of them if you wish). You will notice that you have a few options to contend with for each one before they are enabled. You can make some fairly common-sense decisions regarding these, and the following screenshot shows how the forums menu item has been set up:

Home » administer » menus

edit menu item

Title:*

> forums

The name of the menu.

Description:

> Go to the Forums

The description displayed when hovering over a menu item.

Path:
forum

☑ Expanded

If selected and this menu item has children, the menu will always appear expanded.

Parent item:

> Navigation ▾

Weight:

> 0 ▾

Optional. In the menu, the heavier items will sink and the lighter items will be positioned nearer the top.

[Submit]

Select Parent item carefully, as you may not always want a menu item to be displayed on the top level. For example, there is a Search box present at the top-right of the screen (for now), so you might not want the search menu item to appear alongside the other main menu items as this would be fairly redundant.

The Path option allows you to check that this menu item points to the correct content, allowing you to click on the link below (in this case, forum) to see which page is brought up. This is useful if the menu item has been manually added and you are uncertain as to whether the target URL for the item was correctly entered.

Once you are done, you will find that the items you have enabled are now available in the menu on the left-hand side.

It is possible that you will need to create your own menu at some stage—perhaps to provide a more focused navigable area. In such a case, use the add menu tab on the menus page to enter the name of a new menu, like so:

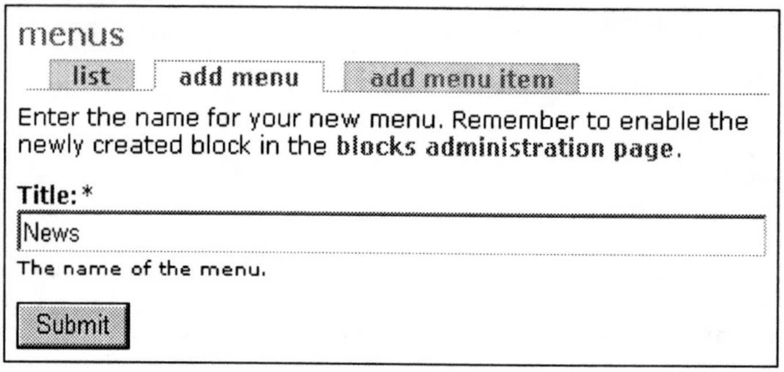

menus

list | add menu | add menu item

Enter the name for your new menu. Remember to enable the
newly created block in the **blocks administration page**.

Title: *

News

The name of the menu.

Submit

After submitting this, it is then easy to add new menu items using the **add menu item** tab:

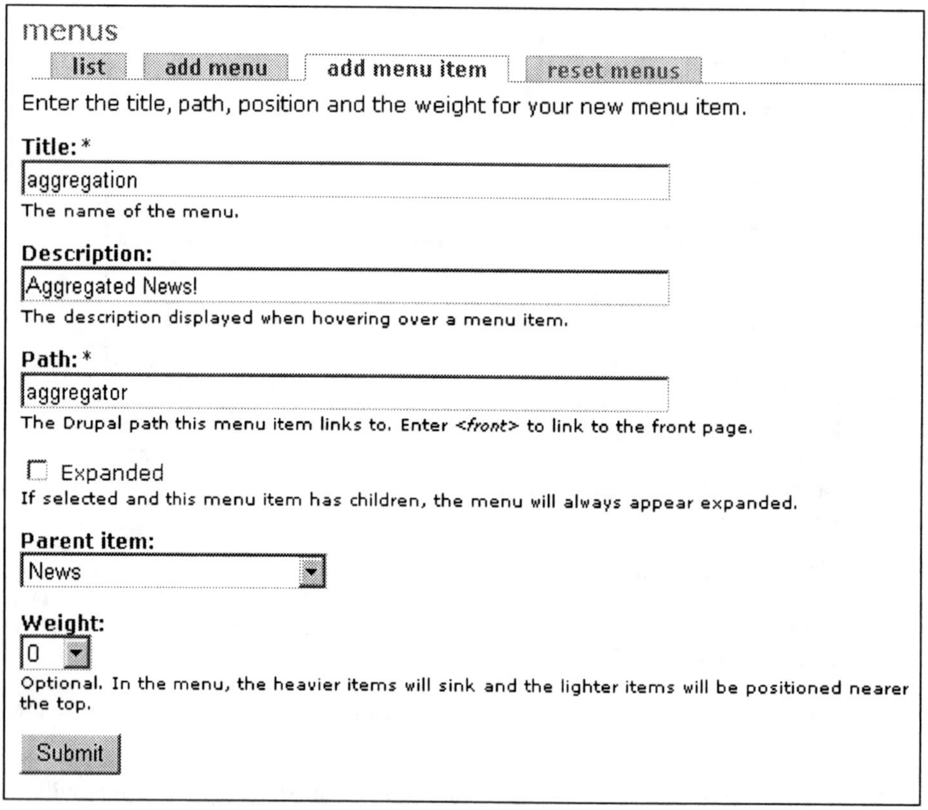

menus

list | add menu | add menu item | reset menus

Enter the title, path, position and the weight for your new menu item.

Title: *

aggregation

The name of the menu.

Description:

Aggregated News!

The description displayed when hovering over a menu item.

Path: *

aggregator

The Drupal path this menu item links to. Enter *<front>* to link to the front page.

☐ Expanded

If selected and this menu item has children, the menu will always appear expanded.

Parent item:

News

Weight:

0

Optional. In the menu, the heavier items will sink and the lighter items will be positioned nearer
the top.

Submit

From the screenshot above, you can see that we are adding a menu item entitled **aggregation** to the
News parent item. The Path we have chosen to link the menu item to is **aggregator**, as this will
display all the aggregated news available on the site (assuming this is set up). If you don't have
aggregator enabled for now, link it to something else—anything will do! Once this is done, you
can view the new menu at the bottom of the menu page:

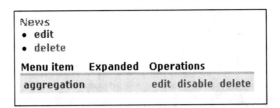

If you would like to have this menu displayed somewhere on your site, then it is a simple matter of enabling it in the blocks section of the main menu under administer. Blocks are discussed in detail later in this chapter under the section entitled *Working with Blocks*, so we won't go any further with this particular topic other than to show you this (the result of adding the News menu, with its aggregator menu item to the left sidebar):

With that out of the way, we need to look at how to configure the primary links, which appear by default at the top right-hand side of each page. We have already clicked on this link in order to bring up the menu section that we used in this section, but we have not yet taken a look at what configuration options we have available for the primary links.

Head on over to the menus link that appears under the settings menu item in the main menu. You will notice that the page is divided into two halves. The first provides a drop-down list for the menu options associated with both primary and secondary links as shown here:

As you can see, the fact that the latest addition to the available menus, News, is present in this list should give you a clue as to how this page is used. In actual fact, we can select whatever menu item we wish to display here. In this case, Navigation is the menu of choice, and after saving these settings, the Navigation menu items are displayed along the top of each page, like this:

create content | my account | my blog | forums | administer | log out

Search

Now, recall that we enabled the forums menu item within the Navigation menu a little earlier in this section, so it appears along with all the other primary links in this menu item. Drupal doesn't stop there, because right below the first drop-down list, we have a second one that can be used to display secondary links.

Selecting Navigation, as shown here:

causes all the secondary links in the given menu item to be displayed. In this case, the administer primary link has a large number of secondary links associated with it; so the header section now looks a bit crowded:

access control | blocks | categories | comments | content | forums | input formats | localization | logs | menus | modules | settings | themes | users | help

create content | my account | my blog | forums | administer | log out

Search

Having the ability to create whatever menus you like and then display them wherever you want is a very powerful tool. There are a multitude of different combinations for you to try out. For example, you might wish to create a content menu that contains a listing of all the different types of content on your site—blogs, forums, stories, polls, and so on. You can then attach this menu to the primary links as a kind of *quick navigation* tool for users. Very powerful and very flexible; I'm sure you'll agree!

Using Modules

So now we have a whole bunch of configured modules just waiting to be used. The content-related modules should be present in the main menu (or at least forums) because we have edited the primary links to allow them to be shown (alternatively, you might have created your own menu to allow navigation of content). We still need to take a quick look at one of the modules here just to prove that everything is in order. One of the more powerful examples of how customizable Drupal is can be demonstrated quite nicely with the locale module, so let's look at that.

Assuming you are a registered user, and the site is configured to allow for localization (by having several languages enabled in the localization page under administer), you could simply log on, click the my account link, and then select the edit tab on that page. Scrolling down, the option to select the interface's language as shown here is now available:

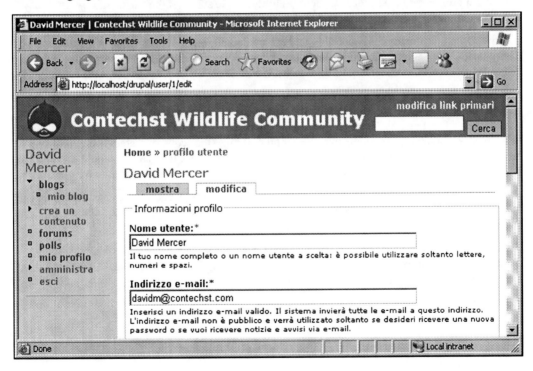

After making a language selection, in this case Italian, click Submit at the bottom of the page, and you will find that, depending on how well the translation has been done, your site is more or less presented in the language of your choice. Now, whenever you log out the site goes back to its default language, in this instance English, but on login the site is re-rendered in Italian, like this:

This is a fairly impressive and powerful feature of Drupal, and hopefully, regardless of whether you need this particular module, you are getting excited about the many possibilities that lie ahead.

It is strongly recommended that you now work with all the modules you have enabled before continuing, and get a feel for what is happening behind the scenes. One question you will ask yourself sooner or later is *How do I go about presenting all my modules on the site?* This is obviously a fairly important question; so we will deal with it right now...

Working with Blocks

As we saw briefly in Chapter 2, blocks contain information or related data that is visible in various places around the site—depending on where you choose to show them. Blocks are often generated by modules, but it is also possible to create them manually. Since many modules generate blocks automatically, it is always wise to pay the blocks section a visit whenever a new module has been enabled, because chances are that you have some new settings to play with.

OK, we know what blocks are, so *what are we discussing in this section?* Well, when we talk about working with blocks, what we are really saying is *"How do we want to present the functionality of the site to the user?"* Naturally, everyone should strive to make a striking and unique site, and layout configuration is a big part of that—especially since it governs how functionality is organized on the site's interface.

Keep in mind at all times that the overriding factors, which govern the way you set things up when it comes to presenting the site, are all about usability. Make sure that the site is intuitive and easy to follow and never sacrifice clarity and ease of use for artistic reasons.

Luckily, Drupal is already fairly sensibly laid out by default, but that doesn't mean that there is not plenty to do. You have an exceptional amount of control over where and how everything is displayed and correspondingly, quite a lot to work on.

For the moment, we are only concerned with *where* functionality is going to be presented on the page. In other words, we are dealing with the part of the interface design that is directly concerned with the site's functionality. For example, a theme would work with such things as color and font, or even background images and layout, among other things (the scope of themes is actually very broad but for the time being it is fine to look at things in this way), whereas we would still need to enable and add blocks to certain parts of the site regardless of what template/theme we were using.

But where do we begin? Well, one of the best ways to find out how you want things done is by looking on the Net and seeing how other people have made sites that work nicely. If there is something you like, see if it can be imitated on your site.

Another way to learn about how you are ultimately going to set out your site is to actually play around and see what works. This section will concentrate on this method and leave the first method for you to research.

Adding Blocks

Under the administer menu item, click blocks to bring up the list of blocks that are available for the site at present. Remember that as you add and change things on your site, this list will change—you will probably have to revisit it more than once. Looking over the blocks page, you will see a list of the available blocks and several options for each one. Drupal gives you the ability to place any of these options pretty much anywhere on the page, but your choices shouldn't be quite so random.

Try to make the site intuitive to use. In order to do this, it is a good idea to group related information into the same places on the site, so that users can get a feel for where they might look for a specific type of content. For the purposes of the demo site, the following settings were made for the time being (remember that as the site develops, it is likely that this will change):

Block	Enabled	Weight	Placement	[more help...] Operations
Left sidebar				
Navigation	☑	0	left sidebar	configure
User login	☑	0	left sidebar	configure
Footer				
Who's online	☑	1	footer	configure
Who's new	☑	2	footer	configure
Right sidebar				
Active forum topics	☑	4	right sidebar	configure
Search form	☑	1	right sidebar	configure
Most recent poll	☑	2	right sidebar	configure
Recent blog posts	☑	3	right sidebar	configure
Disabled				
New forum topics	☐	0	left sidebar	configure
Primary links	☐	0	left sidebar	configure
Recent comments	☐	0	left sidebar	configure
Syndicate	☐	0	left sidebar	configure

There is one interesting point to note about the Weight settings. If you look at the previous screenshot, you will see that the blocks in the right sidebar have weightings of 1 to 4. *What do I do if I want to add two new blocks above these?* Fortunately, the Weight drop-down list (under blocks) has negative numbers that allow you to give weightings of less than 0 so that you don't have to redo all the weightings to insert one above. Accordingly, if you wanted to add two more blocks to the top of the right sidebar, you could give them weights of –1 and 0 without changing anything else.

Moving on, notice that information about *other users*, like Who's new and Who's online, is confined to the footer area of the page in the previous screenshot. This is because obviously the main area of concern for the site is not who is online, but rather content relating to wildlife. This information is therefore assigned to the bottom of the page where people who are interested in taking a look at who's around can take the trouble to check, without it detracting from the main content of the site. It's a good idea to put all information like this at the bottom of your pages.

What else? All content-related issues are grouped into the right-hand sidebar. This means that if people want to quickly take a look at what new content has been added to the site, they can find it by looking here. As well as this, information is structured such that polls appear above all other information (because we generally want to encourage people to take the time to answer a poll), but we have left the search form at the top of the page, because we envisage this to be the most useful tool once the amount of content on the site has become substantial.

Of course, some blocks remain disabled as the site does not need them for now. It is always easy to add or remove blocks at a later date. Provided you make sure there is a nice logical layout for the various blocks, you can chop and change what is and is not displayed as and when required. But try not to *chop and change* too often as this will hurt the usability of the site and may lead to frustration among users once it has gone live.

Taking a look at your homepage once these changes have been saved (by clicking Save blocks), you will see that the various blocks have been inserted into your web pages as you requested. It's easy enough to move things around until you are totally happy with the way the page looks.

Some of you may also have noticed that there is an add block tab at the top of the blocks page. Clicking this brings up a page that can be used to insert your own blocks into your site, as shown here:

Block title:

Quote of the Day!

The title of the block as shown to the user.

Block body:

```php
<?php

$file = "quotes.txt";
$handle = fopen($file, "r");
if (!$handle){
echo "I'm speechless!!";
}else{
$quotes = fread($handle, filesize($file));
$results = explode("\n", $quotes);
fclose($handle);
$choose = (rand(1, sizeof($results)) - 1);
echo "<i>";
print_r($results[$choose]);
echo "</i><br> David Mercer";
}
```

The content of the block as shown to the user.

Block description: *

Display Quotes

A brief description of your block. Used on the block overview page.

In this case, we are adding a little block of PHP code that takes a quote out of a file from the drupal folder in the file system (quotes.txt), breaks it up into an array of lines, picks one at random, and then displays it in a special font. Don't worry about understanding the PHP code for the moment. This is really just here to give you an idea of why you might wish to add a block to the site in future. If you then view the new block on the website you should get something like this (depending on what quotes you have added to your quote.txt file):

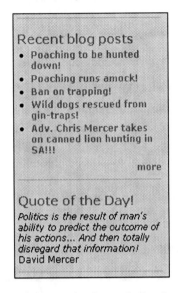

Adding silly quotes is of course something quite fun to do, but hopefully you appreciate how easy it is to include new blocks in your pages. The situation becomes more complex when we start thinking about whether certain people should be allowed to access a block or not, or whether the block should be displayed on all pages or only on selected pages. In order to find out how to deal with these issues, we must look at block configuration in some detail.

Configuring Blocks

Drupal allows us to control when a block is displayed through the configure link at the right-hand side of each block in the list. This configuration page is split up into three sections that deal with:

- Block specific settings
- User specific visibility settings
- Page specific visibility settings

Combining these three sections provides a sophisticated method of controlling when a block is shown, and to whom. Of course, some modules don't require any specific settings of their own; so you might find that you are only required to make specific decisions about users and pages more often than not.

A good example for configuring a block can be shown by the Who's online page. This page allows us to decide how long users can be inactive, before we no longer consider them online, as well as, the maximum number of people to show at any one time. That's easy enough to deal with, and really depends on the needs of the site. The next two options give us something to think about though:

▾ User specific visibility settings

Custom visibility settings:

○ Users cannot control whether or not they see this block.

◉ Show this block by default, but let individual users hide it.

○ Hide this block by default but let individual users show it.

Allow individual users to customize the visibility of this block in their account settings.

▾ Page specific visibility settings

Show block on specific pages:

◉ Show on every page except the listed pages.

○ Show on only the listed pages.

○ Show if the following PHP code returns TRUE (PHP-mode, experts only).

Pages:

```
<front>
```

Enter one page per line as Drupal paths. The '*' character is a wildcard. Example paths are *'blog'* for the blog page and *blog/* * for every personal blog. *<front>* is the front page. If the PHP-mode is chosen, enter PHP code between <?php ?>. Note that executing incorrect PHP-code can break your Drupal site.

As you can see, the settings above allow users to edit their own preference for whether they can see the Who's online block—although, it is visible by default. While you might find that most of your casual users don't really mind, regular users often appreciate being given some control over how they set up their pages.

With these settings in place, users editing their account information are presented with the following checkbox that allows them to enable the block or leave it disabled:

▾ Block configuration

☑ Who's online

Allowing users to make their own choices is one thing, but what if we don't want to display a certain block on a certain page ever? Well, the next section allows us to do exactly this, and if you look at the screenshot before last, you will see that the Show on every page except the listed pages option has been selected and the text <front> has been entered in the Pages text area. This means that whenever someone visits the site, they aren't shown who is online. This information only becomes available once they have logged in or begun using the site by looking over content or adding material.

More advanced users can add some code to determine whether or not the block is displayed. This could be in the form:

```
if (some_condition_is_true){
 return TRUE;
}else{
 return FALSE;
}
```

You will probably find that you only need to come back to this section later on, when there are specific reasons to show or not show information. As always, it is recommended that you play around and attempt to show a module on a certain page but not others. *For example, can you show a block only when someone is using the forums?* The answer is of course to select Show on only the listed pages option, and then enter forum or forum/* into the text area. Make sure this is correct by trying it out on your own machine.

Now you know how to configure a block. It is simply a case of going through each one you have enabled, and making the appropriate decisions about when, where, and to whom they will be displayed.

Summary

With the general configuration tasks out of the way, we knuckled down to the all important topic of adding functionality and organizing it on the site. This is one of the most important tasks you will undertake during the development phase. Selecting and implementing the right functionality is a subtle task, but hopefully you found that Drupal makes it quite easy to implement once you have made up your mind about what goes where.

As well as this, we got a taste of what it's like to have an entire development community to draw from, when we downloaded and installed a contribution module. Contribution modules are an invaluable resource for extending the functionality of a site. This valuable facility comes with the express warning that you need to safeguard the security of your site by making backups before implementing any changes.

Drupal's power and elegance shone through brightly when we talked about how easy it is to customize the site's menu and navigation. Having a powerful tool, combined with the flexibility of the menu system, is an extraordinary help when it comes to creating a well designed and easy-to-use site. Hopefully, the relationship between how menus are created and how they relate to the functionality provided by the modules became clear to you over the course of the latter stages of the chapter.

One of the most important things you hopefully learned from this chapter is that, because Drupal is so flexible and customizable, there are a large number of settings that are held at different places. Keeping track of all of these might seem quite daunting at first, but you will become more familiar with them as you work with Drupal. Eventually, you will be able to find your way around with ease.

For now though, sit back and take a quick break, happy in the knowledge of a task well done. In the following chapter we will begin looking at how to work with users and permissions—another topic crucial for your success as a Drupal administrator.

5
Users, Roles, and Permissions

It's time to look at an entirely different aspect of running a Drupal website. Up until now we have focused on adding and organizing the site's basic functionality. We have not yet given any thought to how this functionality is to be accessed, or by whom. As the site grows, you will most likely feel the need to delegate certain responsibilities to various people. Alternatively, you might organize a team of people to work on specific aspects of the site. Whatever your needs, at some stage you will have to make decisions about who can do what, and the good people at Drupal have made sure that it is possible to do precisely this.

In the same vein as the previous chapter, having Drupal simplify the implementation of your access control policies does not mean that the task is a trivial one. There is still much thought that needs to go on behind the scenes in order to create a sophisticated, and above all, effective policy for controlling access to the site. Because of this, we will spend a bit of time exploring the ramifications of the various choices available, instead of simply listing them. Taking a holistic approach to your access control policy will ensure you don't end up with any nasty surprises down the line.

Since we have now been working with Drupal for a little while we will start spreading our wings a bit and use some slightly more advanced methods provided by contributed modules. Specifically, this chapter will look at the following topics:

- Planning an access policy
- Roles
- Permissions—including the use of the *Taxonomy Access Control* module
- Users
- Access rules

Before we continue, it is worth pointing out that at the moment you are more than likely using the administrative user (user number 1) for all the site's development needs. That is absolutely fine, but once you have finished making any major changes to the site, you should begin using a normal administrative user that has only the permissions required to complete your day-to-day tasks. The next section will highlight the general philosophy behind user access, which should make the reason for this clear.

Planning an Access Policy

When you think about how your site should work, you need to focus in on what will be required of yourself, other community members, or even anonymous users. In other words, *will there be a team of moderators working to ensure that the content of the site conforms to the dictates of good taste and avoids material that is tantamount to hate speech and so on? Will there be subject experts who are allowed to create and maintain their own content? How much will anonymous visitors be allowed to become involved, or will they be forced to merely window shop without being able to contribute?*

Some of you might feel that you want the use of the site to grow organically with the community, and so you want to be extremely flexible in your approach. However, you can take it as given that your site and access policies are already flexible, given how easy it is to make changes in Drupal. This means that no one is exempt from building a proper access control plan to begin with. If you need to change it as time goes by, so be it, but at least there will be a coherent set of roles from the start.

So where do we begin? The first and foremost rule of security that can be applied directly to our situation is to:

> Grant a user permissions sufficient for completing the intended task, and no more!

Our entire approach is going to be governed by this rule. With a bit of thought you should be able to see why this is so important. Obviously, the last thing anyone wants is for an anonymous user to be able to modify the personal blog of a respected industry expert. This means that each type of user should have carefully controlled permissions that effectively block their ability to act outside the scope of their role.

One upshot of this is that you will find it better to create a larger number of specific roles rather than create a generic role or two, and allow everyone to use those catch-all permissions. Drupal gives us fine-grained control over what users can accomplish, and you should make good use of this facility. It may help to think of your access control using the following figure (this does not necessarily represent the actual roles on your site—it's just an example):

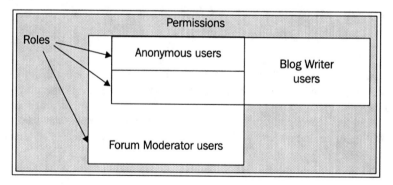

The shaded region represents the total number of permissions available for the site. Contained within this set are the various roles that exist either by default, like the Anonymous users role, or those you create in order to cater for the different types of users the site will require—in this case, the Blog Writer users and Forum Moderator users roles. Each role can then contain any number of users.

From the previous diagram you can see that the Anonymous users have the smallest set of permissions because they have the smallest area of the total diagram. This set of permissions is totally encapsulated by the Forum Moderator users and Blog Writer users—meaning that forum moderators and blog writers can do everything an anonymous user does, and a whole lot more.

Of course, the blog writers have a slightly different remit. While they share some common permissions with the forum administrators, they also have a few of their own. Your permissions as the primary or administrative user encompass the entire set, because there should be nothing that you cannot control.

It is up to you to decide on which roles are best for the site, but before you attempt this it is important to ask: *What are roles and how are they used in the first place?* To answer this, let's take a look at the practical side of things in more detail.

Roles

It may seem a bit odd that we are not beginning our practical look at access control with a discussion on users. After all, it is all about what *users can* and *cannot* do! The problem with immediately talking about users is that the focus of a single user is too narrow, and we can learn far more about controlling access by taking a more broad view using roles. Once we have learned everything there is to know about roles, actually working with users becomes a trivial matter.

A user role, in Drupal, is akin to a character in a play. In a play, an actor must always be true to their character—in other words, there is a defined way to behave and the character never deviates (no matter which actor portrays the character), otherwise the illusion is broken. In the same way, Drupal allows defined roles that determine the behavior of a user. Creating a role in Drupal is very easy! Simply click the access control link under administer and select the roles tab to bring up the following simple interface:

Name	Operations
anonymous user	locked
authenticated user	locked
	Add role

As you can see, we have two roles already defined by default—the anonymous user and the authenticated user. It is not possible to change these, and so the Operations column is permanently set to locked. To begin with, the anonymous user (this is any user who is browsing the site without logging in) has very few permissions set, and you would more than likely want to keep it this way despite the fact that it is possible to give them any and all permissions.

Similarly, the authenticated user, by default, has only a few more permissions than the anonymous user, and it is also sensible to keep these to a minimum. We will see in a little while how to go about deciding who should have which permissions.

In order to add a new role, simply type in a name for the role and click Add role, and you're done! *But what name do you want to add?* That's the question! If you are unsure about what name to use, then it is most likely you haven't clearly defined what purpose you want that role to serve. To see how this is done, let's assume that the *Contechst Wildlife Community* requires a forum moderator who will be a normal user in every way except for the ability to work directly on Conservation forums (to take some of the burden of responsibility off the administrator's hands) to create new topics and to edit the content if necessary.

So, to get the ball rolling, we type in Forum Moderator user and click Add role—actually, you might even want to be more specific and use something like Conservation Forum Moderator user in this case, but you get the general idea. That's it! We have added the role successfully. Now, when you are presented with the roles page you should be able to view the new role, with the option to edit it shown on the right-hand side of the page. You can click edit in order to change the name of the role or delete it completely.

Our work is just beginning, because now we need to grant or deny the various permissions that the Forum Moderator user role will need in order to successfully fulfill its purpose. New roles are not given any permissions at all to begin with—this makes sense if you think about it, because the last thing we want is to create a role only to find that it has the same permissions as the administrative user.

The chances are you will need to add several roles depending on the needs of the site. For the moment, let's move on and take a look at how we flesh out this new role by setting permissions.

Permissions

In order to work with permissions, click the permissions tab on the access control page and you should be presented with a screen much like this (notice the new Forum Moderator user role on the right-hand side of the page):

Permission	anonymous user	authenticated user	Forum Moderator user
block module			
administer blocks	☐	☐	☐
use PHP for block visibility	☐	☐	☐
blog module			
edit own blog	☐	☐	☐
comment module			
access comments	☐	☑	☐

As you can see, this page lists all of the available permissions down the left-hand column and allows you to enable or disable that permission by checking or un-checking boxes in the relevant column. It is easy enough to see that one simply goes down the list selecting those permissions required to be given for each role. What is not so easy is actually determining what should and shouldn't be enabled in the first place.

Notice too that the permissions given in the list on the left-hand side pertain to specific modules. This means that if we change the site's setup by adding or removing modules, then we will also have to change the permissions on this page. What this means is that:

> Most times a module is added, you will need to ensure that the permissions are set as you require them for that module, because by default no permissions are granted.

What else can we learn from the permissions page shown in the previous screenshot? Well, what does each permission precisely mean? There are quite a few verbs that allow for completely different actions. The following lists the more common, generic ones although you might find one or two others crop up every now and then to cater for a specific module:

- administer: gives the user the ability to affect the function of a module. For example, granting administer rights to the locale module means that the user can add or remove languages, manage strings, and even export .po files. This permission should only ever be given to trusted users, and never to anonymous users.

- access: gives the user the ability to make use of a module without being able to affect it in any way. For example, granting access rights to the comment module allows a user to view comments without being able to delete, edit, or reply to them.

- create: gives the user the ability to create content of some sort. For example granting rights to create stories allows users to do so, but does not also give them the ability to edit those stories.

- edit own: gives the user the ability to work with the content *they have created*. For example, granting edit own rights to the *story* module means that the user can modify their own stories at will.

There are also other module-specific permissions available, and it is recommended that you play around and understand any new permission(s) you set—most are pretty self explanatory.

Now, as the permissions given to the default roles are pretty sparse, you will probably want to take a look at what those users can do at the same time as you work on any new roles. More than likely, you will want to allow anonymous users to access much of the site's content, without allowing them to modify it in any way. I'll leave those choices up to you. But how do we go about setting up the required permissions for the Forum Moderator user?

If we look down the list of permissions shown on the Permission page, we see the following forum-related options (at the moment, the Forum Moderator user permissions are those in the outermost column):

forum module			
administer forums	☐	☐	☑
create forum topics	☐	☐	☑
edit own forum topics	☐	☐	☑

Enabling these three options and then testing out what new powers are made available should quickly demonstrate that this is not quite what we want.

If you are wondering how to actually test this out, you will need to register a new user and assign them to the Forum Moderator user role. The following section on *Users* explains how to create new users and administer them properly, so if you are unsure as to how to do this, jump ahead quickly and check that out so that you have a new user to work with.

The following point might make your life a bit easier:

Use two browsers to test out your site! The demo site's development machine has IE and Firefox. Keep one browser for the administrator and the other for anonymous or other users in order to test out changes. This will save you from having to log in and out whenever testing new permissions.

Assuming you are happy to test out the new permissions one way or another, you will find that the forum moderator can access and work with *all of the forums*, and we want to confine this particular user to only the Conservation-related topics. We need something more specific— *perhaps in one of the other modules?*

Looking over the remaining permissions we can see that there is an administer nodes option— let's try that. Disable the administer forums option and enable the administer nodes option for the anonymous user before saving and logging out. You should now find that the Forum Administrator user can edit *any posts* to the forum quite easily by selecting the content link in the main menu. *So, what's the problem?* Well, for a start this user can now also configure all the different types of content on the site, as well as edit any type of content including other people's blogs. This situation is worse than the first one!

Oh dear, despite the fact that we have quite a bit of control over who does what at the moment, there is already an indication that there are some things that are not easily done without help from elsewhere. In order to complete this task we will need to make use of the *Taxonomy Access Control* module that we downloaded and installed in the previous chapter, because the solution to the current problem lies in forcing Drupal to define users who can access and manipulate content based on its category.

Setting Permissions with Taxonomy Access Control

Assuming you have this module enabled, head on over to the access control section under the administer link (you will need to be logged in as the administrator again). You should notice that there is a new tab on this page entitled category permissions. This page *should* contain a list of the available roles and the ability to edit their category permissions. Straight off the bat, however, it probably won't work because you need to enable the module first. If this is the case, the following link should be shown:

They're the boss! Head on over to the taxonomy_access page under settings and enable the module. Now when you view the category permissions page in access control, you will see a list of the available roles, ready for you to work with. Click the Forum Moderator user in this list to see the permissions for any and all types of categorized content (incidentally, don't worry if you are unsure about content taxonomy and categories as yet—all this will be discussed in the following few chapters), like this:

There is a lot to think about here! Now there is a taxonomy access help page at taxonomy_access under help in the administer section, which you should read along with this. Let's take a quick look at all of these options in action as well.

The first three column-options available are View, Update, and Delete. These are fairly self explanatory and allow the user to view, work with, or remove content respectively. The next option, Create, allows users to fix the specified term to a post. List causes the specified term to be displayed on a posting's page, in a category list or even in the breadcrumb navigation. Ensure that you have List enabled if you want that term to actually appear in, on, or around your pages— leaving it disabled could have some unexpected results.

The first three options have three settings to choose from:

- Allow (A): Grants the user the associated permission for any given category
- Ignore (I): Effectively denies the user the associated permission but can be overridden by using other Allow commands
- Deny (D): Denies the user the associated permission for any given category

The second bullet in this list brings us to an important point concerning precedence:

> The Deny directive takes precedence over Allow!

Why is this important? Think about what would happen if at some stage a posting is linked to several categories (this scenario is possible, and we will come across it later in the book). If permissions are set up such that a user has the Allow directive set for a term in one *vocabulary* (vocabulary, and other taxonomy-related terms are all discussed in detail in Chapter 7 on *Advanced Content*), but Deny set for that term in the other, then the Deny directive takes precedence. This is why Ignore is so important because it allows you to effectively deny a permission for a term in one category without affecting others.

> Use Deny only if you are sure that a given role will *never* need access to that term.

The drop-down lists shown at the top of each vocabulary allow you to make generalized statements that influence the entire column. For example, you might want to allow a user to view all the terms in a vocabulary rather than have to change each and every setting manually. If this is the case, simply select Allow all from the drop-down list and away you go. Below the drop-down list is the Default option, which causes any new terms in that column to be automatically endowed with the permission you set here—if you are not sure what you want here, stick to Ignore.

Now, if you attempted to access the forums using your Forum Moderator user with the default permissions set, you will more than likely be disappointed:

Home
No forums defined

This is really to be expected (despite the fact that we know that the forums do exist) because by default the forum moderator has only Ignore directives set. Set your page to look like the following, and ensure that your Forum Moderator user has permission to create forum topics and edit own forum topics (set on the permissions tab of the access control page):

▾ Forums Category	View			Update			Delete			Create	List
Forums	-- ▼			-- ▼			-- ▼			-- ▼	-- ▼
	A	I	D	A	I	D	A	I	D		
Default	○	◉	○	○	◉	○	○	◉	○	☐	☐
Conservation	◉	○	○	◉	○	○	◉	○	○	☑	☑
-Commercial Fishing	◉	○	○	◉	○	○	◉	○	○	☑	☑
-Commercial Hunting	○	◉	○	○	◉	○	○	◉	○	☐	☐
-Initiatives	○	◉	○	○	◉	○	○	◉	○	☐	☐

Clicking Save category permissions captures these settings, and you can now try out the new permissions. Specifically, we need to check whether this user can perform the expected operations. *What are the expected operations?* Given the settings, we want the user to be able to access only the Commercial Fishing forum within the Conservation container. The user should be able to post to this forum as well as edit any posts within this forum (even if they are not the user's own posts).

Looking at the Forums page from the perspective of the forum moderator, we get the following:

Forums

- **Post new forum topic.**

Forum	Topics	Posts	Last post
Conservation			
Commercial Fishing	2	2	1 hour 17 min ago by Dave

This is perfect! The user can only access the one forum as expected, but the real test lies in whether we can edit someone else's posts. In this case, I used my administrator user to post a note to this forum, and accessing it via the Forum Administrator user brings up the following page:

Japan

| view | edit |

Commercial Fishing

Apparently, the government is getting behind whaling so that it enjoys the support of 'all of Japan' instead of a few small interest groups... They are thinking of adding endangered species to their list!

Whaling ›

» add new comment

From this you can see that the List directive that was enabled is working correctly because the taxonomy term Commercial Fishing is displayed. Obviously, the View and Update directives are working fine because we can see the post and can edit it. If you would like to confirm that the Delete directive is working, simply click on edit and check that the option to Delete the post is available at the bottom of the page.

This is great news! Having tested the simplest case of granting permissions on a single forum, you now have to go back and set all the permission that will be needed. In doing so, it is likely that you will come across a few other interesting points. I will cover a couple of them here in detail—ultimately, you need to practice working with taxonomies and permissions to be able to achieve exactly what you want. I suggest waiting until we have covered taxonomies in more detail before diving in, though.

Go back to the category permissions page for the Forum Moderator user, disable all of the Create directives, and save your settings. Now try post a new forum topic using the Forum administrator user. You should be presented with a page like this:

Submit forum topic

Subject: *

Administrator's welcome note..

Body: *

```
Hi everyone,

I just wanted to drop you a line to say that I will be moderating
this forum in the future. I look forward to working with you
all...
```

What's the problem? Submit this message and then go back to the forums to view it. *Do you see the issue?* We have disabled Create, so we are not given the option of specifying which term this post should be associated with. So, because we can only view the Conservation container and the Commercial Fishing forum, the new content is not available to us. *"But we would ultimately allow the forum moderator to "View" all of the forum topics anyway"*, you might counter. This is true, and doing so would certainly make the post accessible, but it wouldn't help the forum moderator to actually post to the forum he or she is in charge of.

This has hopefully demonstrated that choosing your settings is quite a subtle task. Re-enabling the Create directive and attempting the post again brings up the following extra option, which then does the trick:

Subject: *

Administrator's second welcome note...

▼ Categories

Forums: * -Commercial Fishing ▼

Body: *

Hi,

Apologies! I forgot to send my first note to the right forum.
Don't panic, everything is under control...

Now when this content is submitted, it is correctly displayed in the Commercial Fishing forum. We will leave taxonomy permissions there because we have yet to discuss taxonomy in any detail, and you will be able to practice more effectively once we have discussed the ins and outs of taxonomies. Some of you may be wondering, for example, how to post this note to *all* the forums within the forum administrator's remit instead of *one at a time*—tasks like this will be dealt with in Chapter 7.

Once you are happy that you can control the Forum Moderator user, let's try something slightly different. Click the permissions tab of the access control page under administer and ensure that your anonymous user has all the available forum module permissions selected. Save these changes and log out of Drupal. Now, you have already seen what these permissions do; the anonymous user, most likely, will be able to administer all the forums. Sure enough, the main menu shows us the link to go to the forums as well as a link to administer forums. Click on the bottom link, which leads to the administration page for the forums. You should notice something fairly odd, like this:

forums

list | add container | add forum | configure

This is a list of existing containers and forums that you can edit. Containers hold forums and, in turn, forums hold threaded discussions. Both containers and forums can be placed inside other containers and forums. By planning the structure of your containers and forums well, you make it easier for users to find a topic area of interest to them.

[more help...]

Name   **Operations**

There are no existing containers or forums. You may add some on the add container or add forum pages.

Hmm, that's strange because we know there are forums there. Let's try the other forum link in the main menu. This time, following that link simply brings up a blank page. That's very odd, we have full administrative permissions on the forums, yet Drupal is acting like they don't exist. *Can you figure out why?*

As the administrator, remove the forum module permissions for the anonymous user in the access control section and save the settings. Now, click on the category permissions tab and then select the edit link for the anonymous user. You will be presented with the same untouched settings page that we initially saw for the Forum Moderator user. The answer should now be apparent. As the anonymous user has no permissions set here, we were effectively giving Drupal conflicting instructions by saying that this user is a forum administrator who is not allowed to access anything related to the taxonomy terms within the forums.

In our case, we would like anonymous users to be able to view all the content in the forums (although, if there were any topics you wanted to hide you could simply leave them unchecked) so we choose Select all from the List drop-down and Allow all in the View column drop-down and save the settings. Take a look at the results as the anonymous user. You should find that it is possible to view all the forums as expected, but you are required to login in order to post anything.

This has exemplified the need to thoroughly test your site regularly so that unforeseen changes don't have disastrous effects. You may have asked yourself at some stage during the discussion on permissions: *Can one user belong to several roles?* The follow-up question to this is of course *What permissions does a user who belongs to more than one role receive?* In order to answer these very important questions, let us take a look at the next topic in our discussion.

Users

A single user account can be given as many or as few permissions as you like via the use of roles. Drupal users are not really anything unless they already have a role that defines the manner in which they can operate within the Drupal framework. Hence, we discussed roles first.

Users can be created in two ways. The most common way is by registering on the site—if you haven't already, go ahead and register a new user on your site by clicking the Create new account link on the homepage just to test things out for yourself. Remember to supply a valid email address otherwise you won't be able to sign in properly. This will create an authenticated user, with any and all permissions that have been assigned to the authenticated user role.

The second way is to use your administrative user to create a new user. In order to do this, log on as the administrative user and click on users under administer. Select the add user tab and follow the instructions on that page—you will need to supply Drupal with usernames, email addresses, and passwords. Once you have a couple of users to play around with, it's time to begin working with them.

Administering Users

As the site's administrator, you are given complete access to the other users' account information. By clicking on the edit link shown to the right of each user account (under the Operations column heading) in the users page under administer, you can make any changes you require to a given user.

Now, we have already looked over this page briefly when we initially set up our administrative user in Chapter 2, but it is worth looking over it in slightly more depth now as it has an important setting that was not there the first time round. If you scroll down the page a bit, you will notice that you now have the option to stipulate which roles this user belongs to. At present the demo site's Roles section looks like this:

Roles:

☑ Forum Moderator user

The user receives the combined permissions of the *authenticated user* role, and all roles selected here.

Reading the lines below the checkboxes in this screenshot, you can see that whenever you add a user to another role, the user obtains the combined permissions of these roles. So, that answers the questions we had in the earlier section on *Permissions. But what's all the fuss about?* By knowing this, you should go about delegating roles in the following fashion:

1. Define the most basic user of the site by setting the anonymous user permissions.
2. Set permissions for a basic authenticated user—most likely for people who have registered on your site.
3. Create special roles by only adding the *specific additional permissions* that are required by that role, and no more. Don't re-assign permissions that the authenticated user already has.
4. Create new users by combining whatever roles are required for their duties or needs.

If you follow the steps above, you will be sure to always give the correct permissions to each role. This is because you are building up a user's permissions from the most basic to the most complex without having to assign every single permission each time. It should be obvious that a forum moderator would have all the permissions of an anonymous and authenticated user plus a few more. So, if you look back to the first diagram in the chapter you can see that, in this case, we would:

1. Define the anonymous user and authenticated user role permissions—an authenticated user should have all the permissions of an anonymous user, plus whatever else is needed by your basic site user.
2. Create new roles with only the additional permissions needed for both the Forum Moderator user and Blog Writer user other than those given to the authenticated user
3. Assign blog writers to the Blog Writer user role (they are automatically given the permissions granted to an authenticated user), and do the same for forum moderators and their role.

Other than using that strategy for assigning roles to users, the information in this section is pretty easy to intuit; so let's move on.

Configuring Users

This section really discusses how the site treats users rather than discussing what users can and cannot do. However, you will find that some of the information in this section is important for the look and feel of the site. Click on settings under the administer link and then click users. You will be provided with set of options beginning with user registration settings as follows:

User registration settings

Public registrations:

○ Only site administrators can create new user accounts.

◉ Visitors can create accounts and no administrator approval is required.

○ Visitors can create accounts but administrator approval is required.

User registration guidelines:

```
Please submit the following information in order to
register as a user for this site. You will then be sent an
email to confirm you address and following that you will be
able to access more content and become involved in the
community.
```

This text is displayed at the top of the user registration form. It's useful for helping or instructing your users.

You might want to consider which of the first three options to select quite carefully depending on how you envisage the site functioning. For example, you might wish to allow everyone to read and post comments to the forums, or do whatever, without needing to register first. If this is the case, then it is likely that the only people who would need to register are going to be performing some sort of administrative duties, in which case you would probably want to select the first option, or at least the third option.

For the demo site's sake, the second option is fine as we would like to make it easy for as many people as possible to become involved in the community without allowing absolutely everyone to post content and potentially cause problems. A helpful message is also added to explain the registration process to potential users.

The next section on this page deals with the process of user email customization. There is an interesting facet to this however, in that Drupal makes certain variables available for use within the static text that is entered. Let's take a look at how to modify a line or so in order to get the feel for how this works.

By way of example, we will change the Subject of welcome e-mail text from:

Account details for %username at %site

to a slightly sprightlier:

Congratulations %username, you have registered with the %site on %date!

Nothing too complicated here! The keywords preceded by the % sign are simply placeholders for other values, which are inserted into your email according to how they are set at that particular time. This gives you the ability to personalize your correspondence. In this case, the subject of the welcome email for a user registered as David is now displayed as follows:

```
┌─────────────────────────────────────────────────────────────────────────────┐
│ ✉ Congratulations David, you have registered with Contechst Wildlife Community on Thu, 20... _ □ X │
├─────────────────────────────────────────────────────────────────────────────┤
│  File  Edit  View  Insert  Format  Tools  Actions  Help                       │
├─────────────────────────────────────────────────────────────────────────────┤
│  ℞ Reply   ℞ Reply to All  ℞ Forward  🖨 🖺  ▼  🖳 ✕  ▲ · ▼ · A  🔲 .          │
├─────────────────────────────────────────────────────────────────────────────┤
│  From:    staff@contechst.com                        Sent:  Thu 12/01/2006 11:45 │
│  To:      edit@contechst.com                                                  │
│  Cc:                                                                          │
│  Subject: Congratulations David, you have registered with the Contechst Wildlife Community on Thu, 2006-01-12 11:45! │
├─────────────────────────────────────────────────────────────────────────────┤
│ David,                                                                      ▲ │
│                                                                              │
│ Thank you for registering at Contechst Wildlife Community. You may now log in to │
│ http://localhost/drupal/user using the following username and password:     ▼ │
└─────────────────────────────────────────────────────────────────────────────┘
```

As you can see, the %username, %site, and %date placeholders have been correctly changed to reflect the contents of the variables for that particular setup. There are settings available for several standard emails such as password recovery and welcome (awaiting admin approval). The defaults are of course fairly sensible and easy to change should you need to. Remember the placeholders that are available for each piece of text are mentioned below the text area so play around with them until you are comfortable with their usage.

The final section deals with Pictures. Now, if you wish to enable Picture support for users, then select Enabled from the list, provide a default picture if you want one, and click Save configuration (the other settings are fairly self explanatory and sensible, and you can come back at any stage to change them if they are not suitable for you).

Drupal will set up a `pictures` folder to hold all of the pictures within the `files` folder in your Drupal installation. Once everything is done, users will have a new section added to the edit tab of their my account page, like so:

```
┌─ Picture ──────────────────────────────────────────────────────────────────┐
│                                                                             │
│  Upload picture:                                                            │
│  ┌────────────────────────────────────────────────────┐ ┌──────────┐        │
│  │ C:\Documents and Settings\David Mercer\Desktop\use │ │ Browse...│        │
│  └────────────────────────────────────────────────────┘ └──────────┘        │
│  Your virtual face or picture. Maximum dimensions are 85x85 and the maximum size is 30 │
│  kB.                                                                         │
│                                                                             │
└─────────────────────────────────────────────────────────────────────────────┘
```

When the picture has been successfully uploaded, it will appear on the my account page, and with the user's blog and forum posts on the site.

If the image does not appear and you end up seeing a link, something like this:

```
┌─────────────────────┐
│   Dave's picture    │
└─────────────────────┘
```

then you will need to ensure that you set the correct upload module permissions on the access control page, as follows:

upload module			
upload files	☐	☐	☐
view uploaded files	☑	☑	☐

Remember that since the Forum Administrator user automatically receives all the permissions of the authenticated user, it is not necessary to enable the view uploaded files permission for the Forum Administrator as this would be redundant and would make the purpose of your user less clear.

Allowing users to incorporate pictures into a site is a good way for people to be able to personalize their contributions, and also gives everyone something visual to associate posts with. This is a great way to foster a community, as it helps give different users an identity of sorts.

Editing the picture is easy! Simply modify it in the Picture section of the user's edit page as shown here:

That is pretty much the end of the line for configuring users. There are still a few more things we need to discuss with regards to security before we can move on though.

Access Rules

So far it should seem like Drupal has things more or less covered when it comes to ensuring that it is possible to control who does what on the site. This is certainly the case, but there are a few more situations that we have not yet discussed, and may well end up affecting the site at some stage. For example, *what happens if you find that there is a company that repeatedly spams your forums with advertisements and marketing information?* Or, *what happens if you want only people from a certain company to access your site?*

Problems of this nature can really be a thorn in your side. Access problems can even end up driving community members away—unless you have the ability to set access rules.

There are some techniques that can be used to set access rules via the access rules tab on the access control page under the administer main menu item. To implement any access rules you will need to select the add rule option, which brings up the following page:

access control

permissions | category permissions | roles | access rules

list | add rule | check rules

Set up username and e-mail address access rules for new *and* existing accounts (currently logged in accounts will not be logged out). If a username or e-mail address for an account matches any deny rule, but not an allow rule, then the account will not be allowed to be created or to log in. A host rule is effective for every page view, not just registrations.

Access type:

○ Allow

◉ Deny

Rule type:

○ Username

◉ E-mail

○ Host

Mask: *

bad_user@contechst.com

%: Matches any number of characters, even zero characters.
_: Matches exactly one character.

Add rule

From this you can see that I am in the process of making a rule that denies access based on an email address. Before we continue on this line, it is important to note that there are both Allow and Deny options available, and these will act based on a supplied Username, E-mail, or Host address given in the Rule type section. The final option, Mask, allows you to specify the actual name of the user or host to which the rule will apply.

In the above case, the email address bad_user@contechst.com will have a deny rule created after Add rule has been clicked.

Go ahead and create a rule like this one, and once you are done you will see that the rule now appears under the list tab. Now that there is a deny rule in place, *how do we go about using it?* The answer is that it is already being used. If someone tries to register with the email address supplied in the rule, they will be denied access. As it stands, this is probably not very helpful, because it is unlikely you will know ahead of time what specific email addresses to block.

In order to cater for the times when you aren't entirely sure of the specific address, there are two wildcard characters provided that can serve as generic strings or characters. Let's say that you wanted to ban someone who runs a small spamming business. Simply blocking their current email address is not really sufficient, because they can simply create another address and use that one to register with Drupal. If you know that the addresses come from one location, such as:

```
<some characters>@irritating_spammer.com
```

You could use the % character to match whatever characters are present before the @ sign, effectively stopping anyone from that email server from registering, like so:

```
%@irritating_spammer.com
```

If you have a Hotmail account, or something similar, try blocking any address that ends in @hotmail.com and then attempt to register an account on the site. You should find that Drupal presents you with the following message:

A new problem rears its ugly head when it so happens that you don't want to allow Hotmail addresses on the site with the exception of a close personal friend who is traveling around the world and can only access a Hotmail address. In this case, you need to set an Allow rule as well. If it so happens that the email address of the person is good_friend@hotmail.com, then you could set the allow rule by selecting the appropriate options to cater for this on the add rule page.

Your rules would then look something like this:

Access type▲	Rule type	Mask	Operations	
deny	e-mail	bad_user@contechst.com	edit	delete
deny	e-mail	%@hotmail.com	edit	delete
allow	e-mail	good_friend@hotmail.com	edit	delete

What this does is ban all Hotmail addresses on the site. However, because *an allow rule takes precedence over a deny rule*, the one and only Hotmail address specified in the single allow rule shown in the screenshot will work fine. Now when your good friend attempts to register, everything will go swimmingly well.

After some time, you might find that the set of rules that are in place can become slightly confusing, or alternatively, it is simply not feasible to continue attempting to register new names all the time to ensure that they work according to plan. In this case, use the check rules tab on the right-hand side of the access rules page. This allows names of users, email addresses, and hosts to be entered in order to check whether they have access or not. Simply compare these results with your expectations to determine if everything is working as planned.

One final thing to bear in mind is that if you deny access using the host criteria, then this will be enforced throughout the site and not just on the registration pages. For the case of the spammer, you would probably want to deny access to the site in general; so you would select the host option with something like this for the Mask:

```
%irritating_spammer%
```

This would then match to any host with `irritating_spammer` in it. For example:

```
www.really_irritating_spammer.com
www.mildly_irritating_spammer.com
www.extremelyirritating_spammer.org
www.unbelievably_irritating_spammer.comms.org.co.sz
```

and so on. Remember to check that all the rules you add have the desired affect on the site's access policy. It would be a shame to make a rule that prevented potentially valuable community members from accessing content, causing them to go elsewhere.

I would be remiss if I didn't mention, before finishing off, that there are a number of other user access/authentication-related modules available on the Drupal website. It is probably worthwhile to check these out at `http://drupal.org/project/Modules/category/74` in case there is something you find that is particularly suited to your needs.

Of special interest are the *node privacy byrole* and *Path Access* modules, which provide an alternative method of controlling access to content. Having seen how the *Taxonomy Access* module worked, you should feel confident enough to work with any of these contributions assuming you are not able to achieve precisely what you want already.

Summary

This chapter has given you a good grounding in the basics of controlling access to your site's content. You have seen that Drupal comes with a large number of facilities and options to ensure proper maintenance of the site by retaining overall control with the administrative user, as well as delegate important jobs to trusted users via the use of roles.

We looked at how to go about planning an access policy. This is not only an important requirement, in terms of making sure the site runs smoothly, but also helps to solidify how the site will eventually work by forcing you to consider many eventualities. Following this, a tour of the fundamental aspects of access control in Drupal saw us discussing roles, permissions, and users, and learning how to plan and implement an access policy based on the requirements of the site.

A discourse on how to use the contributed module that controls access based on taxonomy showed us how to implement even further fine-grained control over the content's access permissions. However, you probably also found out that creating a well-designed and coherent access policy takes a bit of time. Planning, and above all, testing, will help ensure that everything works as intended.

Access rules were then introduced as a further way of controlling who gets into the site, with a discussion on how to use the wildcard characters effectively. With that, we are done with access control although you are strongly urged to spend some time playing around with the various options until you are comfortable with being able to make changes and knowing their effects.

The next two chapters take an in-depth look at content—the beating heart of Drupal!

6
Basic Content

Everything we have dealt with so far, as important as it may be in terms of creating our own unique site, must take a back seat when it comes to the topic of content and content management in Drupal. After all, content *is* what this is all about! With the explosion in the number of sites offering dynamic content, it is now an absolute necessity to provide meaningful, dynamic, and relevant information on your site in order to prosper. How this is done behind the scenes is really of no concern to a site's users, but if you can make their browsing experience hassle free and relevant to them, they will stick with you.

What does hassle free mean in this context? Content needs to be easy to find, which in turn means it needs to be well organized. It needs to be well presented and easy to interact with—in other words, simple to use. Most of this is taken care of already by Drupal, and for very little additional effort, we can provide some very powerful functionality. However, before we look at adding more functionality, we should really ensure that we have a good grasp of how to use what is already in place.

To this end, this chapter will provide a good grounding in the basics of content management before it moves on to look at a few interesting and powerful features of Drupal. Specifically, we will look at the following:

- Content types
- Working with content
- Content-related modules

Once we are done here, it will be time to look at how to put together some neat pages using HTML and PHP, as well as the all important task of working out how to classify and categorize all your data to provide a sophisticated and intuitive content management system. All this is to come in the following chapter. For now, let's get on with familiarizing ourselves with Drupal and its content.

Content Types

You have already been exposed to some of Drupal's content types' structure and usage. This is actually fairly useful because it means we can spend time focusing on more important issues in lieu of giving a broader overview of content and content management in Drupal. That's not to say that everything in this section, and the one that follows, has already been covered, though.

For a start, we need to have a good idea of the types of content that can be created in Drupal, and then we need to look at the various ways these content types can be put to use. Knowing this will help you determine the best way to go about implementing whatever functionality you have in mind for your site.

The following table lists the content types that ship with Drupal by default:

Content Type	Description
blog entry	A blog, or weblog, is an author-specific content type that is used as a journal or diary, among other things, by individuals. In Drupal, each blog writer can, depending on the site's settings and their permissions, add attachments, HTML, or PHP code to their blog.
	A good example of a blog can be found at: `http://googleblog.blogspot.com/`, which demonstrates an interesting use of the blog content format.
Book Page	A *book* is an organized set of book page types (actually any type can be used nowadays), which are intended to be used for collaborative authoring. Book pages may be added by different people in order to make up one single book, which can then be structured into chapters and pages, or in whatever structure is most appropriate, provided it is in a hierarchical structure.
	Because pretty much any data type can be added to a book, there is plenty of scope for exciting content (think of narrated or visual content complementing dynamic book pages, created with PHP and Flash animations, to create a truly unique Internet-based book—the possibilities are endless!).
	A good example of a book is the documentation provided for developers on the Drupal site, found at: `http://drupal.org/node/316`. This has been built up over time by a number of different authors.
	You will notice that if you have the book module enabled, an additional outline tag is presented above all/most of the site's posts. Clicking on this tab allows you to add that post to a book—in this way, books can be built up from content posted to the site.
Comments	Comments are slightly different in that they aren't really nodes like the other types. In other words, you can't create a comment in the way that you create any other content. Instead, you can tack comments on to other content types, and these are very popular as a means to stimulate discussion among users.
	You can see comments in action by logging in to the Drupal forums, `http://drupal.org/forum`, and posting or viewing comments on the various topics there.
forum topic	Forum topics are the building blocks of forums. Forums can only consist of forum topics and their comments, unlike books, which can consist of pretty much any content type. Information in forums is categorized in a hierarchical structure, and they are extremely useful for hosting discussions as well as community-based support and learning.
	Forums are abundant on the Internet and you can also visit the Drupal forums to get a feel for how they operate.
page	The page type is meant to allow you to add basic, run-of-the-mill web pages that can be found on any site. *About us* or *Terms of use* pages are good candidates for the page type, although you can spruce these up with a bit of dynamic content and HTML.
	Just look on any website to see examples of such pages.

Content Type	Description
poll	The poll type provides the facility to ask questions, and supply a set of answers that are then presented in graph format. Many different enterprises make use of polls in order to collect political or marketing information, or to conduct research, among other things.
	Polls by nature generally have a limited life span; so you will have to search for your own examples. Many news sites such as Time magazine conduct polls to determine public opinion; so these may be your best bet for seeing how polls can be put to good use.
story	A story page is more or less the same thing as a standard page type. However, you might want to distinguish the two by using story types for short-lived pages, such as news or notices.

The following table looks at some of the content types that are available as contributions:

Content Type	Description
Acidfree	Albums and media item types provided with the Acidfree contribution allow you to work with image and video content. The contribution also provides facilities to manage your media files.
Daily	The daily contribution provides two new node types, called daily item and daily container. These are used to facilitate browsing of content items by date, or even controlling when content items are made available on the site in the future.
Flexinode	This contribution allows users to define and edit their own content types.
Front Page	While not technically a node/content type, Front Page does allow users to create a front page, which does not have to conform to the standard page layout of the rest of the Drupal site. Useful if you would like to add an introductory page to your site.

Every time you create new content for your site, there are several options available for you to make the appropriate decisions over, and these are displayed in the list that appears below the body of the post. Depending on the permissions of a given user, they will also have some, although hopefully not all, options available to them. For example, if upload permissions are enabled for authenticated users, then they will be able to decide whether to attach a file to any content they create.

As the administrator, your powers are more substantial; so let's go through the default options available when creating a standard page content type. Be aware that different types of content may also have additional options available for them. For example, if you create a new poll, you will have to decide how long the poll is to run for by setting the Poll duration in the poll type's unique Settings section.

The content options discussed in the following section are representative of most types.

Working with Content

Knowing *what* is and is not available for use in terms of content doesn't necessarily mean that you automatically know *how* to work with the content. This section will therefore take a slightly more in-depth look at how to both edit and configure content to reflect the needs of the site. We have already worked with content in previous chapters, and so are familiar with bits and pieces of this section already. However, the intention here is to give you a single, cohesive point of reference from which to learn.

There are a few different aspects to working with content, and we will begin by looking at how to set up the correct default options whenever you create something new. Following this, it is important to look at the content administer facility, and to round everything off, we will have brief discussion on issues to look out for in general since working with content can be quite confusing at times.

Content Options

When creating new content, we have the Input format section presented as follows (if the Input format link is minimized, click on it to bring up the full version):

```
▼ Input format

⦿ Filtered HTML
    • Allowed HTML tags: <a> <em> <strong> <cite> <code> <ul> <ol> <li> <dl> <dt> <dd>
    • Lines and paragraphs break automatically.

○ PHP code
    • You may post PHP code. You should include <?php ?> tags.

○ Full HTML
    • Lines and paragraphs break automatically.

More information about formatting options
```

By default, the Filtered HTML option is selected. Unless you have a good reason to use one of the other options available, stick to this. Especially be wary of allowing any user to add PHP to their content, as this could put your site at serious risk. Remember that even Filtered HTML is not entirely safe, as users could still add links to malicious web addresses to their pages, which amounts to the same thing as having it on your site.

Here's an example of how a user could gain information about your site (assuming the PHP code option is enabled) before making an attack. In the body text of a page, add the following snippet of code to your page:

```
<?
Phpinfo();
?>
```

Ensure the PHP code option is enabled, and after supplying a Title for the page, click Preview. You should see something like this:

While the server information in this screenshot may not be clear enough to read, it is certainly clear enough for someone viewing the page online to find out everything about your server. In this case, it is better to be safe than sorry, and you should leave the default option for this type of setting as Filtered HTML. All this goes to reiterate a point we discussed earlier when we looked at users and permissions:

> Make sure you only give trusted users just enough permissions to fulfill their roles—and no more!

Before continuing, I should mention that in the following chapter we will discuss how to create custom input formats, because the default options might not always be suitable for the site's requirements.

Following on, Authoring information has only two options. The first names the author of the content, and the second gives the date on which the content was first created. Naturally, modifying the content will not change the Authored on date. If, however, you were modifying a page that has already been created, then you would come across a logging option (this may also be available when the content is first created).

For example, a typical log message might be something like the following:

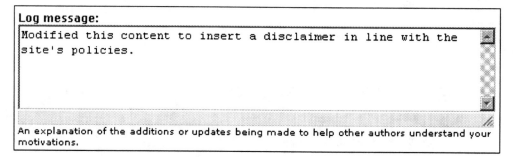

If you are wondering why I have not bothered to add a date to this log message, it is because Drupal will make this clear when viewing revisions of the content automatically. Wait until we have discussed revisions before taking a look at the effect that log messages have on their content.

This log facility is quite simple, but should suffice for most people's needs. It is possible that a new, more sophisticated system of logging will be introduced for Drupal in the future, so keep an eye out for that.

The Publishing options can be tricky to get right, depending on how things are set up. This is what they look like at the moment:

As you will see in the following section on *Administering Content*, it is possible to decide whether content of certain types coming from certain users needs to be moderated before it can be allowed on to the site for general consumption. If this is the case, you or a designated user will have the ability to go through a moderation queue in order to confirm that any and all the content meets the site's requirements.

In the previous screenshot, the content being added is being published directly without the need for moderation. Enabling the second option, In moderation queue, would force the content to be approved before publication. The third option has been selected, and this will cause the content being created to appear on the front page of the website when it is first published (unless you have set a specific node to be displayed here already).

It is unlikely that by default you would want, for example, new book pages to appear on the front page ahead of say blogs from industry experts; so enable this option only for the content types that should steal some of the limelight.

The fourth option, Sticky at top of lists, causes the node to remain at the top of its list regardless of how many other postings there are. This is extremely useful for posting important messages to forums. For example, if there is some confusion about how to do something on a given forum, write a note explaining how things are done, and select this option to pin it to the top of the forum. In this way you ensure that it is the first thing everyone sees when they access that forum.

The final option, Create new revision, causes Drupal to create a new version of the content if it is being updated or revised. This means that you maintain the old version of the content as well as making a new version. This is useful if you want to keep track of what changes are being made to your documents. If a new revision has been created and tracked, then the next time you look at the content (assuming you have sufficient permissions) you will notice a new revisions tab on the page as follows:

Using this revisions page, it is now possible to work with your content quite easily. For example, you can decide which revision should be the active one (displayed to others) by clicking on revert, or you can delete revisions altogether. Notice that the log message that was added to the content type is also displayed at the bottom of each revision. From this you can see that they are actually quite important for maintaining good version control in content that is often modified. In this case, the log message for the revised version of the book page content mentions a change in the title.

Moving along, the next section, Comment settings, simply allows you to determine whether other users will be able to add comments to the content or not, as shown here:

The first option, Disabled, is useful if you are posting content for which comments are not appropriate—perhaps, like me, you are averse to criticism about your poetry, or something similar. The second allows only those with administration rights to post comments to this content, although other users can view the comments, and the final option allows all users with sufficient permissions to pass comment on your wonderful poetry (or whatever).

The following set of options deals with adding content to a menu. The next screenshot shows how a typical about us page might be added to the Navigation menu:

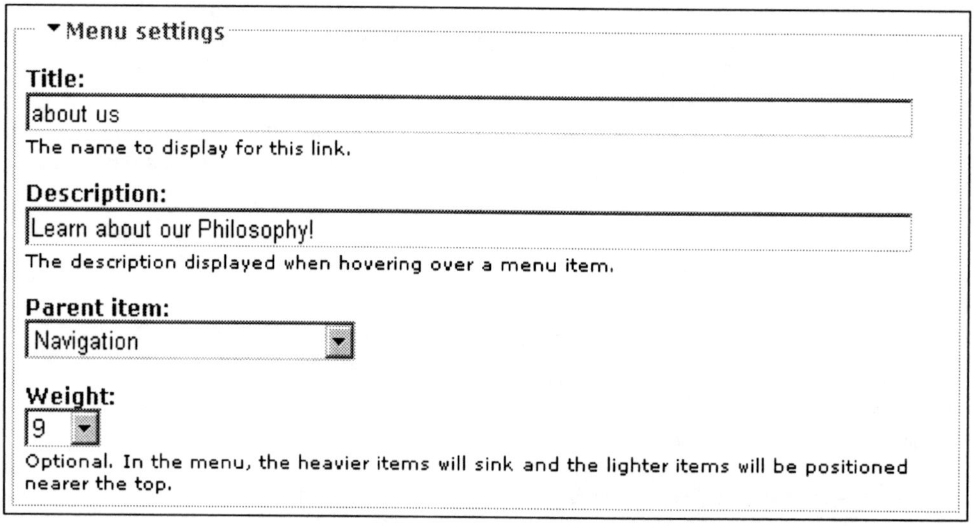

In this case, a fairly hefty weight has been assigned to this page as we only ever want it to be shown after the actual content posts so that is doesn't detract from the main focus of the website. If you now take a look at the main menu and hover the cursor over the new about us link, you'll see the following:

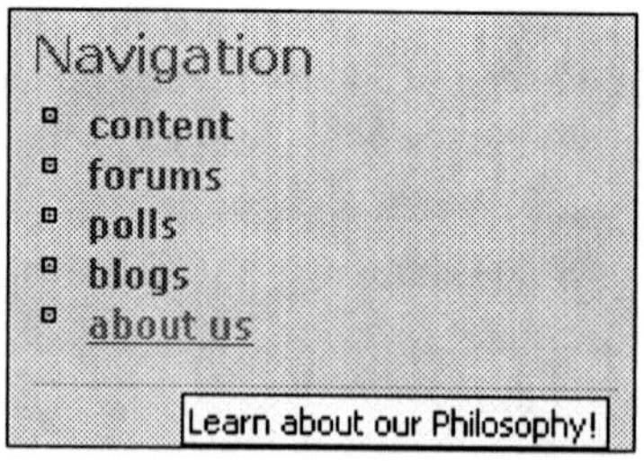

If you ever wish to remove or edit this menu item again, simply look at the same Menu settings section, and there will be a new checkbox, automatically available, to delete it.

The final option available concerns the use of file uploads; it is easy to work with and we have already seen it in action, and so we'll discuss it no further here. That about wraps it up for default content options—there's plenty more to learn, however, so keep your thinking cap on as we venture into the world of content administration.

Administering Content

We saw in Chapter 4, that in the settings section, under administer, it was possible to set default options for a content type. Head back over there, and disable all the Publishing options with the exception of In moderation queue for the page content type (or any type that can be created using the authenticated user) and save the changes. Log out of the administrator account and log in using a standard account, and then create a new page.

Assuming the authenticated user does not have administer permissions enabled on nodes, he or she will not have the power to modify the Publishing options, and will simply have to click Submit in order to send their page for moderation. Now look through all the available content on the site; the page just submitted will not appear yet because it has not been published. In order to see what's going on, we need to visit the content page under administer, which shows a list of all the content on the site along with a variety of options in order to work with it, like so:

content

list   search

Below is a list of all of the posts on your site. Other forms of content are listed elsewhere (e.g. comments).

Clicking a title views the post, while clicking an author's name views their user information.

[more help...]

Show only items where

⦿ status	is	published	▼	Filter
○ type		blog entry	▼	
○ category		Conservation	▼	

Update options

| Approve the selected posts | ▼ | Update |

	Title	Type	Author	Status	Operations
☐	Administer me!! new	page	David	not published	edit
☐	This page must go for moderation...	page	David	not published	edit
☐	I think this is ok...	page	David Mercer	not published	edit
☐	about us	page	David Mercer	published	edit
☐	Chapter 1		David Mercer	published	edit

Notice that in this screenshot the top two submissions were posted by the user David (whereas, in the case of the demo site, the administrator is David Mercer). Neither of these page nodes has yet been published because the default settings require them to first be moderated. Notice also that new has been tacked onto the latest submission to distinguish it from posts we have already seen—useful when you have tonnes and tonnes of nodes to go through.

Now, the content filter shown towards the top of the page, above Update options, is a very important tool in your administrative workshop. It allows you to display only those nodes that satisfy certain requirements. There are three filter criteria provided: status, type, and category. These allow you to filter the whole list, presenting only those items that meet the specific requirement set in the drop-down list to the right of the selected method.

If we wanted to locate a node that has already been published, we would check the status criterion, and then select the published option from the drop-down list (as shown in the previous screenshot) before clicking Filter. The displayed list would then be filtered and only the relevant results displayed on the page. Easy enough to do!

That's all good and well, *but where is the moderation queue?* Well, if you look at the drop-down list provided with the status criterion, you will notice that there is an in moderation option. Selecting this and clicking Filter will present us with the following results:

Title	Type	Author	Status	Operations
☐ Administer me!! new	page	David	not published	edit
☐ This page must go for moderation...	page	David	not published	edit
☐ I think this is ok...	page	David Mercer	not published	edit

None of these pages have been published yet, because the publishing option was disabled and in moderation queue was set for all of them.

> Note that is possible to use the filters several times in order to refine your results!

It is now possible for the administrator to edit the node, and once all is well, the node can be published. Doing this is simple enough! Let's say we wanted to allow the Administer me page to be published because after a bit of editing we are happy with it. Simply select the box to the left of the Title, and then, in the Update options section directly above the list, select the relevant option as shown here:

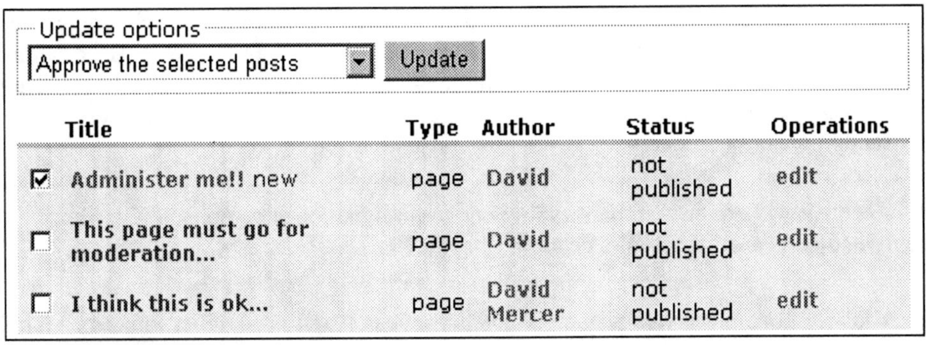

Update options				
Approve the selected posts ▾	Update			

Title	Type	Author	Status	Operations
☑ **Administer me!! new**	page	David	not published	edit
☐ **This page must go for moderation...**	page	David	not published	edit
☐ **I think this is ok...**	page	David Mercer	not published	edit

Clicking on Update will ensure that the page is now published as intended. You can confirm this by logging out and viewing the page as either an anonymous user or as an authenticated user depending on your permissions.

It's worth noting that there are quite a few options available when it comes to updating posts. You can promote the posting to the front page, or can demote it if you so choose. You can make the post sticky (in other words, it will stick to the front of its list) as shown here:

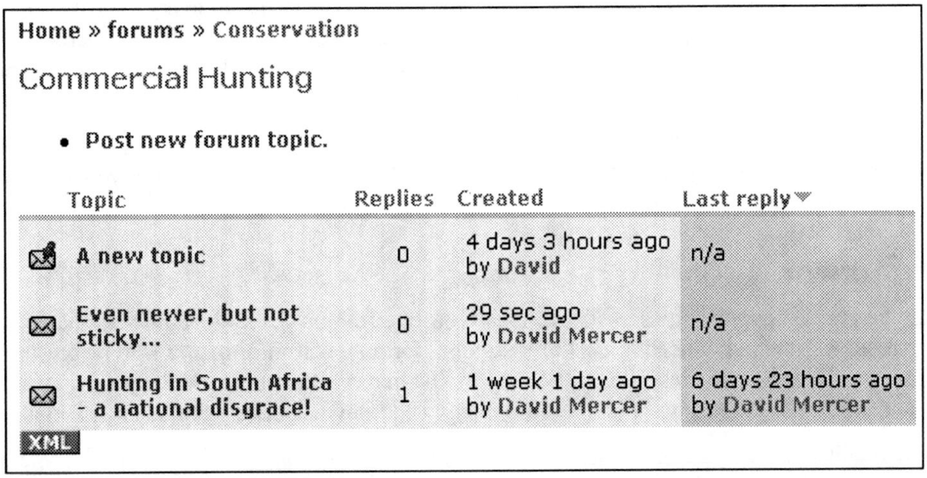

Home » forums » Conservation

Commercial Hunting

- **Post new forum topic.**

Topic	Replies	Created	Last reply ▾
✉ **A new topic**	0	4 days 3 hours ago by David	n/a
✉ **Even newer, but not sticky...**	0	29 sec ago by David Mercer	n/a
✉ **Hunting in South Africa - a national disgrace!**	1	1 week 1 day ago by David Mercer	6 days 23 hours ago by David Mercer

XML

With the Make the selected posts sticky under Update options enabled for the A new topic forum post, you can see that there is a pinned icon to the left and that the latest post, which is not sticky, appears below it. You can also unpublish and delete posts, both of which prevent users with insufficient permissions viewing the post on the site. The difference is that the Delete the selected posts option removes the post from the system entirely, whereas an unpublished post can be re-published at a later date—useful for simply taking a post offline in the event you need to correct or modify it without getting rid of it.

Finally, in the event that it is not possible to easily locate content, there is a search tool provided under the search tab of the content page, which allows you to search by keyword. Bear in mind that you can make use of the * wildcard character to match any characters in order to broaden your search. The Advanced search link on this page also provides you with several other options to specify conditions for your search.

> New content will not be searchable until your cron run has been completed! Cron and scheduled tasks are discussed in detail in Chapter 10.

Finally, you are strongly urged to play around with the search options in order to become familiar with how each option functions.

Content-Related Modules

As well as talk about content-related modules, this section will also serve to give you a better idea of what is available to work with, and therefore what is possible to accomplish using both default and contributed modules.

We already know how to install modules, so we won't show how to install every contribution we discuss. If and when there are any noteworthy deviations from the usual installation methods they will be mentioned here—otherwise, please install and enable each module, remembering to check if there are any special permissions that need to be set as you go.

Chapter 9 deals with more advanced topics, and it is there that we discuss the *Flexinode* module, which constitutes the last bit of information directly related to content; so remember to also check there before *closing the book* on content.

Aggregator

One of the greatest opportunities available to web-based communities is the ability to share information. All you really need is a set of guidelines for how that information is to be presented, and once you have that, the rest is easy. So easy in fact that it is now possible for you to include news and articles of interest on your site from many well known sources with just a few clicks.

What makes it so easy to include other people's news, documents, articles, or any other content easy is a standard called **Rich Site Summary** (**RSS**). This allows aggregators (programs that consume RSS feeds) to understand how to present content on web pages due to the way in which the RSS feed is structured. Drupal comes with one of these aggregators built in—simply enable it in the modules section under administer, and you will find that a few extra menu items pop up, allowing you to administer and view the content once it has been added.

Let's assume that the demo site would like to provide some news relating to wildlife from the *National Geographic* website. We pop along to the news site at http://news.nationalgeographic.com/ and look for where the RSS feed icons are presented on the site. In this case they look like the following:

Clicking on the RSS link here will bring up the following page—luckily Drupal takes care of all the dirty work for us, and we don't even need to understand the XML in order to consume this feed:

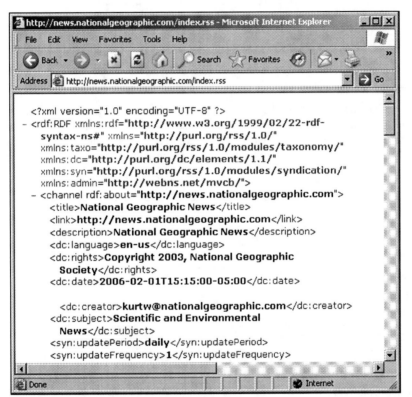

This may not mean much to you at the moment, but it serves to confirm that there is a feed available for use at the address given in the URL. Knowing this, we can now head over to our site and look for the aggregator link under administer in order to begin adding this feed to the site. This will bring up the as yet blank list of feeds along with everything else we need. On this page, clicking on the add category tab brings up the following form:

```
aggregator
   list    add category    add feed

Categories provide a way to group items from different news feeds together. Each
news category has its own feed page and block. For example, you could tag various
sport-related feeds as belonging to a category called Sports. News items can be
added to a category automatically by setting a feed to automatically place its item into
that category, or by using the categorize items link in any listing of news items.

Title:
Commercial

Description:
This category contains items which are produced by commercial
organisations - feeds produced by individual activists or
organizations, which rely on donations for their survival
should be added to other categories.

Submit
```

Assuming you intend to make use of a variety of feeds, it is probably prudent to categorize your content right from the start. Remember, providing access to timely and interesting news is a value-added service for your site and encourages users to return time and again. With this in mind, it is probably quite valuable to have a variety of relevant feeds available.

Once you are done, click Submit, and then click on the add feed tab to bring up the following:

```
aggregator
   list    add category    add feed

Add a site that has an RSS/RDF feed. The URL is the full path to the RSS feed file. For
the feed to update automatically you must run "cron.php" on a regular basis. If you
already have a feed with the URL you are planning to use, the system will not accept
another feed with the same URL.

Title:
National Geographic News
The name of the feed; typically the name of the web site you syndicate content from.

URL:
http://news.nationalgeographic.com/index.rss
The fully-qualified URL of the feed.

Update interval:
1 day
The refresh interval indicating how often you want to update this feed. Requires crontab.

Categorize news items:

☑ Commercial

New items in this feed will be automatically filed in the checked categories as they are received.

Submit
```

As you can see, we have:

1. Specified a title for the new feed
2. Supplied Drupal with the location of the RSS feed (check this against the URL of the RSS feed page we visited on the actual *National Geographic* site a bit earlier)
3. Given an Update interval of one day, making this a daily news feed
4. Associated this feed with the newly created Commercial category

There are a number of things to consider when filling out this form. First, you need to ensure that you are not infringing any licensing issues that will be supplied by the creator of the source feed. If there are restrictions as to what can and cannot be done with the feed, please ensure you abide by those restrictions.

Next, there is no point in setting an update interval of one hour if you are only running the cron script once a day—the cron can at most only update the script once a day in this case. By the same token, there is no point in using the cron to update your feed every ten minutes if the feed itself is only updated on a weekly basis—check with the providers of the feed how often they recommend you update your feed.

Having taken these factors into account you can now click on Submit to add the feed to your site. Now the aggregator homepage has something to tell us, and should look something like this:

aggregator

| list | add category | add feed |

Thousands of sites (particularly news sites and weblogs) publish their latest headlines and/or stories in a machine-readable format so that other sites can easily link to them. This content is usually in the form of an RSS feed (which is an XML-based syndication standard). To display the feed or category in a block you must decide how many items to show by editing the feed or block and turning on the feed's block.

[more help...]

The feed has been updated.

Feed overview

Title	Items	Last update	Next update	Operations		
National Geographic News	0 items	never	never	edit	remove items	update items

Category overview

Title	Items	Operations
Commercial	0 items	edit

As yet there are no items in the feed because the cron.php script hasn't been run. You can either wait for it to be accessed by your scheduled task or crontab, or if you are not keen to hang around, simply navigate to http://localhost/drupal/cron.php in your browser (if the path to your cron.php script is different, ensure you change this URL to suit your site). Remember that cron.php is just a script, with no HTML; so you will not see anything displayed on this page even if it is working correctly.

Once you have done that, click refresh on the aggregator page to see the results. You should get something like this, assuming everything has worked correctly:

Feed overview						
Title	**Items**	**Last update**	**Next update**	**Operations**		
National Geographic News	9 items	6 sec ago	23 hours 59 min left	edit	remove items	update items

Success! From this you can see that the feed now contains 9 items as of the last update, which occurred 6 sec ago. As well as this, you can edit the feed, remove items from the feed, or manually update the feed by clicking update items—in this case, the feed can be modified to reflect any changes on the source site. That's all there is to it!

You can, of course, now view the content of the feed on the site. For the demo site, permission to access the feeds has been granted to anonymous and authenticated users alike. So when someone visits the site and clicks on the news aggregator link in the main menu, they are presented with something like the following:

---

news aggregator

Kidnapping Penguins May Be High on Hormone, Study Says
National Geographic News - 2 min 40 sec ago

A *March of the Penguins* mystery may be solved. Parental chemistry might help explain why some female emperor penguins that have lost babies kidnap chicks.

Categories: Commercial

The End of Oil? Breakthrough Turns Coal Into Clean Diesel
National Geographic News - 2 min 40 sec ago

As oil prices hit record highs, scientists have unveiled a technology that can turn coal, natural gas, and biomass into a fuel that burns cleaner than gasoline.

Categories: Commercial

Video: Baseball's Louisville Slugger, Behind the Bat
National Geographic News - 2 min 40 sec ago

As baseball season gears up again, get a grip on the facts and the legends about the sport's best known bat.

Categories: Commercial

Shorebirds Face Extinction Due to Crab Decline
National Geographic News - 2 min 40 sec ago

Some species of migratory birds that feed on the eggs of horseshoe crabs may soon disappear. Can the rapid decline in the numbers of crabs be reversed in time to save the birds?

Categories: Commercial

Now all users have instant access to all the content provided by *National Geographic*. Nothing stops you from gathering information from any number of other feeds, and what is interesting is that provided you are not infringing any licenses, you can make your feeds available to other sites. Doing this is easy (remember to enable the syndication block before trying to work with it)! Scroll down to the bottom of the page until you see a small icon that looks like this:

Clicking on it brings up the feed page that is provided at the following URL (in the case of the demo site): `http://localhost/drupal/aggregator/rss`, and in this way content can be syndicated. You aren't limited to syndicating online feeds you have obtained—any content can be syndicated.

It's worth noting that your sources can be revealed in the navigation column by clicking on the **sources** link under **news aggregator**. In this case, we are presented with the following; note that I have added a feed from the WWF (World Wide Fund for Nature, formerly World Wildlife Fund):

sources

National Geographic News

- **Meat-Eating Dinosaur Was Bigger Than T. Rex** *10 min 26 sec old*
- **Photo in the News: Volcano Threatens Indonesian Island** *10 min 26 sec old*
- **Shorebirds Face Extinction Due to Crab Decline** *10 min 26 sec old*

more

WWF

- **New species of freshwater stingray discovered in Thailand** *1 week 13 hours old*
- **Amur tiger cubs born in southeast Siberia for first time in over 100 years** *1 week 3 days old*
- **Western Australia signs on to national water initiative** *1 week 6 days old*

more

`XML`

This presents us with a nice summary of feeds from each source. So far so good, but *what does the more link do?* Clicking on the more link for the WWF source brings up the following page:

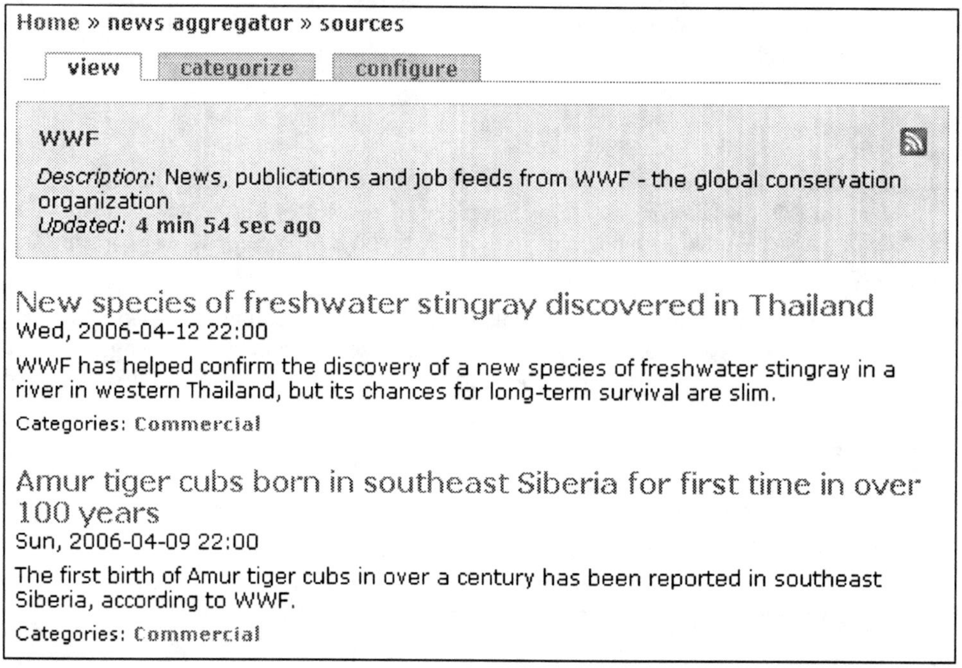

Home » news aggregator » sources

| view | categorize | configure |

WWF
Description: News, publications and job feeds from WWF - the global conservation organization
Updated: 4 min 54 sec ago

New species of freshwater stingray discovered in Thailand
Wed, 2006-04-12 22:00

WWF has helped confirm the discovery of a new species of freshwater stingray in a river in western Thailand, but its chances for long-term survival are slim.

Categories: Commercial

Amur tiger cubs born in southeast Siberia for first time in over 100 years
Sun, 2006-04-09 22:00

The first birth of Amur tiger cubs in over a century has been reported in southeast Siberia, according to WWF.

Categories: Commercial

From here it is possible to click on the name of the feed in order to go to the source website, in this case http://www.panda.org. The feeds associated with this source are listed on the page below the title box for easy access to feeds by source. Clicking on the orange syndicate icon at the top right of the box takes the browser to the actual feed page. In this case it is http://www.panda.org/rss/news.cfm?Press%20Office.

As well as this, there are two tabs at the top of the page. The categorize tab opens up the following screenshot, which allows us to put individual feed items into a variety of categories (assuming you have a variety of categories available).

This screenshot shows the second feed item being assigned two categories, namely Commercial and Special. In this case, the Special category was created with a specific purpose in mind. Because there is news every now and then that warms one's heart, all items that are tagged in the Special category should be displayed in a special block on the website so that every user can see the good news when viewing any page on the site.

| view | categorize | configure |

WWF

Description: News, publications and job feeds from WWF - the global conservation organization
Updated: 10 min 35 sec ago

Categorize

New species of freshwater stingray discovered in Thailand
Wed, 2006-04-12 22:00

WWF has helped confirm the discovery of a new species of freshwater stingray in a river in western Thailand, but its chances for long-term survival are slim.

Categories: **Commercial**

☐ Charitable
☑ Commercial
☐ Special

Amur tiger cubs born in southeast Siberia for first time in over 100 years
Sun, 2006-04-09 22:00

The first birth of Amur tiger cubs in over a century has been reported in southeast Siberia, according to WWF.

Categories: **Commercial**

☐ Charitable
☑ Commercial
☑ Special

The final tab on the sources page simply brings up the same page that was used in order to create the feed. From here you can make any changes you require to the feed with ease.

Since we have not yet covered taxonomy and categorization, you may wish to come back to what follows in this section once you have read Chapter 7 as there may be a few things that are not clear now. For example, we add a module to display content based on its category later on in this chapter, which is why we can work with the Special category in the manner shown next. The information presented here is simply to give you an idea of what you will be able to do—hopefully it will not be too confusing now.

Remembering that it is entirely possible you would like to display some of the latest feeds in a block somewhere on the site, head on over to the blocks category under the administer link and enable one of the new blocks so that it displays its latest items—notice that it also possible to display the latest feeds in a category too:

Right sidebar				
Recent blog posts	☑	0 ▾	right sidebar ▾	configure
Who's new	☑	0 ▾	right sidebar ▾	configure
Special category latest items	☑	2 ▾	right sidebar ▾	configure

Once this is done, you will see the new feed, along with a selection of its items on your web pages. You can configure the number of news items displayed in the Block specific settings on its configuration page (click on configure to open this up)—for our purposes, the default option of five feeds is just fine.

Now, assuming that a user has blogging permissions and the feed license allows your site to do so, you can add feed items to blogs, by clicking on the little b icon that appears next to each item, as shown here:

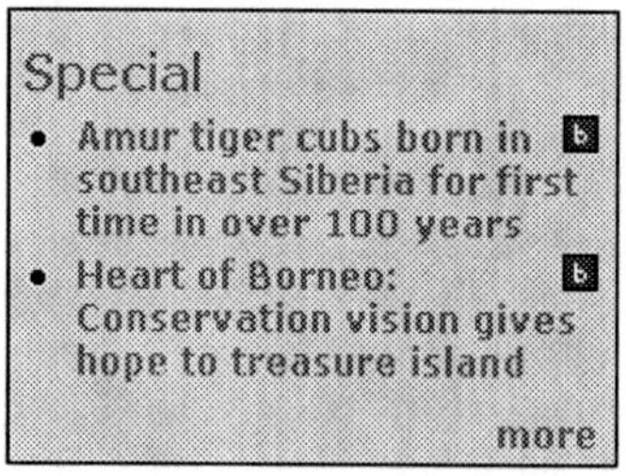

Adding a news item to your blogs gives the article more permanency as it will not be lost when or if the list of items in the feed is cleared. Of course, if you are going to build up lots of content over time, then it is highly likely that you will need to make use of the archive module.

The aggregator has one more important section to look at—configuration! If you click on aggregator under the settings link in the main menu, the following page is displayed:

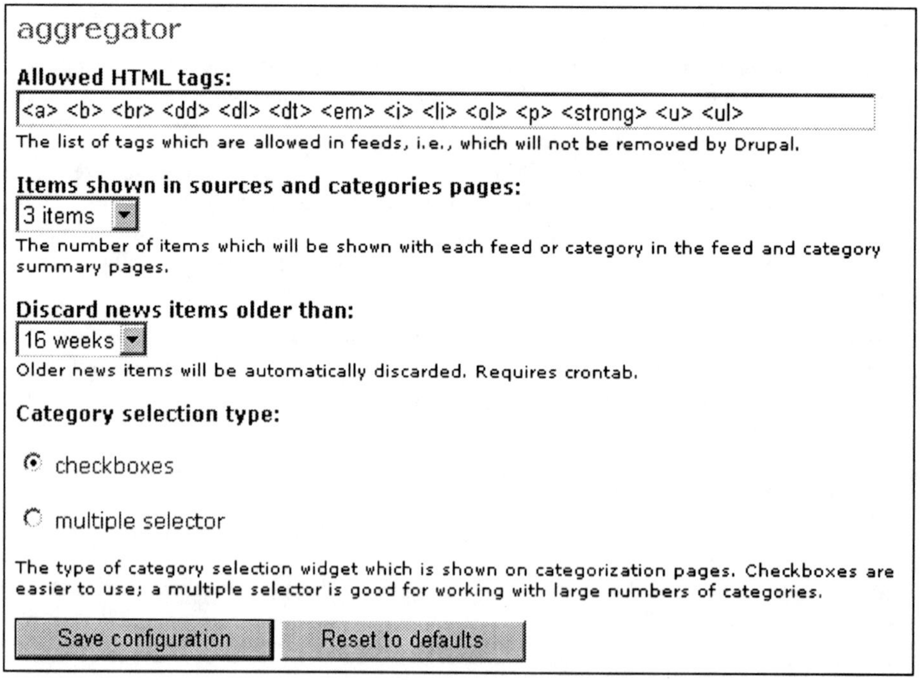

This interface provides control over the type of HTML that is allowed within the feeds that are to be consumed by your site. This should be sufficient for most if not all the feeds you want to aggregate, but on the off chance that there are problems with some feeds, it is likely that they are using tags that are not specified in this section. When in doubt, leave it as is!

Next, the number of items to be shown with each feed in general as well as how long to hold on to old feed items are presented, and it is easy enough to make sensible selections here. The final section stipulates whether the category selection interface (on the categorize tab of the sources page) should use checkboxes or the multiple selector. We have already seen checkboxes in use, and they are fine for the purposes of the demo site. If, however, multiple selector was enabled, the category selections would look like this:

Before we move on, it is worth mentioning again that if at some stage you feel the urge to syndicate your site's content, you can enable the syndicate block to force Drupal to show the orange syndicate icon. Further, if you would like to enhance the control of the site's syndication, you can take a look at the syndication module provided at `http://drupal.org/project/syndication`.

Archive

The **archive** module is simple and to the point! Enable it in the modules section under administer. Then, go to the blocks section and enable the option entitled Calendar to browse archives, placing it wherever is most appropriate, and away you go. In the case of the demo site, it is envisaged that a lot of content will be added on a daily basis, so the archive calendar will be a great way to locate content chronologically. For this reason, the Calendar to browse archives block was given a low rating so that it always appears on top of the right-hand sidebar. Once the changes are submitted, the user can navigate to an item by searching through the calendar for when it was posted:

Not that much to it; however, it is worth noting that clicking on a date or changing the month shown on the calendar will immediately bring up a form in the content section allowing users to search using drop-down lists like so:

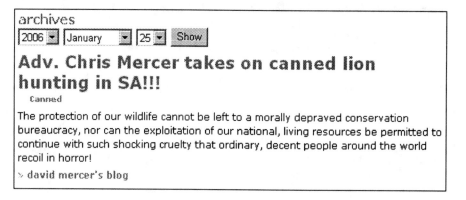

It's a testament to the excellent design of Drupal that such powerful functionality can be so easily implemented. If this doesn't impress you, not much will!

Similar Entries

I don't know about you, but I often find that when reading news stories I end up following the similar/related stories links in order to try to find out more about a given bit of news, or simply get a more rounded view on whatever it is I am looking at. Having the ability to display related items is fairly useful functionality to have, and it should come as no surprise that it is very easy to use on Drupal by installing the **Similar Entries** module.

Download the module from the Drupal website and extract it to your modules folder. With that done you need to now enable the module in the modules section under the administer menu item—search for the new module entitled similar. It is important to go through the readme file in this case as it may affect how you install this module depending on your system's setup.

The next task is to decide how many related items you would like to display on the site, among other things. In order to do this, head on over to the blocks section under administer and click on configure adjacent to the Similar entries block to set the number, before enabling the block and setting its Placement and Weight. The demo site used the default settings:

'Similar entries' block

▼ Block specific settings

Include teaser text:

⦿ No

○ Yes

Number of similar entries to find:

5 ▾

Node types to display:

☑ blog

☑ page

☑ story

▼ Taxonomy category filter

Filter by taxonomy categories:

⦿ No category filtering

○ Only show the similar nodes in the same category as the original node

○ Use global category filtering

By selecting global filtering, only nodes assigned to the following selected categories will display as similar nodes, regardless of the categories the original node is or is not assigned to.

▼ Taxonomy categories to display

Forums: Commercial Fishing
Forums: Conservation
Forums: Environment
Forums: Research

Hold the CTRL key to (de)select multiple options.

If certain content types are not available for selection, then this is most probably because there is no content of that particular type on the site yet. As soon as you create content of a certain type, it will appear in the node types to display drop-down list. Further, assuming the taxonomy module is enabled (which it should be), there are three options related to how the Similar Entries module finds its related content. The default options are fine in this case as we are not concerned about category filtering. If, however, I wanted to show related content only from the Conservation forum container, then the following settings would need to be made:

```
▼Taxonomy category filter
  Filter by taxonomy categories:

  ○  No category filtering

  ○  Only show the similar nodes in the same category as the original node

  ◉  Use global category filtering

  By selecting global filtering, only nodes assigned to the following selected categories will
  display as similar nodes, regardless of the categories the original node is or is not assigned
  to.

      ▼Taxonomy categories to display
      ┌─────────────────────────────────┐
      │ Forums: Commercial Fishing      │
      │ Forums: Conservation            │
      │ Forums: Environment             │
      │ Forums: Research                │
      └─────────────────────────────────┘
      Hold the CTRL key to (de)select multiple options.
```

The rest of the settings on this page are standard for each and every block, and we have already seen how to work with these. With the configuration out of the way, simply enable the block and place it where you want. Now when users view any content on the site, the module presents any related content by searching for other posts with similarities. For example, when viewing the following post, notice that there is now a new block present in the right-hand sidebar:

```
Home » my blog                                              Similar entries
An article on canned lion hunting                           • Canned Hunting News...
  [ view ] [ edit ] [ outline ]                             • Adv. Chris Mercer takes
  Hunting | hunting | bear traps                              on canned lion hunting in
                                                               SA!!!
canned lion hunting. Snaring and gin-traps were some        • Wild dogs rescued from
of the topics under debate yesterday...                       gin-traps!
 » david mercer's blog | add new comment                   • hunting
                                                            • Snaring in Africa - A
                                                              global controversy!
```

As you can see, three of the five related items presented have hunting in their titles, so we expect them to be shown in this list. *What about the other two?* If you look closely, the content of the post mentions both snaring and gin-traps, which relate to the titles of the two items that do not explicitly mention hunting.

So, from this we can see that in order to present a list of similar posts or items, the Similar Entries module searches all the titles posted to the site and lists those that have any similarities in the title. Not content with that, it also searches the posts' body content for similarities, and presents those (assuming there is enough space in the block). This is obviously very useful for people doing research, or for a news-like site.

Taxonomy Block

The final module we will discuss here relates to the **taxonomy** module. Unfortunately, this relies on the fact that categorization is enabled on your site already. Because of this, you may want to skip this section until you have read through the chapter on *Advanced Content*, which follows directly after this one.

Like the previous module discussed, this module also presents similar topics to the user, depending on what they are viewing. In this case, though, *taxonomy block* displays a list of recently posted items based on their category. Now, you should think carefully about whether you prefer this module or the previous one to provide readers with related topics. Having both displayed on your page will create some redundancy as there will obviously be some overlap in the content of the blocks.

> Functionality must reflect and meet the requirements of the site. Anything else is redundant!

In other words, don't clutter up your web pages with information or functionality that is not really necessary; this hurts the usability of the site, and therefore, indirectly, its popularity.

The installation of the module is fairly basic—simply extract the contents of the download to the `modules` folder. You will need to execute a `.mysql` script against your database, so once again, ensure you have a recent backup before making any changes like this. You can run the script by executing the following command at the command line (remember to use the correct username and database for your system):

```
$ mysql -u<username> -p drupal <
C:\apache2triad\htdocs\drupal\modules\taxonomy_block\taxonomy_block.mysql
```

Change the file path to the one that suits your system if this is not where the `taxonomy_block.mysql` script is held on your machine. Assuming that the command executes without any hassle, you can now head on over to the modules section to enable the new addition to the site—look for taxonomy_block in the list. Once the module is enabled, you will need to decide where it should be presented on the site, using the blocks page under administer.

Unlike other modules, the taxonomy block doesn't automatically appear in the list of blocks to be enabled—instead you will find a link to it in the main menu underneath the blocks menu item. This link opens up a block creation page, from which you can stipulate the type of information you would like to display based on which category you wish to associate this block with, like so:

Taxonomy Block Administration

Current Blocks

Create Block

Block Name:

Canned hunting

This is the name of your block.

Block Description: *

Recent canned hunting posts

This is the description of your block. It is not displayed to users.

Teaser Length:

50

This is the length of node body content to display under each title in characters. Leave blank for none.

Node Count: *

3

This is the number of nodes to display.

Category: *

Hunting - Canned

Select taxonomy type to display

Create Block

In this case, we have chosen to present a block containing information relating to the contentious issue of canned lion hunting. The Block Description option allows you to enter the name of the block as it will appear in the list of blocks on the parent blocks page. The Teaser Length sets the number of characters you wish to show for each post that appears in the block. In this case, I have decided to show 50 characters for each post, but limit the number of related topics shown to only 3 in order not to take up too much space with this block. Finally, the block is associated with the Hunting - Canned category as expected.

Clicking on Create Block saves these changes, and now we can venture to the blocks page in order to enable the block and have it displayed on the site. Search through the list of Disabled blocks for the Block Description you entered on the previous page. Once you have found it, make your choices regarding where it should be displayed and what weight it holds, and click on Save blocks. You now have taxonomy-based related content up and running on your site. In the case of the demo site, the similar entries block was disabled and this one enabled in its place.

Now when a user views anything related to canned hunting, they see something like this:

Of course, you can have wildly varying results depending on the way in which you create the block. You might find that you simply want to leave out the teaser entirely, in which case you will end up with only the titles of each post being displayed. Whatever your choice, you now have some fairly powerful functionality at your disposal. Just remember not to get carried away and add blocks simply because they work nicely.

Summary

Knowing how to deal with content efficiently and quickly is a highly desirable trait when it comes to working with CMS systems such as Drupal. To this end, this chapter set the foundation for you to work from by giving an overview of the fundamentals as well as a taste of what else is available. To start with, we took a brief look at the various types of content that can be implemented using Drupal and then discussed how to work with that content using the administration tool.

One of the most important jobs you will take on when running a website is administering the content of the site. At the moment it might seem fairly straightforward, but as the site grows larger, the job becomes slightly harder. Ensuring that you spend time learning your way around the content-related administrative areas of the administer menu will ensure that you stay on top of things as and when your site becomes more widely used, or when you begin attempting more complex content-oriented tasks.

The second half of this chapter demonstrated some of the powerful functionality that ships with Drupal or is provided by contributions. We saw that it is possible to aggregate RSS feeds with relative ease, and in turn syndicate content so that it is made available to other sites to consume. Having the ability to do this with only the minimum of fuss is a quantum leap for the Internet as a whole and hopefully you will spread the good word about how easy it is to work with Drupal.

Armed with a solid understanding of how to work with content as well as the type of things available to use, we are now ready to look at some slightly more advanced content issues. The next chapter will talk about how to create your own dynamic and attractive content, as well as talk about how to categorize content through the use of the taxonomy module.

7
Advanced Content

Most of our dealings with content so far have been fairly basic in that they require us only to learn which settings to enable and what text to enter. There is a fundamental difference between this and what is coming in this chapter, mainly because the content in this chapter requires us to think ahead and plan what we want ahead of time, in order to prevent things going awry at a later date.

At this point, after hearing so much about taxonomy and categorization in previous chapters, you might be wondering what all the fuss is about. The main reason for concerning ourselves with categorization is that in order to make Drupal's classification system so powerful, it must be left for us to decide how best to implement. This might sound a little strange at first, but we will see later on in the chapter why this faculty of Drupal is one of the things that distinguish it from everything else out there—it's really a good thing!

Accordingly, this chapter discusses the following subjects:

- HTML, PHP, and Content Posting
- Categorization

Don't be fooled by the fact that there are only two items listed here as they both represent a step up in complexity from all the other topics we have discussed so far. However, once these topics are under your belt, you will be more or less on the home straight in terms of the site's development—with only the topic of theming to come before we can begin looking at more administrative-type tasks.

As well as this, the skills learned during the process of honing your content creation and management techniques will prove useful not only for this website but also in other aspects of your life—whether it is creating and managing office reports for your boss, building a new website, or even writing a book. The reason for this is because, by and large, we are now going to learn *how content should be managed and created* rather than how to click buttons and links to enable or disable settings.

In any case, I'm sure you're eager to get on with it.

HTML, PHP, and Content Posting

We briefly touched upon the fact that it is possible to include HTML or PHP within our posts earlier in Chapter 3, where we added some formatting and a hyperlink to some of our text—we also saw a short PHP script in the section on Adding Blocks in Chapter 4, which provided the site with nice *Quote of the Day* functionality. So, at this point you should be comfortable with the fact that given sufficient permissions, it is possible to post some fairly unique and interesting content.

It is likely that at some stage you will want to upgrade at least some of your content from plain text to something that looks a little *out of the ordinary*. If it's layout you are talking about, then HTML is what you need to know. Alternatively, if you want to create some dynamic content, which can change depending on the state of your site, or respond to user interaction, then PHP is the way forward. More than likely, you will end up using a combination of both, once you have gained a bit of experience.

Unfortunately, we can't possibly hope to give you a comprehensive introduction into either technology in the space we have here. However, there are tons of online resources available where you can learn about HTML and PHP for free and we will list a bunch of them throughout this section.

For now, we will look at how to achieve some fairly useful tasks by way of demonstrating how to create an *about us* page that will contain links to other useful sites, pictures of the *imaginary team* as well as some dynamic content.

Input Formats and Filters

The first thing you need to understand is that it is necessary to stipulate which type of content we will be posting, in any given post. This is done through the use of the input format setting, which is displayed when posting content to the site—assuming the user in question has sufficient permissions to post different types of content. In order to control what is and is not allowed, head on over to the input formats link under the administer main menu item. This will bring up a list of the currently defined input formats, like this:

Home » administer

input formats

| list | add input format |

Input formats define a way of processing user-supplied text in Drupal. Every input format has its own settings of which *filters* to apply. Possible filters include stripping out malicious HTML and making URLs clickable.

Users can choose between the available input formats when submitting content.

Below you can configure which input formats are available to which roles, as well as choose a default input format (used for imported content, for example).

Default	Name	Roles	Operations
⦿	Filtered HTML	anonymous user, authenticated user	configure
○	PHP code	No roles may use this format	configure delete
○	Full HTML	No roles may use this format	configure delete

| Set default format |

At the moment, you might be wondering why we need to go to all this trouble to decide whether people can add certain tags to their content. The answer to this is that because both HTML and PHP are such powerful internet technologies, it is not hard to subvert even fairly simple abilities for malicious purposes. For example, you might decide you would like to allow authenticated users the ability to link to their homepages from their blogs. Using the ability to add a hyperlink to their postings, a malicious user could create a virus or some other harmful content, and link to it from an innocuous and friendly looking piece of HTML like this:

```
<p>Hi Friends! My <a href="link_to_virus.exe">homepage</a> is a great place to
meet and learn about my interests and hobbies. </p>
```

This snippet simply writes out a short paragraph with a link, supposedly to the author's homepage, but in reality the hyperlink reference attribute points to a virus, link_to_virus.exe. That's just HTML; PHP can do a lot more damage—to the extent that if you don't have proper security or disaster-recovery policies in place, then it is possible that your site can be rendered useless or destroyed entirely. Security is the main reason why, as you may have noticed from the previous screenshot, anything other than Filtered HTML is unavailable for use by anyone except you as the administrator.

Again, it is important to re-iterate the tenet:

> Never allow users more permissions than they require to complete their intended tasks!

As they stand, you might not find the input formats to your liking, and so Drupal provides us with some functionality to modify them. Click on the configure link adjacent to the Filtered HTML option, and this will bring up the following page:

'Filtered HTML' input format

view | **configure** | **rearrange**

Every *filter* performs one particular change on the user input, for example stripping out malicious HTML or making URLs clickable. Choose which filters you want to apply to text in this input format.

If you notice some filters are causing conflicts in the output, you can rearrange them.

Name: *

Filtered HTML

Specify a unique name for this filter format.

---Roles---
All roles for the default format must be enabled and cannot be changed.

☑ anonymous user

☑ authenticated user

☑ Forum Moderator user

---Filters---
Choose the filters that will be used in this filter format.

☑ HTML filter
Allows you to restrict if users can post HTML and which tags to filter out.

☑ Line break converter
Converts line breaks into HTML (i.e.
 and <p> tags).

☐ PHP evaluator
Runs a piece of PHP code. The usage of this filter should be restricted to administrators only!

Save configuration

The view tab provides you with the option to alter the Name property of the input format; the Roles section in this case cannot be changed, but as you will see when we come round to creating our own input format, roles can be assigned however you wish. The final section provides us with a checklist of the types of Filters we would like to apply when using this input format. In this case the first two have been selected, and this causes the input format to apply the HTML filter (discussed in a moment) as well as the Line break converter, but not the PHP evaluator.

The line break converter simply makes it easier for users to format their content because it means that they do not have to explicitly enter <br> or <p> HTML tags in order to display new lines or paragraph breaks. If this is disabled, then unless the user has the ability to add the relevant HTML tags, you might end up with all your content looking like this:

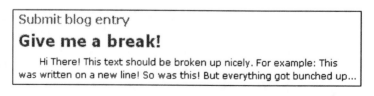

Submit blog entry
Give me a break!
Hi There! This text should be broken up nicely. For example: This was written on a new line! So was this! But everything got bunched up...

The PHP evaluator simply causes posts to be sent for PHP processing, so that any code that falls between the PHP delimiters <?php and ?> gets executed properly. This should not be enabled for anyone other than yourself or a highly trusted administrator who needs it to complete his or her work. There is, however, no other work to be done for either of these options. The only additional settings we need to look at here are for the HTML filter.

Click on the configure tab at the top of the page in order to begin working with the HTML filter. You should be presented with something like this (once you have clicked on the HTML filter link to expand its content):

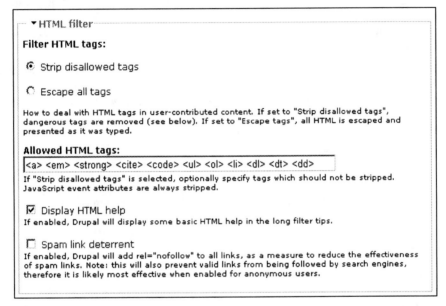

To start with, it is possible to decide, using the first two options, whether you would like to strip HTML tags that are disallowed, or simply ignore all tags from any posts (Escape all tags causes any tags that are present in the post to be displayed *as is*). Remember that if you strip all the tags from the content, you should enable the Line break converter so that users can at least paragraph their content properly. Which tags are to be stripped is decided in the following section, where you can enter a list of all the tags that *are* to be allowed—anything else gets removed!

In the previous screenshot you can see that there are eleven different types of tags allowed in this input format. Notice that the first one is in fact the <a> tag, which can be used to insert links into content—so be wary of this!

Following on, the next setting allows us to specify whether users are given HTML help when posting content—try enabling and disabling this option and browsing to this relative URL in each case to see the difference: filter/tips. There is quite a bit of helpful information on HTML in the long filter tips; so take a moment to read over those. The Spam link deterrent is a useful tool if you find that the site is being used to bombard members with links to products not sanctioned by you.

This is not the end of the story, because we also need to be able to create input formats in the event we require something that the default options can't cater for. In this case, let's assume that we want to add some picture files to the *about us* page, which we will create in due course. Now, there are several ways in which this can be done, but there are two main criteria that need to be satisfied before we can consider creating our page. We need to be able to:

1. Upload image files and attach them to the post.
2. Insert and display the image files within the body of the post.

We have already seen how to perform task number one when we discussed *Upload* in Chapter 4 on *Adding Functionality*. So assuming that you are able to attach files to your posts, this leaves us to deal with the second criterion. There are several methods for displaying image files within your posts. The one we will discuss here does not require us to download and install any contribution modules such as *Img_assist*. Instead we will use HTML directly to achieve this—specifically, we will need the <img> tag.

Take a look at the previous screenshot that shows the configure page of the Filtered HTML input format. You will notice that the <img> tag is not available for use. Let's create our own input format to cater for this instead of modifying this default option. Head on back to the main input formats page under administer and click on add input format. This will bring up the following page, from which you can build your new input format as shown:

Since we will need to make use of some PHP code a bit later on, we have enabled the PHP evaluator option, as well as prevented the use of this format for anyone but ourselves—normally you would create a format for a group of users who require the modified posting abilities, but in this case we are simply demonstrating how to create a new input format; so this is fine for now.

Clicking Save configuration adds this new format to the list, and it can now be configured by clicking on the configure link adjacent to its name in the list in order to bring up its configuration pages. Now, the only difference between this input format and the default Filtered HTML in terms of HTML is the addition of the <img> tag followed by a space in the Allowed HTML tags list, as follows:

Allowed HTML tags:

<img> <a> <em> <strong> <cite> <code> <ul> <ol> <li> <dl> <dt> <d

There is one other thing we need to look at before we are done with this input format. As things stand at the moment, we will run into problems with adding PHP code to any content postings. This is because at the moment the HTML filter has its way with the content first, and mangles the code for the PHP evaluator. *What can be done about this?*

Simply click on the rearrange tab when configuring your input format and give the PHP evaluator a lighter weight, as shown here:

'Inline Images' input format

view   configure   rearrange

Because of the flexible filtering system, you might encounter a situation where one filter prevents another from doing its job. For example: a word in an URL gets converted into a glossary term, before the URL can be converted in a clickable link. When this happens, you will need to rearrange the order in which filters get executed.

Filters are executed from top-to-bottom. You can use the weight column to rearrange them: heavier filters 'sink' to the bottom.

Name	Weight
PHP evaluator	0
HTML filter	10
Line break converter	10

Save configuration

Now, the PHP evaluator gets *dibs* on the content and can process the PHP properly. For the purposes of adding images to your posts, this is all that is needed for now. Once that has been done, save the changes before using this to create the *about us* page. Before you do, though, it is probably most useful to have a short discourse on HTML since you will find that you need to be able to work with HTML as you attempt more complex postings.

HTML

For your browser to render the neatly laid out and colorful pages that we are used to seeing everyday, it needs instructions on what goes where and what color to give everything. This is the domain of **HyperText Markup Language (HTML)**, and Drupal is no exception in its use of HTML here.

Let's have a quick crash course on various aspects of HTML before we go any further:

- **Simplicity**: From tables and frames to lists and images, as well as specifying fonts and styles, HTML is a convenient and readily understandable convention for web-page creation and layout.

- **Platform independence**: HTML is platform independent (although not all browsers are exactly the same), which makes sense if you think about it; the last thing you would want, as the builder of a website, is to have to cater for every different type of machine that could make use of HTML.

- **Tags**: HTML comes in the form of opening and closing tags, which tell your browser how to display the information enclosed within them. For example, the title of a page would be enclosed within the title tags like this: `<title>My Title Page</title>`. Notice that a forward slash is used to distinguish a closing tag from an opening tag.

- **Attributes**: Tags can have attributes, which can modify or define certain aspects of a tag's behavior. For example, the `size` attribute in the following HTML snippet defines the size of the font, `<font size="2">I have a font size of 2</font>`, when it is rendered in a browser.

- **Sections**: An HTML page is enclosed within `<html></html>` tags and is divided into `<head></head>` and `<body></body>` sections. The body tags enclose the bulk of the page and contain the information seen on the actual web page. In our case, we need not worry about this because all content is automatically posted between the `<body>` tags.

This gives us a fair overview of what HTML is and does, but for practical purposes it is important to see what can be achieved right here and now using the HTML that is available to us. Actually, all HTML tags are available for you as the administrator to use, but recall that you should only use this account during development; once your site has gone live, you should post content using an input format that you have designed for the task. Because of this you will need to know what the tags actually do.

The following table discusses each of the default allowed tags along with the `<img>` tag that has just been added. Bear in mind that it is not really practical to show each and every attribute for each tag here, so if you would like to learn more about each tag individually, then please take a look at `http://www.w3schools.com`, which is an excellent resource for all things HTML and more.

Tag	Important Attributes	Description
`<img>`	`src`: gives the path to the image file `alt`: holds a description of the image	The `<img>` tag, unlike other tags, does not require a closing `</img>` tag. It is used to display images within HTML pages, and through the use of optional attributes can accurately control the appearance and layout of images.

Tag	Important Attributes	Description
`<a>`	`href`: specifies the destination URL of the link `name`: allows bookmarks to be created within web pages. `target`: defines where to open the link—most often this is a new page, `_blank`, or the same page, `_self`.	The anchor element facilitates the creation of hyperlinks or bookmarks, which can be navigated by users.
`<em>`		The emphasis tag converts standard text to italics.
`<strong>`		The strong tag renders text in bold.
`<cite>`	`title`: can be used to specify the source or author of the citation in question	The citation tag allows text to be referenced as coming from another source or author. It is often rendered in italics.
`<code>`		The code tag changes the style of the enclosed text to mimic computer code's style.
`<ul>`	`type`: defines the type of bullet point to be used: `disc`, `square`, or `circle`.	The unordered list creates a list of bullet points—it requires the use of the `<li>` tag to stipulate items in the list.
`<ol>`		The order list creates a numbered list of bullets—it requires the use of the `<li>` tag to stipulate items in the list.
`<li>`		The list item tag creates a new item within either an ordered or unordered list; because of this it is contained within `<ul></ul>` or `<ol></ol>` tags.
`<dl>`		The definition list tag creates a structured list of items that are defined by the `<dt>` and `<dd>` tags.
`<dt>`		The definition term tag creates a term within a definition list. It is contained within `<dl></dl>` tags.
`<dd>`		The definition description tag creates a description of its parent term—it is contained within `<dl></dl>` tags.

This table really only lists a fraction of all the tags that are available to you to use. Most tags also have a wide variety of required, optional, or event-based attributes that you can play around with in order to achieve the desired effect. There is one other tag that we will need to make use of in order to lay out pages properly, and that is the all important `<table>` element. Tables are used to order and place content within a page and make use of the `<tr>` tag, which defines a new row in the table, and `<td>` tags, which define new cells within that row. As an exercise, head on back to your newly created input format, and add these tags.

With that out of the way, we are ready to begin creating a slightly more advanced posting than all the previous ones.

Creating a Feature-Rich Page

One of the cool things about creating a new page like this is that once it is done, you can reuse the code pretty much anywhere else, substituting in only those values or content that need to change. Obviously, you want the site to look fairly uniform and this supports the principle of code reuse— at least in terms of HTML.

It is quite likely that at some stage you will want to create more than just one standalone page. If this is the case, simply cut and paste whatever page you have created here and make whatever modification you need, before posting. Doing things in this way will lend all your pages a similar look and feel above and beyond the attributes already given to them by the current theme.

The *about us* page is going to have the following features:

- Well-structured content
- List of objectives
- Inline pictures of the team
- Information about the project
- List of important links
- Some dynamic, PHP-based content
- Advertising

In order to meet the requirements stated, we are going to need to make use of the following tags:

- `<table>`
- `<ol>`
- `<ul>`
- `<img>`
- `<a>`

along with a few others, which we will use to demonstrate the various types of font styles available. In order to create a slightly more complex page like this, you should consider working with a proper code/HTML editor (something like EditPlus, `http://www.editplus.com`, will do— alternatively, a simple search on Google will turn up many results, some of which are free) that can indent your code automatically as well as color code the various tags and content, to make life easier.

OK; we are pretty much ready to begin. I am going to list the entire page's code piece by piece instead of all at once because there are quite a few important things that are worth discussing as we go. However, nothing here is too complicated once you have the hang of HTML and PHP. Before we begin, it is better that we look at the resulting page to get a good idea of what we are working towards. The following screenshot shows the bulk of the page:

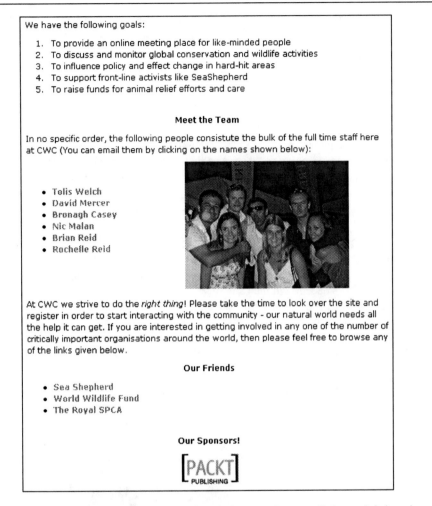

We have the following goals:

1. To provide an online meeting place for like-minded people
2. To discuss and monitor global conservation and wildlife activities
3. To influence policy and effect change in hard-hit areas
4. To support front-line activists like SeaShepherd
5. To raise funds for animal relief efforts and care

Meet the Team

In no specific order, the following people consistute the bulk of the full time staff here at CWC (You can email them by clicking on the names shown below):

- Tolis Welch
- David Mercer
- Bronagh Casey
- Nic Malan
- Brian Reid
- Rochelle Reid

At CWC we strive to do the *right thing*! Please take the time to look over the site and register in order to start interacting with the community - our natural world needs all the help it can get. If you are interested in getting involved in any one of the number of critically important organisations around the world, then please feel free to browse any of the links given below.

Our Friends

- Sea Shepherd
- World Wildlife Fund
- The Royal SPCA

Our Sponsors!

[PACKT]
PUBLISHING

I hope you'll agree that this page is fairly pleasing to the eye! For very little work it is quite easy to achieve a look and layout such as this. What isn't apparent from this page is that the list of names given here, along with their email links, was provided by a short PHP script that was embedded into the HTML page.

Let's get on with the code—to start with, we have the following:

```
<table border="0" cellpadding="5">
  <tr>
    <td align="center" colspan="2">
    <strong>The CWC</strong>
    </td>
  </tr>
  <tr>
    <td colspan="2">
    The <em>Contechst Wildlife Community</em> was started by a group of
    individuals in <cite title="South Africa">Cape Town</cite>. Through
    hard work, dedication and plenty of play time, they have built a truly
```

```
    international community that strives to effect change with regards to
    all things related to our biosphere.
  </td>
</tr>
<tr>
  <td colspan="2">
  <br>
  We have the following goals:

  </td>
</tr>
```

This first section is used to declare the table, which will ultimately be responsible for laying out all the content in the places we want to put it. Notice that I have used two table attributes here. The first one, border, is set to 0, which means that the border is invisible. *Why have I done this?* It's a good idea while you are building your table to set the border to 1, so that you can see what you are doing. When you begin making complex, nested tables and so on, you will find that errors sometimes creep in. Being able to see what your table border looks like is a great help in this case. Once you are finished, simply set the border value to 0 to remove the frames from the page.

The next option, cellpadding, gives each cell in the table a bit of space (or padding, if you prefer) so that content doesn't appear all bunched up together. You can also see that we have a series of table rows and table cells declared in the form of <tr> and <td> tags. However, the first <td> tag has two attributes, which control where the content is placed within the cell (align) and how many columns this cell spans (colspan). This was necessary because at a later stage the image to be added took up a cell on the right-hand side of the table, but the rows above and below still needed to fill the whole page (the whole page being two columns in this case, hence the setting colspan="2").

To get a clearer picture of what I mean, take a look at the following screenshot with the border attribute set to 1:

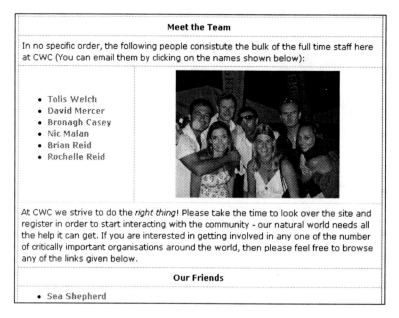

Notice how the rows, above and below, all span both columns of the center rows. You will often need to play around a bit in order to get things right when working on more complicated tables.

If you look past this snippet of code in the previous listing you will notice the use of the `<cite>` tag, with a `title` attribute defined. This is here to show you a novel use for providing references. If a user hovers their cursor over the text contained within the `<cite>` tag (in this instance, Cape Town), the text defined in the `title` attribute (in this case, South Africa) will be displayed on screen. In this way you can clarify or explain important terms without cluttering up your pages.

Continuing along, we get the following ordered list of goals:

```
<tr>
  <td colspan="2">
  <ol>
    <li>
      To provide an online meeting place for like-minded people
    </li>
    <li>
      To discuss and monitor global conservation and wildlife activities
    </li>
    <li>
      To influence policy and effect change in hard-hit areas
    </li>
    <li>
      To support front-line activists like SeaShepherd
    </li>
    <li>
      To raise funds for animal relief efforts and care
    </li>
  </ol>
  </td>
</tr>
```

As you can see, each list item contains exactly one line of content (or one goal, in this case), and all are contained within the `<ol>` and `</ol>` tags. This is simple enough, but is fairly effective as I am sure you will agree. The next section is where we meet some PHP code as well as insert our image of the team:

```
<tr>
  <td align="center" colspan="2">
  <strong>Meet the Team</strong>
  </td>
</tr>
<tr>
  <td colspan="2">
    In no specific order, the following people constitute the bulk of the
    full-time staff here at CWC (You can email them by clicking on the names
    shown below):
  </td>
</tr>
<tr>
  <td>
  <ul>
<?php
    $team = array('Tolis Welch', 'David Mercer', 'Bronagh Casey', 'Nic Malan',
'Brian Reid', 'Rochelle Reid');
    foreach($team as $item){
    $name = explode(" ", $item);
    echo '<li><a href="mailto:' . $name[0] . '@cwc.org">' . $item .
'</a></li>';
    }
?>
```

```
            </ul>
            </td>
            <td align="center">
            <img src="files/bnmv.jpg" alt="The Team" width="250">
            </td>
        </tr>
        <tr>
```

In this case, we have been quite sneaky, as you will see! To summarize, in this section we:

1. Created an unordered list with the <ul> tag

2. Opened up a PHP script by using the <?php tag

3. Created an array of team member names

4. Used a foreach loop, to iterate through each name in the array

5. Obtained the first name of each member by using the built-in explode function

6. Echoed the results, replete with HTML tags to the screen

The actual email links were created using the <a> tag and the special mailto option within the href attribute. The email addresses were built from the first name of the team member so the first two addresses are Tolis@cwc.org and David@cwc.org. This is slightly contrived as you might not have such an ordered system to your email addresses, but it serves to demonstrate how PHP can be embedded into your pages quite nicely.

Once the email addresses have all been listed, we create a table cell adjacent to them and use the image tag to insert the picture of the team. As you can see, there are three attributes used here to get things done. The first, src, gives the path to the image file to be displayed; the second gives a description of the photo so that if someone hovers their cursor over the picture, the text The Team will be displayed; finally, we picked a size for the width of the photo in order to fit it to the page properly. Take note:

> Keep image files small! You can reduce their quality and size using image editing software—large images slow down your site.

The following section of HTML prints out a list of links to a few other organizations that may be of interest to users:

```
        <td colspan="2">
            At CWC we strive to do the <em>right thing</em>! Please take the time
            to look over the site and register in order to start interacting with
            the community - our natural world needs all the help it can get.<br><br>
            If you are interested in getting involved in any one of the number of
            critically important organizations around the world, then please feel
            free to browse any of the links given below.
        </td>
        </tr>
        <tr>
            <td align="center" colspan="2">
            <strong>Our Friends</strong>
            </td>
        </tr>
        <tr>
            <td colspan="2">
            <ul>
```

```
<li>
  <a href="http://www.seashepherd.org" target="_blank">Sea Shepherd</a>
</li>
<li>
  <a href="http://www.worldwildlife.org" target="_blank">World Wildlife
Fund</a>
</li>
<li>
  <a href="http://www.rspca.org.uk" target="_blank">The Royal SPCA</a>
</li>
</ul>
</td>
</tr>
```

This part is fairly straightforward, with the exception of the fact that we are now using a new attribute for the <a> tag. Because we would rather have people remaining on the site without moving off to visit our friends, we have set the target attribute to _blank to force the browser to open up a new window to display the target URL. Other than that, this section is pretty clear, so we move on to the last item on the page—the advertisement:

```
<tr>
  <td align="center" colspan="2">
  <strong>Our Sponsors!</strong>
  </td>
</tr>
<tr>
  <td align="center" colspan="2">
  <a href="http://www.packtpub.com" target="_blank">
  <img src="files/PacktLogosmall.png" alt="Packt Publishers">
  </a>
  </td>
</tr>
</table>
```

This makes use of both a hyperlink and an image file. In effect, we have turned the image, the *Packt* logo, into a hyperlink by enclosing it within <a> and </a> tags. This means that people can not only view the sponsor's logo, but if they wish, they can also visit the sponsor's site directly by clicking on the image. If your sponsors wished to track how many times people followed links from your site, they might require you to modify the target URL to provide them with some additional information. For example, you might end up making the hyperlink reference something like this:

```
<a href="http://www.packtpub.com?referrer=cwc" target="_blank">
```

Actually, things like tracking banner ads can get fairly complicated, but that is a whole other story; so we won't go into it here!

With that done, you not only have a nice, shiny new *about us* page, but you also have a rough template from which to make other pages with a similar look and feel. There is actually a lot more that goes into giving your pages their look and feel, but this involves the use of themes, which we have not yet discussed (these will actually be discussed in detail in the following chapter).

With the page completed, we are not quite finished yet, because it still needs to be added to the site. In order to do this, we need to look at how to actually work with the content we are adding.

Posting a Feature-Rich Page

We saw earlier in the *Working with Content* section how to post pages, although we didn't really have any fairly complex pages to work with at that stage. This brief section will show you the process for getting your more complex pages up and on the site. The following list shows the steps required:

1. Create a new content post, or edit one that is to be modified. In our case, we have an *about us* page already, so as the administrator we can simply click on the edit tab when viewing the about us page.

2. Enter or modify the title of the page accordingly.

3. Select the correct input format. In this case we have a specially created format called Inline images.

4. Copy and paste the HTML created in your HTML or code editor into the Body text area.

5. Ensure the Authoring information and Publishing options are all correct.

6. Upload any image files that are needed for this post and ensure that you enter the correct file path and name into your code. For example, the File attachments section of the about us page looks like this:

In this case, I have not decolorized the bnmv.jpg image as I wanted to preserve its quality for the purposes of the book—however, you should probably aim for image sizes under 10KB.

Compare the file paths shown in this screenshot to the ones presented in the code (these file paths are what you would expect when the download method for files is set to Public):

```
src="files/bnmv.jpg"
src="files/PacktLogosmall.png"
```

Notice that in the code, we need to give only the relative file path and not the fully qualified one. Because the page is being called from the drupal directory, which contains the files directory, we need to show only the file path and name from files onwards.

If you find that instead of getting a file path like the ones shown in this demonstration, you get something like `http://localhost/drupal/system/files?file=PacktLogoSmall.png`, then it is because you have the Download method set to Private in the File system settings section of the settings menu item under administer.

This means that files are uploaded somewhere outside of the document root (this is set in the same section under File system path), and you need to enter the fully qualified file path instead of simply the relative file path as we did here.

7. For something like the *about us* page it is probably best to disable comments as you really want this to be a standalone page and not subject to any debate from the rest of the community.

8. Next, ensure that the menu settings are appropriate for the page you are adding. In this case, we have the following settings in place:

▼ Menu settings

Title:

about us

The name to display for this link.

Description:

Provides information about the CWC team and its philosophy

The description displayed when hovering over a menu item.

Parent item:

Navigation

Weight:

10

Optional. In the menu, the heavier items will sink and the lighter items will be positioned nearer the top.

☐ Check to delete this menu item.

You may also edit the advanced settings for this menu item.

That's it! Once you are ready to view the page, click on Preview, and if everything looks in order, submit it. You can easily edit it again if anything is wrong; so don't fret too much about getting everything just right before you look at it on the site.

So, this section should hopefully have you feeling quite good about how easy it is to create really nice pages for your site. Obviously, if you are not familiar with either HTML or PHP, you will need to practice a bit with these, but the following links should give you a good start:

*   `http://www.php.net`
*   `http://www.phpbuilder.com`
*   `http://www.htmlgoodies.com`
*   `http://www.w3schools.com`

Now that you know how to post and work with content, it is important that you learn how to classify and organize that content so that the archive of information that piles up on your site over time doesn't simply become an unsorted heap of laundry, but instead becomes an intuitive and easy-to-use resource of information. In order to achieve this, we need to discuss...

Categorization

At first glance it might seem that categorization and taxonomy are yet more terms used as indicators that your job is going to be more complex for some reason or other. After all, it's perfectly reasonable to set up a website facility to allow blog writers to blog, forum posters to post, administrators to administer, or any other type of content producer to produce content and leave it at that. With what we have covered so far this is all quite possible, so *why does Drupal insist on adding the burden of learning about new concepts and terms?*

If you know that your site is never going to gather a substantial amount of content, then spending time working with taxonomies and so on is probably not going to bring much advantage—you can simply go ahead and enable whatever content types you require and let users add whatever they please. However, our aim is not generally to remain in obscurity when creating a website, so assuming that you want to attract a large community of users, you will find that the method of categorizing content in Drupal makes it one of the most sophisticated content management systems around—no kidding!

Take the time to master working with categories and taxonomy in Drupal, because not only will this help you to work out how to manage your content better, but it will also really set your site apart from others because of the flexible and intuitive manner in which the content is organized. You will also find that you can manage a site of pretty much any size imaginable (just in case what you are working on is what becomes *the next big thing*), because of the manner in which content is associated with terms and categories.

What and Why?

Taxonomy is described as the science of classification. In terms of how it applies to Drupal, it is the *method by which content is organized* using several distinct types of relationship between terms. Simple as that! This doesn't really encompass how useful it is, though, but before we move on to that, there is a bit of terminology that we should pick up first:

- **Descriptor**: A term used to describe content (also known as a *term*)
- **Vocabulary**: A grouping of related descriptors
- **Category**: A synonym for vocabulary
- **Thesaurus**: A categorization of content, which describes *is similar to* relationships
- **Taxonomy**: A categorization of content into a hierarchical structure
- **Tagging**: The process of associating a term (descriptor) with content
- **Synonym**: Can be thought of as *another word for* the current descriptor

It may help to view the following diagram in order to properly grasp how these terms inter-relate:

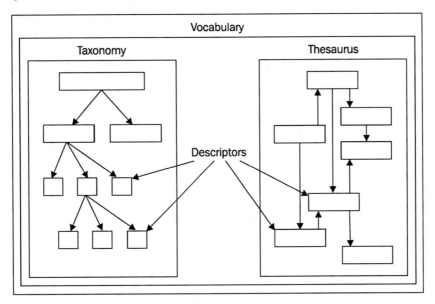

This serves to illustrate the fact that there are two main types of vocabulary. Each type consists of a set of descriptors, but the relationship between them are different in that taxonomy deals with a hierarchy of information, and thesaurus deals with relationships between terms. The descriptors (shown as small boxes) and their relationships (shown as arrows) play a critical role in which type of vocabulary you use.

We have already seen an example of a taxonomy when the forum module was discussed. In this case there was a hierarchical relationship between forum containers and the forum topics they contained. *But what would we need thesauri for?* Well, if you were working on creating a scientific document and you wanted to allow plenty of references between terms so that users could browse related pages, which didn't necessarily have child-parent relationships, then you would go for this type of structure.

So we know that we can classify content in Drupal, but *why is this useful?* One of the things that makes the Drupal taxonomy system so powerful is that it allows content to be categorized when it is created. This removes the burden on the administrators of the site in terms of manpower, because it is no longer necessary to moderate every bit of content coming into the site in order to put it into pre-determined categories.

It is also possible to tag a given node more than once. This means that content can belong to several vocabularies at once. This is very useful for cross-referencing purposes because it highlights relationships between descriptors or vocabularies through the actual nodes.

Implementing Taxonomies in Drupal

The best way to talk about how to implement some form of categorization is to see it in action. As you might expect from Drupal by now, there are quite a few settings to work with and consider, in order to get things up and running. Let's assume that the CWC demo site has enlisted a large number of specialists who will maintain their own blogs on the website so that interested parties can keep tabs on what's news according to the people in the know.

Now, it is assumed that some people will be happy with visiting their blog of choice and reading over any new postings there, but some people might want to be able to search for specific topics in order to see if there are correlations or disagreements between bloggers on certain subjects. Since there is going to be a lot of content posted once the site has been up and running for a few months, we need some way to ensure that specific topics are easy to find regardless of who has been discussing them on their blogs.

Introduction to Vocabularies

Let's quickly discuss how categories are dealt with in the administration tool in order to work out how to go about making sure this requirement is satisfied. If you click on the categories link under administer, you will be presented with a page listing the current vocabularies. Assuming you have created a forum during the last few chapters, you should have something like this:

categories

| list | add vocabulary |

The taxonomy module allows you to classify content into categories and subcategories; it allows multiple lists of categories for classification (controlled vocabularies) and offers the possibility of creating thesauri (controlled vocabularies that indicate the relationship of terms), taxonomies (controlled vocabularies where relationships are indicated hierarchically), and free vocabularies where terms, or tags, are defined during content creation. To delete a term, choose "edit term". To delete a vocabulary and all its terms, choose "edit vocabulary".

[more help...]

Name	Type	Operations	
Forums	forum topic	edit vocabulary	edit terms

Before we look at editing terms and vocabularies, let's take a look at how to create a vocabulary for ourselves. Click on the add vocabulary tab to bring up the following page, which we can use to create our first vocabulary manually:

categories

list **add vocabulary**

When you create a controlled vocabulary you are creating a set of terms to use for describing content (known as descriptors in indexing lingo). Drupal allows you to describe each piece of content (blog, story, etc.) using one or many of these terms. For simple implementations, you might create a set of categories without subcategories, similar to Slashdot.org's or Kuro5hin.org's sections. For more complex implementations, you might create a hierarchical list of categories.

Vocabulary name: *

| Hunting |

The name for this vocabulary. Example: "Topic".

Description:

| This tag associates your content with the general topic of hunting. |

Description of the vocabulary; can be used by modules.

Help text:

| If you have created an entry on any of the above topics, please use |

Instructions to present to the user when choosing a term.

Types: *

☑ blog entry

☐ book page

☐ forum topic

By way of example, this vocabulary will deal with the topic of hunting, and there are a couple of friendly notes to guide users when they intend to submit a blog entry. This only applies to blog entries because that is the only content (or node) type for which this vocabulary is enabled—you can select as many or as few as you like, depending on how many content types you want this vocabulary to apply to.

Looking further down the page, there are several other options, which we will discuss in more detail shortly. Clicking on Submit adds this vocabulary to the list, so that the main page now looks like this:

Created new vocabulary *Hunting*.

Name	Type	Operations	
Forums	forum topic	edit vocabulary	list terms
Hunting	blog entry	edit vocabulary	list terms

So far so good, but this will not be of much use to us as it stands! We need to add some terms (descriptors) in order to allow tagging to commence.

Dealing with Descriptors

Click on list terms and then select the add term tab to bring up the following page:

```
list terms
    [ list ] [ add term ]
    
    Term name: *
    [ Trapping                                    ]
    The name for this term. Example: "Linux".
    
    Description:
    [ Trapping is an insidious practice! Many animals suffer
      untold cruelty - more commonly lost limbs, infections,
      starvation, thirst, and of course, ultimately, death.
                                                              ]
    A description of the term.
    
    Synonyms:
    [                                                         ]
    Synonyms of this term, one synonym per line.
    
    Weight:
    [ 0  ▼]
    In listings, the heavier terms will sink and the lighter terms will be positioned nearer the
    top.
    
    [ Submit ]
```

The term Trapping has been added here, with a brief description of the term itself, which can be used to guide contributors. We could, if we choose, associate the term Snaring with Trapping by making it a synonym. In this case, the term Snaring (or any other synonym you care to add) gets treated as the term Trapping. Edit the term Trapping so that the Synonyms option looks like this:

```
Synonyms:
[ Snaring                                        ]
Synonyms of this term, one synonym per line.
```

Synonyms don't actually do anything useful at the moment, unless you make use of the *Glossary* module—while it is not covered here, feel free to download and try it out for a bit of practice. Add a few more terms of your choice to this vocabulary so that your list looks something like this:

Hunting
| list | add term |

Name	Operations
Canned	edit
Poaching	edit
Trapping	edit

Now it's time to make use of these terms by posting some blog content.

Posting Content with Categories Enabled

Using any account with the requisite permissions to add blog content, attempt to post to the site. You should now be able to view the newly inserted Categories section as shown here:

▼ Categories

Hunting:

| Canned ▼ |

If you have created an entry on any of the above topics, please use this tag to make it easy for others to locate your posting.

Now comes the really, really clever bit! Once this blog node has been posted, users can view the blog as normal except that it now has its tagged descriptor displayed below the title as shown here:

Notice there is a pop-up window that holds the description of the term that will be displayed if the user hovers the cursor over the descriptor's link. *Talking of which, where does the descriptor link take us?* If you click on the term, in this case, Canned, you will be taken to a page listing all of the content that has been tagged with this term. This should really have you quite excited about using Drupal, because with very little work, users can now find focused content without having to look that hard—this is what content management is all about!

Hierarchies

What we have seen thus far is really only the start of things. As you can imagine, you can build an entire hierarchy of terms in a vocabulary to give you a fairly complex taxonomy. Remember that if it is a hierarchy you are building, then the broadest terms should be towards the top of the pile with the more focused terms near the bottom. At the moment, though, we don't really have a *hierarchy*, but rather, more of a *flat* structure.

What if we wanted a set of more specific descriptors, which would allow bloggers to tag their content (which focuses on specific types of Trapping, for example)? The answer lies in editing the vocabulary to select a Hierarchy (under categories) option as follows:

Hierarchy:

○ Disabled

◉ Single

○ Multiple

Now, if we wanted to add a term entitled Snaring to our vocabulary, specifically, under the term Trapping, we would simply click on the add term tab and select the relevant parent from the new Parent drop-down list that should now be available:

edit term

Parent:

Trapping ▼

Parent term.

Term name: *

Snaring

The name for this term. Example: "Linux".

With this addition saved, the list of terms looks like this:

Name	Operations
Canned	edit
Poaching	edit
Trapping	edit
-- Snaring	edit

That was fairly easy to do, and now we are free to create as complex a structure as we require by adding terms to their correct place in the hierarchy. You might expect Drupal to show you a breadcrumb trail of the hierarchy, but alas this functionality is not yet present. It is possible to add it manually, but that requires some PHP coding and modifications to the source files, which

fall outside the scope of this book. If you are feeling adventurous, take a look at
`http://www.greenash.net.au/posts/thoughts/basic_breadcrumbs_and_taxonomy`, which
outlines a process to include the full hierarchy breadcrumb into your content pages.

But what happens if your topic is slightly more complex than a straightforward hierarchy? For
example, snaring is also a commonly used method of poaching, so it should also appear under
Poaching in the hierarchy. This is easily achieved by selecting the Multiple option under the
Hierarchy section when editing your vocabulary. Once this change is saved, you can edit the terms
that you would like to fall under multiple categories, by holding down the Shift or Control key
when making your selection in the Parents section of the edit term page as follows:

That takes care of how the Hierarchy options affect the structure of Drupal's content. But it's not
the end of the story yet.

Content Structure

What if, in the demo site's case, we have the term Trapping *available to tag content (blog posts in
this case) with, but someone is really talking about something other than hunting entirely and
there happens to be some sort of content overlap?* An example scenario might be as follows:

- Several specialists are contracted to maintain blogs about the African continent.
- They tag their content using a new Africa vocabulary, which contains terms like
  nature, gazelle, predators, lakes, rivers, mountains, hunting, weather, and tourism.
- You wish to be able to allow material that is created from the Africa blogs to be
  cross-referenced by hunting-related topics in the Hunting specialists' blogs.

In order to achieve this it is necessary to create a new vocabulary called Africa. Attach this
vocabulary to the blog content type, and then create several descriptors, ensuring that one of them
is entitled Hunting as follows:

Africa

| list | add term |

Name	Operations
Rivers	edit
Hunting	edit
Tourism	edit
Weather	edit

Now when users attempt to post content, they are presented with not one but two options to classify their content, and assuming you have used the Weight option correctly, you can apply a kind of hierarchy to your tags. For example, a blog post on poaching by one of the Africa bloggers might look like this:

Submit blog entry

Title: *

```
Poaching to be hunted down!
```

▼ Categories

Africa:
```
Hunting ▼
```

Hunting:
```
Poaching ▼
```

Body: *

```
I have received word from a member of the latest round of
talks! It seems the government will divert funds to help
improve the efficacy of the trans-frontier game parks...

Good news indeed! I am personally grateful to all those people
who dedicated their time to help us with this project.
```

Once this is posted to the site, it is then possible to view both categories on the content page instead of just one. In other words, the node has been tagged with several descriptors in what is known as **faceted tagging**. Basically, faceted tagging uses a *bottom up* system of classification, where facets or properties of the content are described by the terms. In this way a very intuitive method of classifying content can be created without users needing to understand the top-down path of a content hierarchy in order to find the content they are after. Ironically, in this case, the specific method of tagging used here helps to elucidate the hierarchy of terms too.

Taking a look at this posting on the site confirms that users can now go directly to both the Hunting and Poaching category pages by clicking on the links provided in the posting.

There is something slightly more subtle in all of this though. *Can you see it?* Drupal, by default, and at the time of writing, doesn't provide us with a breadcrumb trail of categories so that we can view any category further up the hierarchy simply by viewing its content type. However, structuring your hierarchy using this method does exactly this. Take a look at the poaching post on the page we have just submitted:

Poaching to be hunted down!

| view | edit |

Hunting | Poaching

I have received word from a member of the latest round of talks! It seems the government will divert funds to help improve the efficacy of the trans-frontier game parks...

We know already from the Hunting vocabulary that it is the parent of Poaching. Yet, using only the single vocabulary, there is no way that a user could tell which category the Poaching term fell under. Doing things this way allows users to effectively navigate up a level by visiting Hunting, or staying at the same level by visiting Poaching. But there's a problem with this too.

What happens if one of the Hunting bloggers simply wants to make an entry and tag it with the Canned term from the Hunting vocabulary without having to first specify that this content also belongs to the Africa vocabulary? The answer lies once again in editing the vocabulary page, which contains a Required checkbox right at the bottom. If this option is enabled, then posters must select at least one tag, but if we leave it unselected, then posters can choose whether to include a term from that vocabulary.

Talking of new options, there are three others present here that we should take a look at quickly. Related terms does nothing on a standard Drupal site at the time of writing, although you might wish to play around with the *Glossary* module, which makes use of this feature. A related term can be considered to be a kind of cross-reference at the *vocabulary level*—as opposed to a synonym, which works at the *term level*. Free tagging is an interesting option because it allows posters to decide on their own terms for their content. Enabling this option for the Hunting vocabulary, for example, means posters are given the following category options when creating a blog entry:

Notice that there is a red asterisk superscript above the Hunting category. This is because despite the fact that we are using free tagging, the Required option on the edit vocabulary page is still enabled—so something *has* to be entered here. Secondly, there is a drop-down list of all the tags available (starting with whatever letter you type). This means that giving people free reign to type in their own tags is not as random as it may at first seem, because they can still be guided as to what terms are already available using this drop-down list. In this way, Drupal can encourage a more coherent body of descriptors.

Free tagging has some pros in that it is far more flexible to allow free tagging because people can really tag their content exactly as they please—making the tagging system fit the content far more snugly. The problem is, however, that your vocabulary may well become unwieldy, because similar content could be tagged with entirely different descriptors, making it hard for users to find what they are looking for. If you are to allow this option, then you should ensure that the people who are using it are made aware of the fact that they should tag their content sensibly and in as uniform a manner as possible.

At any rate, if we were to continue with our posting on hunting, we might end up with something like this:

In this case, we have entered four descriptors for this blog entry; so when someone visits the site, they are presented with all four tags associated with this post, like so:

You should make note of the fact that it is not possible to create a hierarchy of terms using the free tagging system because every new tag is on the same level as all the other tags. So what you end up with is really a thesaurus instead of a taxonomy.

This can be very useful for someone who is using the content as reference material because if, for example, they clicked on the descriptor name of a post, which was only tagged with clamps, the page that displays all the posts associated with that tag would no doubt display the post we have just added. Because of this, the person would be able to see that Trapping, bear traps, and gin-traps are all related topics, and would be able to research related material by hopping around from post to post.

The final option available to us on the edit vocabulary page is Multiple select. This relates to free tagging in that if you have free tagging enabled, it is possible to enter more than one descriptor for each post—you simply separate each descriptor with a comma. However, if you want to allow for a more thesaurus-like structure of descriptors for your content, without enabling free tagging, you would simply enable Multiple select, and this would allow users to tag their posts with as many descriptors as are made available by the creator of the vocabulary. Effectively, this is a middle ground in terms of allowing some flexibility in the tagging while retaining control over how content is tagged.

With Multiple select enabled, and Free tagging disabled, you would then select the terms you would like to tag a post with in the same way as you selected multiple parents in the hierarchy section earlier:

Hunting:
bear traps
Canned
clamps
gin-traps
Poaching
-Snaring
Trapping

With that we come to the end of the discussion on categorization. As mentioned when we first began working on this section, it may take a little while to get the hang of things, because the way in which the categorization works in Drupal is atypical and not obviously intuitive. However, once you have mastered it you will find that your content is readily accessible and well organized with little effort.

Summary

With this chapter out of the way, you will hopefully have a good understanding of the tasks that lie ahead in creating a fully functional, content-focused website. If you are not already familiar with HTML and PHP, then I recommend you spend some time learning a bit about HTML before continuing on with the next chapter. That said, you have seen how to create input formats to allow different types of HTML or PHP content into your posts, as well as looking at how to create a fairly nice HTML-based dynamic web page.

While this is certainly important in terms of creating an aesthetically pleasing site, the real nuts and bolts of your content management lesson came with the discussion on categorization. Drupal's taxonomy system sets it apart from other CMS technologies and provides the flexibility and power to implement pretty much any type of structure that we can imagine for our content. With powerful features like free tagging available at the click of a button, you are sitting at the controls of one of the best systems around.

Just because it is useful doesn't make it easy though, and you will no doubt need to spend some time putting into practice what has been discussed here. Once you are confident that you have set things up in line with the site's envisaged needs, you should also be able to make any modifications that might be required along the way with the minimum of fuss.

With much of the hard work out of the way, we can turn our attention to the most creative and, in my opinion, fun part of creating a Drupal site. The following chapter will discuss themes and how to create a unique and appealing look for the new site.

8
Drupal's Interface

Working on your site's interface to make it distinctive and attractive not only requires some technical know-how when it comes to Drupal, but like any design-like task, it also needs some creativity. Your site as it stands at the moment is fully functional and doesn't look awful—it's a bit plain, but it will get the job done! As you will see, however, with a bit of effort creating something entirely new is not out of your reach, and as you might expect, Drupal comes with a host of features to make our lives easier.

If, like me, you enjoy working on the more creative aspects of a website, then this is really the chapter you have been waiting for. It's time to design, plan, and implement the visual environment in which users will *be immersed*—if you can succeed in creating a pleasing atmosphere in which to interact, then you will certainly have done a lot in terms of ensuring users are happy with your site.

However, like everything else in this book, we can't simply dive in headlong and learn to swim once we have begun working. There are plenty of interesting things to think about and learn before we begin customizing Drupal's interface.

You also have the luxury of having a website already set up for you, which frees you to simply make changes here and there to achieve your design goals rather than develop the HTML from scratch. To some extent, this luxury actually restricts you because anything short of a total rewrite of the pages will mean your site retains some of the Drupal *flavor*. But that's not a bad thing at all now, is it?

To this end, this chapter will discuss the following:

- Planning a web-based interface
- How Drupal's interface works
- CSS
- Themes

I should warn you that there is quite a lot involved with coming up with an entirely fresh, pleasing, and distinct look for a site. There are lots of fiddly little bits to play around with, so you should be prepared to spend some time on this section because after all, your site's look and feel is really the face you present to your community, and in turn the face of your community to the outside world.

Another thing to remember is that you should take some time to look at what is already out there. Many issues that you will encounter while designing your site have already been successfully dealt with all over the show, and not only by Drupal users of course. Also, don't be scared to treat your design as an ongoing process—while it is never good to drastically change your site on a weekly basis, regular tweaking or upgrading of your interface can keep it modern and looking shiny new.

Planning a Web-Based Interface

The tenet *form follows function* is widely applied in many spheres of human knowledge, ranging from evolution to biokinetics and engineering. It is a well understood concept, which basically says that the way something is built or made must reflect the purpose it was made for. This is an exceptionally sensible thought, and applying it to the design of your site will provide you with a yardstick to measure how well you have designed it. If you, or preferably everyone you ask, can honestly say that your site looks like it is meant to do whatever it is you are doing, then you are doing a good job.

That's not to say your site should look like every other site that performs the same function. In fact, if anything, you want to make it as distinctive as possible without stepping over the bounds of what you believe your target user will consider *good taste* or *common sense.*

How do you do that? The trick is to relate what you have or do as a website with your specific target audience. If you are providing content that has appeal to both sexes of all ages across all nationalities, races, or religions, then obviously you should go with something that everyone can use. If anything, this might be a slightly flavorless site since you wouldn't want to marginalize any group of users by explicitly making your site friendly to another group. Luckily, though, to some extent your target audience will be slightly easier to define than this, so you can generally make some concessions for a particular type of user.

Bear in mind that while these following sections refer to *visual* or *functional* design, what you are really thinking about is the visual or functional aspect of the *interaction* design, which encompasses all visual and functional design. The interaction design is how you envision your audience using and interacting with your site. This is an important distinction because thinking about everything from the perspective of the user will help to define your choices as you go along.

Visual Design

There's no beating about the bush on this issue. Make the site appear as visually simple as possible without hiding any critical or useful information. By this, I mean you shouldn't be afraid to leave a fairly large list of items on a page if all the items on that list are useful, and will be (or are) used frequently. Hiding an important thing from users—no matter how easy it appears to be to find it on other pages—will frustrate them, and your popularity might suffer. A consequence of this is that you should not be afraid to have quite long pages that users must scroll down—rather have information available at the bottom of the page than have a complex navigation structure.

How you make your site look can also have a big impact on how users understand the site's working. For example, if you have several different fonts that apply to different links, then it is entirely likely that users will not think of clicking on one type of link or another because of the different font styles. Think about this yourself for a moment! If you were reading a page of text and the links were all given in the same font as the writing, how would you know on which words to click? This can be summed up as:

> Make sure your site is visually consistent and that there are no style discrepancies from one page to the next.

There are quite a few so-called rules of visual design, which you could apply to your site. These are largely theoretical, and you may or may not wish to read up on these further—might I suggest Google for some good reading matter. Some that might apply to you are: the rule of thirds, which states that things divided up into thirds—either vertically or horizontally—are more visually appealing than other designs; the visual center rule, which states that the visual center of the page (where the eye is most attracted to) is just above and to the right of the actual center of the page.

Language

Now this is a truly interesting part of your site's design, and the art of writing for the Web is a lot more subtle than just saying what you mean. The reason for this is that you are no longer writing simply for human consumption, but also for consumption by machines. Since machines can only follow a certain number of rules when interpreting a page, the concessions on the language used must be made by the writers (if they want their sites to feature highly on search engines).

Before you worry about making your site's text highly optimized for searching, there are a few more fundamental things that you need to get right. First off, make sure your language is clear and concise! This is the most important; rather sacrifice racy, stylized copy for more mundane text if the mundane text is going to elucidate your important points better.

Apart from the actual content of your language, the visual and structural appearance of the copy is also important. Use bold or larger fonts to emphasize headings or important points, and ensure that you space your text out nicely to make the page easier on the eye and therefore easier to read and understand—we saw an example of this in the previous chapter when we posted a well formatted and laid out "about us" page.

Images

Working with images for the Web is very much an art! I don't mean this in the sense that generally you should be quite artistic in order to make nice pictures. I mean that actually managing and dealing with image files is itself an art. There is a lot of work to be done for the aspiring website owner with respect to attaining a pleasing and meaningful visual environment. This is because the Web is the one environment that is most reliant on visual images to have an effect on users because sight and sound are the only two senses that are targeted by the Internet, for now.

In order to have the freedom to manipulate images as required by your site, you really need to use a reasonably powerful image editor. Photoshop or Paint Shop Pro are examples of good image-editing environments, but anything that allows you to save files in a variety of different formats and provides resizing capabilities should be sufficient. Of course, if you have to take digital photographs yourself, then you will need to ensure you make the photos as uniform as possible, with a background that doesn't distract from the object in question—editing the images to remove the background altogether is probably best.

There are several areas of concern when working with images, all of which need to be closely scrutinized if you hope to produce an integrated and pleasing visual environment (not all of these relate to what your customers actually see, funnily enough):

- One of the biggest problems with images is that they take up a lot more memory than text or code. For this reason you need to have an effective method for dealing with large images that will be required for your site—simply squashing large images into thumbnails will slow everything down because the server still has to upload the entire large file to the user's machine.

- One common mistake people make when dealing with images is not working on them early on in the process to make them as uniform in size and type as possible. If all your images are of one size and of the same dimension, then you are going to have things a lot easier than most. In fact, this should really be your aim before you do anything involving the site—*make sure your images are all uniform*.

- Deciding what type of image you actually want to use from the multitude available can also be a bit of an issue because some image types take up more space than others, and some may not even be rendered properly in a browser. By and large there are really only three image types that are most commonly used—GIF, PNG, and JPG.

- The intended use of an image can also be a big factor when deciding how to create, size, and format the file. For example, icons and logos should really be saved as PNG or GIF files whereas photos and large or complex images should be saved in the JPG format.

Three types of image files were mentioned in the bulleted list. Let's take a quick look at those here.

GIF, or Graphics Interchange Format, is known for its compression and the fact that it can store and display multiple images. The major drawback to GIF is that images can only display up to 256 distinct colors. For photographic-quality images, this is a significant obstacle. However, you should use GIFs for:

- Images with a transparent background
- Animated graphics
- Smaller, less complex images requiring no more than 256 colors

PNG, or Portable Network Graphics, is actually designed as a replacement for GIF files. In general it can achieve greater file compression, give a wider range of color depth, and quite a bit more. PNG, unlike GIF files, does not support animations. You can use PNG files for anything that you would otherwise use GIFs for, with the exception of animations.

Incidentally, there is also an MNG format, which allows for animations—you might want to check that out as an alternative to animated GIFs.

JPG, or JPEG (Joint Photographic Experts Group), should be used when presenting photo-realistic images. JPG can compress large images while retaining the overall photographic quality. JPG files can use any number of colors, and so it's a very convenient format for images that require a lot of colors. JPG should be used for:

- Photographs
- Larger, complex images requiring more than 256 to display properly

That about covers it for the planning phase of your site's interface development. Before we begin an in-depth look at themes, which are responsible for just about everything when it comes to your site's look and feel, we will need to take a look at how the various web technologies are combined in Drupal to provide your site with its interface.

How Drupal's Interface Works

Knowing a bit about the theory behind creating an appealing site is one thing; applying this knowledge within the context of a Drupal site is another thing entirely. Because of this it is important that we take some time to understand exactly how everything is tied together. You have already seen that HTML and PHP can and do form part of a site's interface, but many of you will have noticed the themes link under the administer menu item and wondered what all that is about.

Further, some of you might have also been wondering what on earth a theme engine is, and how both themes and theme engines relate to your Drupal site. The following two definitions should clear up a few things:

- **Theme**: A file, or set of PHP files, that defines and controls the layout of Drupal's web pages. The look and feel of these pages is in turn controlled by **CSS** (Cascading Style Sheet) files, also provided by the theme. Various standard images might also be held within the theme for use by the site.

- **Theme engine**: Provides functionality to create your own unique theme, which in turn gives excellent control over the all aspects of a Drupal site, ranging from what functionality to include within a page, to how individual page elements will be presented.

Making use of a theme engine requires some programming know-how, as themes are built using code. Modifying themes, on the other hand, is fairly easy, and once a suitable base theme has been found, creating your own unique site is a matter of modifying the theme accordingly. The following diagram should help you picture how everything works together, and will place the subject matter of this chapter into context:

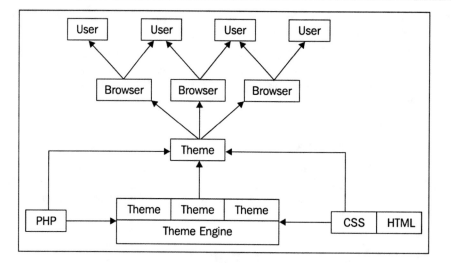

This diagram shows a kind of upside-down waterfall in that the arrows between each level of the diagram represent a contribution of something to the level above. In other words, we can regard PHP, HTML, and CSS as being fundamental technologies that provide the base from which theme engines and themes provide HTML to browsers. Once a theme has provided the HTML to the browser, the browser renders this to the screen for the user to view.

There are several things to make a note of here. Firstly, not all theme engines are pure PHP based. For example, there is a Smarty theme engine available in Drupal for use by people who are familiar with Smarty templates. Second, there are many types of browser out there, and not all of them are created equal. What this means is that a page that is rendered nicely on one browser might look bad, or worse, not even function properly on another. For this reason you should *test your site using several different browsers*!

The Drupal help site has this to say about browsers:

> *It is recommended you use the Firefox browser with developer toolbar and the view formatted source extensions.*

You can obtain a copy of the Firefox browser at `http://www.mozilla.com/firefox/` if you wish to use something other than Internet Explorer.

Now, in terms of how this relates to our situation, we are going to limit ourselves to the selection of a base theme, which we will modify to provide us with the site's interface. This means that for now, you don't have to concern yourself with the intricacies of theme engines. *Can we now move on and look at themes directly?* Not yet; notice that in the previous diagram there is a box containing the term CSS. This is very important in terms of developing our interface, and since we have already seen HTML and PHP in action, let's learn a bit about CSS before continuing.

CSS

The pages in a Drupal site obtain their style-related information from associated style sheets, which are held in the site's theme. Using style sheets gives designers excellent, fine-grained control over the appearance of web pages, and even allows you to produce some great effects. The appearance of pretty much every aspect of the site can be controlled from within a theme, and all that is needed is a little knowledge of fonts, colors, and style sheet syntax.

Before we go any further, it will make life easier if you have a readymade list of the type of things you should look at setting using the style sheet. The following is a list of the most common areas (defined by HTML elements) where style sheets can be used to determine the look and feel of a site's:

- Background
- Text
- Font
- Color
- Images
- Border
- Margin
- Padding
- List

As well as being able to change all these aspects of HTML, you can also apply different effects depending on *whether* certain conditions, like a mouse hovering over the specified area, are met—this will be demonstrated a little later on. You can also specify attributes for certain HTML tags, which can then be used to apply style-sheet styles to those specific tags instead of creating application-wide changes. For example, if you had one paragraph style with a `class` attribute set, like this:

```
<p class="center"></p>
```

you could specify this type of paragraph in your style sheet explicitly by saying something like:

```
p.center { color: green; }
```

Analyzing this line highlights the structure of the standard style-sheet code block, which appears in the form:

- **Selector**: in this case `p.center`
- **Property**: in this case `color`
- **Delimiter**: always `:`
- **Value**: in this case `green`

Note that all the property/value pairs are contained within curly braces, and each is ended with a semi-colon. This introduction to CSS has been very brief, and there are plenty of excellent resources available. If you would like to learn more about this (and it is highly recommended), then visit:

- **CSS Discuss**: http://css-discuss.incutio.com/
- **HTML Dog**: http://www.htmldog.com/

Now that you have an understanding of how Drupal's interface is created through the use of HTML, PHP, CSS, and themes, along with the knowledge of how stylesheets work, we are ready to begin looking at...

Themes

The use of themes makes Drupal exceptionally flexible when it comes to working with the site's interface. Because the functionality of the site is by and large decoupled from the presentation of the site, it is quite easy to chop and change the look, without having to worry about affecting the functionality at all. This is obviously a very useful aspect because it frees you up to experiment however you please knowing that, if worst comes to worst, you can reset the default settings and start from scratch.

You can think of a theme as a *template for your site*, which you can modify in order to achieve the look and feel you want. Of course, different themes have wildly varying attributes; so it is important to find the theme that most closely resembles what you are looking for in order to reduce the amount of work you need to do.

Accordingly, the first task we need to complete is...

Choosing a Base Theme

By default, Drupal ships with a few default themes and there are quite a few more available in the Downloads section of the Drupal site.

> Some themes require the use of a theme engine, in which case, you will need to also download and install the appropriate engine before attempting to use that theme.

Looking at what's already present on the themes page in Drupal, we can see the following:

You might be wondering why it is possible to enable as many themes as you like, yet select only one as the default. The reason for this is that if you enable more than one option, then these options are available for users (assuming they have sufficient permissions) to select by editing their Theme configuration preferences on the edit tab of the my account page as shown here:

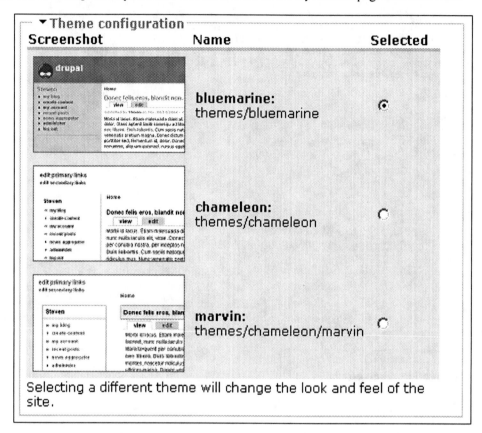

In this case, bluemarine, chameleon, and marvin have all been enabled, with bluemarine selected as the default. Users can then themselves select their preference for how they wish to view the site.

Back to the list of available themes! Enabling the pushbutton theme, and setting it as the default, causes the site, which has been presented in the standard bluemarine theme up until now, to look something like this:

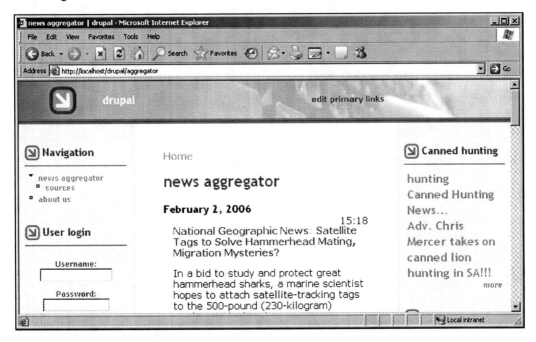

This is a fairly vast change from the previous look provided by the bluemarine theme; however, you should be able to spot the fact that the generic layout hasn't changed much—there are still three columns, there is a heading section containing the site name and logo, there is a navigation section and various boxes, and so forth. What *have* changed are the fonts, colors, and a few images—notice in particular that there is now a background image in the heading section of this theme.

> You should take the time to view each and every theme that is available by default in order to get a feel for what is on offer.

That is not the end of the story, because the Drupal site also has a whole bunch of themes for us to explore, so let's head on over to the themes page at `http://drupal.org/project/Themes` and select the relevant version tab to bring up the themes that are available for your installation of Drupal. Please make note that some of these themes require you to download a theme engine—the Box_grey_smarty contribution is an example of a theme that requires the Smarty theme engine in order to function.

You have already seen how to download and install other modules, and the process for installing themes is no different—simply download and extract the contents of the desired theme to your `themes` folder. For example, the box_grey theme was downloaded, and provides us with two new options in our list of themes, as shown here:

Enabling the box_grey option and setting it as the default causes the site to look like this:

You now have a bunch of default themes to choose from as well as a couple of contributed ones to look over. Once you have decided on one you like, there are a few things to contend with before moving to the next phase. As you might have expected, we can configure the theme by simply clicking on the configure link on the themes page, so let's take a look at that here.

Configuring Your Themes

Clicking on the configure tab at the top of the themes page brings up the global theme options, which will influence each theme regardless of which one is being used—useful if you know that you always want certain features enabled (it's also easy enough to navigate between global and theme-specific settings using the links given at the top of the configure page).

We will concentrate on the global settings page here as this is representative of all the theme configuration pages, so you won't have any problems working on each one individually. Remember that you can override these settings by working on the configure page of a specific theme.

The first section allows you to either use the default logo supplied with the theme, or alternatively, specify a path to your own logo or upload a new logo to the site:

```
┌─ Toggle display ──────────────────────┐  ┌─ Display post information on ──────────┐
│ Enable or disable the display of certain │  │ Enable or disable the submitted by      │
│ page elements.                           │  │ Username on date text when displaying   │
│                                          │  │ posts of the following type.            │
│  ☐ Logo                                  │  │                                         │
│                                          │  │  ☑ blog entry                           │
│  ☐ Site name                             │  │                                         │
│                                          │  │  ☑ forum topic                          │
│  ☐ Site slogan                           │  │                                         │
│                                          │  │  ☐ page                                 │
│  ☐ Mission statement                     │  │                                         │
│                                          │  │  ☑ poll                                 │
│  ☐ User pictures in posts                │  │                                         │
│                                          │  │  ☑ story                                │
│  ☐ User pictures in comments             │  └─────────────────────────────────────────┘
│                                          │
│  ☐ Search box                            │
│                                          │
│  ☐ Shortcut icon                         │
└──────────────────────────────────────────┘
```

In the case of the demo site, we will be making use of a background image to display the logo and name; so this can be unchecked. If you have a site logo, or plan to have one, then simply upload it here.

Drupal also provides us with the ability to specify which content types require post information to be displayed. Now, we have already seen that there are certain types of pages for which we don't need to display this type of information—for example, the *about us* page should be presented as is without informing users precisely who created it.

The reason for the settings as shown in the last screenshot is that it is important to identify a blog posting with the person who posted it, and likewise for forum topics. However, when it comes to things like polls, pages, book pages, or stories, it is less important to do so—often because these sorts of things will be handled by site administrators anyway. For the moment, I have left the page type as the only type to forgo post information.

Please bear in mind that you need to think about what makes sense for your site and apply the settings that reflect *your specific needs*. For example, it may well be important to identify who has contributed certain book pages so that the authors can be contacted in case there is a need to query or modify content on the book page (especially since books are generally collaborative efforts).

The following section allows you to specify Logo image settings and an icon that will be displayed in the site's address bar and in any bookmarks. Once again, what you use here is really up to you. For the purposes of our site, we need not create a specific icon, and we don't yet have a logo to upload; so we can leave things blank for the moment.

The rest of the configure page looks like this as a result:

```
┌─ Logo image settings ─────────────────────────────────────────┐
│                                                                │
│   ☐  Use the default logo                                      │
│   Check here if you want the theme to use the logo supplied with it. │
│                                                                │
│   Path to custom logo:                                         │
│   ┌──────────────────────────────────────────────────────────┐│
│   │                                                          ││
│   └──────────────────────────────────────────────────────────┘│
│   The path to the file you would like to use as your logo file instead of the default │
│   logo.                                                        │
│                                                                │
│   Upload logo image:                                           │
│   ┌────────────────────────────────────────────┬──────────┐   │
│   │                                            │ Browse.. │   │
│   └────────────────────────────────────────────┴──────────┘   │
│   If you don't have direct file access to the server, use this field to upload your logo. │
│                                                                │
└────────────────────────────────────────────────────────────────┘

┌─ Shortcut icon settings ──────────────────────────────────────┐
│   Your shortcut icon or 'favicon' is displayed in the address bar and │
│   bookmarks of most browsers.                                  │
│                                                                │
│   ☐  Use the default shortcut icon.                            │
│   Check here if you want the theme to use the default shortcut icon. │
│                                                                │
│   Path to custom icon:                                         │
│   ┌──────────────────────────────────────────────────────────┐│
│   │                                                          ││
│   └──────────────────────────────────────────────────────────┘│
│   The path to the image file you would like to use as your custom shortcut icon. │
│                                                                │
│   Upload icon image:                                           │
│   ┌────────────────────────────────────────────┬──────────┐   │
│   │                                            │ Browse.. │   │
│   └────────────────────────────────────────────┴──────────┘   │
│   If you don't have direct file access to the server, use this field to upload your │
│   shortcut icon.                                               │
└────────────────────────────────────────────────────────────────┘
```

As you might have guessed, everything has been left blank because we are not specifying anything new and we don't want the default logo or icon to display.

> You will need to ensure that whatever you set here is not unintentionally overridden in the individual theme's configure page.

Customizing Your Theme

Up until now, any settings or changes you have made have been fairly generic. Things are about to change as we begin to implement some more radical modifications that will require amendments to the style sheet in order to get things just right. In the case of the demo site, I have chosen to work with the **box_grey** theme as this most closely resembles the look that is envisaged and has features that are suitable for learning purposes.

Here is some information about box_grey, from their `readme` file:

> *box_ is intended to be relatively easy to modify for those that aren't competent in CSS positioning. Instead of using entirely CSS for layout it is a so called hybrid layout—it uses CSS combined with very simple tables.*
>
> *It is a standard three-column layout using a table for the central three columns with a header above the table and a footer below. This reduces accessibility and adds a little code bloat but has certain advantages:*
>
> - *The content columns won't overlap if a user inserts wide content.*
> - *The content appears in the template (`page.tpl.php`) in the order it appears on the page.*
> - *You can add any sized logo image; the header should expand to fit.*

These features are useful from the point of view of learning how to work with style sheets and this will not only give you an effective means of customizing the look of your site, but also build a platform from which you can attempt some more advanced customizations on other themes when you are ready.

> If you haven't already, now is the time to find a fairly good code editor as you will be looking at code files of one sort or another from here on out.

Navigate to the `themes` folder in your Drupal installation and make a copy of the `box_grey` folder, naming it `box_grey_dev`. This allows us to work on a development version of the theme without putting the original files at risk. Go back to **themes** in your Drupal **administer** section and enable the new **box_grey_dev** theme, setting it as the default. It is important you do this so that you know that you are viewing the correct theme when you check to see what effect any changes you make have on the look of the site.

Now, opening up the `box_grey_dev` folder, you will notice that there are a few `.tpl.php` files, namely:

- `node.tpl.php`
- `page.tpl.php`
- `image_gallery.tpl.php`

which are responsible for the layout of their namesakes. For example, a snippet of the code in
page.tpl.php looks like this:

```
<table id="content">
  <tr>
    <?php if ($sidebar_left != ""): ?>
      <td class="sidebar" id="sidebar-left">
        <?php print $sidebar_left ?>
      </td>
    <?php endif; ?>
      <td class="main-content" id="content-<?php print $layout ?>">
        <?php if ($title != ""): ?>
          <h2 class="content-title"><?php print $title ?></h2>
        <?php endif; ?>
        <?php if ($tabs != ""): ?>
          <?php print $tabs ?>
        <?php endif; ?>

        <?php if ($mission != ""): ?>
          <div id="mission"><?php print $mission ?></div>
        <?php endif; ?>

        <?php if ($help != ""): ?>
          <p id="help"><?php print $help ?></p>
        <?php endif; ?>

        <?php if ($messages != ""): ?>
          <div id="message"><?php print $messages ?></div>
        <?php endif; ?>

        <!-- start main content -->
        <?php print($content) ?>
        <!-- end main content -->
      </td><!-- mainContent -->
    <?php if ($sidebar_right != ""): ?>
    <td class="sidebar" id="sidebar-right">
      <?php print $sidebar_right ?>
    </td>
    <?php endif; ?>
  </tr>
</table>
```

As you can see, this uses HTML to create a table that defines the content of each page. It uses
a bunch of PHP if statements to check whether or not, for example, to display things like the
left-hand sidebar or even the mission statement. The PHP code is embedded within HTML tags,
which have certain attributes associated with them—like id="mission" or id="message". Don't
worry about how these PHP variables are populated; we don't want to alter the way in which the
site functions, we are simply looking at how it is laid out.

But why have they bothered to set the class *and* id *attributes for different sections of the HTML
page?* This is where the power of CSS comes into play. We already know that we want to create a
consistent look for our site. What this means is that every type of related content should have the
same look and feel—in other words, the content of each page should be presented in a similar
manner. This being the case, we can classify a class or id of content to be of a certain type, and
then, using that attribute tag, specify how it should be laid out within the style sheet.

You should be asking for proof, and here it is...

Open up the `style.css` file in the box_grey_dev theme and search for the snippet of code that reads:

```
body {
    color: #000;
    background: #fff;
    font-family: Verdana, Helvetica, Arial, Lucida, sans-serif;
    font-size: 84%;
    padding: 0;
    margin: 0;
}
```

Change this to:

```
body {
    color: #000;
    background: #8E6C63;
    font-family: Verdana, Helvetica, Arial, Lucida, sans-serif;
    font-size: 84%;
    padding: 0;
    margin: 0;
}
```

Save these changes, and refresh the view of your Drupal site in your browser. You should now find that the content on your page has changed so that your pages look something like this:

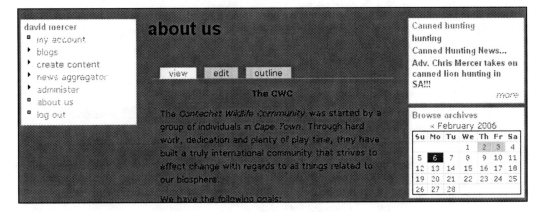

A single change to the body tag in the style sheet has changed the background color throughout each and every page of the whole site. This is quite a powerful and useful property of style sheets, and is precisely why everyone uses them so much nowadays. You can change this back to your original setting or leave it as is—it makes no difference at the moment since it will no doubt change once you have decided on a color scheme for your site.

Now that you know how to implement a change and view the effects of this change on your site, you are ready to continue with modifying the style sheet to reflect how you want the site to look. In the sections that follow, we will discuss several different types of modifications, without grinding through each and every one—and there are a lot of different properties associated with web pages, believe me! Once you have the hang of making changes in one area, it is easy to apply that knowledge somewhere else, so you should find the coverage here sufficient to get you up and running with confidence.

One of the first tasks required for the demo site is to create and upload an image that will serve as the logo and title in the header section of the site.

Images

Images and background images can be tricky to work with because they are generally a fixed width in length, unlike web pages, which can be resized. It can look quite awful if an image stops short of the page size or is in the wrong place, and so we need to work out how to make our images blend into the site so that viewers working on different screens don't end up seeing un-neat images.

In the case of the demo site, I wanted a rough and fairly evocative scene in nature, and what better to use than a sunset shown through African bush (notice that the site's name/logo is actually part of this image, which is why we have done away with the standard site name and logo):

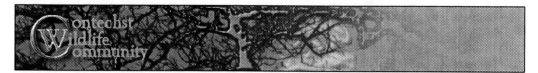

In order to present this on the site, however, we need to do a bit of work with the style sheet. Also, we want this to be presented right up against the top left-hand corner of the page so this will effectively be our site's logo image. Adding this as the site's logo is a simple matter of uploading it in the theme's configure page as shown here:

Upload logo image:

C:\Documents and Settings\David Mercer\Desktop\cwc_header.jpg   Browse...

If you don't have direct file access to the server, use this field to upload your logo.

and ensuring that the Logo option is enabled for this particular theme. Since you have access to the file system, you could also copy the image directly to the files folder and then reference it from the Path to custom logo text box directly above the Upload logo image box:

Path to custom logo:

files/cwc_header.jpg

The path to the file you would like to use as your logo file instead of the default logo.

You could also simply save the new logo image over the old original one, and it will display as normal too.

If you find that you are having problems with viewing this image, then it is most likely that your File system settings in the settings section of the administer menu are at fault. Check them to ensure that you are saving files to the correct places and that you are then attempting to access them from the correct place.

With that done, we can now take a look at the site to see the effect this has had:

Oh dear! This doesn't look very good at the moment, because if you look carefully, the new image is offset to the right (as well as downwards, even though this may not be so noticeable in the screenshot). In order to rectify this we will need to take a look at the cause of the offset. To do this, we need to find out which code is responsible for displaying this area of the page.

Looking near the top of the `page.tpl.php` file we see the following:

```
<div id="header">
  <?php if ($search_box): ?>
  <form action="<?php print $search_url ?>" method="post">
    <div id="search">
      <input class="form-text" type="text" size="15" value=""
name="edit[keys]" /><input class="form-submit" type="submit" value="<?php
print $search_button_text ?>" />
    </div>
  </form>
  <?php endif; ?>
  <?php if ($logo) : ?>
  <a href="<?php print url() ?>" title="Index Page"><img src="<?php
print($logo) ?>" alt="Logo" /></a>
  <?php endif; ?>
```

The highlighted code at the bottom of this snippet is responsible for displaying the site's logo (depending on $logo). As you can see this section uses header as the id attribute for the `<div>` tag, so we should be able to find out what's going on by looking this up in the style sheet. Sure enough, we find the following two header-related tags, which affect our image's position:

```
#header {
  position: relative;
  padding: 1em 0 0 0;
  margin: 0;
}
#header img {
  margin: 0 0.75em 0 1em;
  float: left;
}
```

Both of these can be modified to remove the padding and margin that cause the unwanted offset, as follows:

```
#header {
    position: relative;
    padding: 0 0 0 0;
    margin: 0;
}
#header img {
    margin: 0 0.75em 0 0;
    float: left;
}
```

With these changes saved, you will find that the image is displayed in the desired position. Obviously, you could add padding or change the margins associated with the image as you please.

It is important to realize at this point that changes like this might not be limited only to the area you intend. It may so happen that making a change meant to correct one area actually harms another area—in this case, the loss of padding might have caused images in other areas of the heading, if we were using any, to look bad. *How can this problem be resolved?* You already know that we can add certain attributes to certain tags on a page. To solve this problem, you would add your own custom tag to the area to be altered, and reference it from the style sheet, giving it the properties you require.

Of course, you might want to add a background image to your site too. If you do intend to use background images, make sure that they don't affect the usability of the site. Don't distract or hinder the user in any way from viewing the content. If you are sure that your background image won't be detrimental in any way, then the use of the background property is the way forward.

For example, I modified the body block in the style sheet as follows:

```
body {
    color: #000;
    font-family: Verdana, Helvetica, Arial, Lucida, sans-serif;
    font-size: 84%;
    padding: 0;
    margin: 0;
    background: url(http://localhost/drupal/files/block_background.png) no-
repeat top;
}
```

From this you can see that the background attribute can actually do far more than specify the color to be used—we are not even specifying a background color at the moment because we will deal with colors shortly. In this case, it also sets an address where the background image is to be found. It forces the browser not to repeat the image (we don't want a busy pattern of repeated images in the background cluttering up the site), and finally tells the browser to render the image at the top of the body area. Assuming you have in fact created an image that you want to use (in this case the image is entitled block_background.png) and have ensured that it is small, you would end up with something like this:

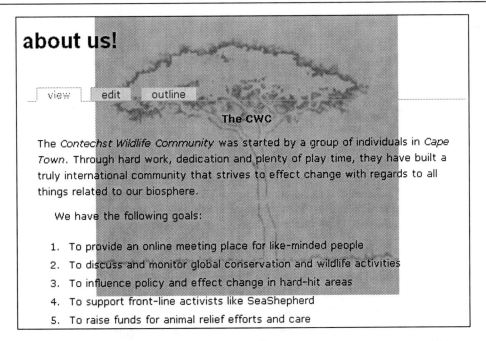

As you can hopefully tell, this background image is fairly unobtrusive and doesn't make it particularly difficult to read any of the content, although, quite clearly, it not the same color as the background yet. Of course, you aren't limited to adding background images to the body of the site—you can add them in other places too. Just check which HTML tags support the `background` or `background-image` options first.

Before we move on to look at colors, it is important to realize that there is an unfortunate problem with the way things have been done here. *Can you spot it?* Think about will happen when these changes are deployed to your live site. *What is the URL of that domain going to be?* It is certain that it will not be `http://localhost/drupal`; so when the time comes for your style sheet to go off in search of your background image by looking for `http://localhost/drupal/files/block_background.png`, it is going to fail.

Consider adding all theme-related images to the actual `theme` folder and not simply uploading them to the standard `files` folder.

Let's try this out by creating an `images` folder under `box_grey_dev`. Insert your background image into this folder and then change the absolute URL `http://localhost/drupal/files/block_background.png` to the relative URL `images/block_background.png` and confirm that you get the expected result.

Now, when the time comes to deploy your site, you won't have the problem of losing images, because the relative URL paths are conserved—it is the absolute paths that change.

Colors

With the new images in place, you might have noticed that neither fits well with the rest of the site because it is currently white by default. In order to rectify this, we are going to change the background color of the site's body tag to the following color:

```
body {
    color: #000;
    background: #BEBEBE url(images/block_background.png) no-repeat top;
    font-family: Verdana, Helvetica, Arial, Lucida, sans-serif;
    font-size: 84%;
    padding: 0;
    margin: 0;
}
```

The site now looks a little better with that modification. The background image integrates seamlessly and the header image now fades into the correct color so that there is a natural transition between the image and the rest of the page as users expand the width of their browsers.

With the change in background color, however, a host of changes need to be made to other colors, especially the colors used for hyperlinks. Of course, it's not even necessary to change the background color! I could have always blended the header image with the default color, or made the background of the background image transparent, but let's continue on with some more changes to get an idea of what can be done.

Now, there can be as many or as few changes as you like to your site's colors. You have already seen that changing the color of an attribute such as background or color is simply a matter of inserting the new color code into the correct place; now we will make a list of the more interesting changes as follows.

Hyperlinks:

```
a, a:link { color: #3A3730; }
a:visited { color: #111111; }
a:hover, a:focus { color: #888888; }
a:active { color: #444444; }
.sidebar .block a:hover { color: #444444; }
#primary a:hover { color: #777; }
```

Sidebars:

```
.sidebar .block {
    background: #E5E5E5;
    border: solid 1px #999;
    margin: 0 5px 5px 5px;
    padding: 0 5px 5px 5px;
}
```

Input:

```
input, textarea {
    background: #E5E5E5;
    color: inherit;
    border: 1px solid #777;
}
```

Footer:

```
#footer {
    color: #666;
    background: #E5E5E5;
    border-top: solid 1px #777;
    padding: 1em 1em 1em 1em;
    font-size: 0.9em;
    text-align: center;
}
```

Primary:

```
#primary {
    font-size: 1.2em;
    border-top: solid 1px #999;
    border: solid 1px #999;
    background: #E5E5E5;
}
```

Once all the color changes have been made, a standard page might look something like this:

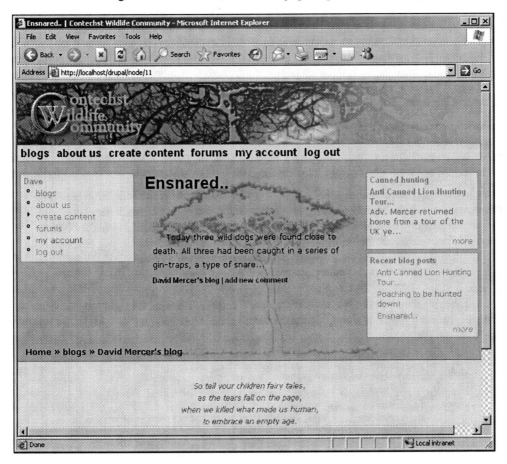

The site as it now stands is easy to use, and hopefully you will agree that the color co-ordination is at least easy on the eye. Remember when making your own adjustments that there are plenty of color-related settings in the style sheet, so you really need to go through your site with a fine-tooth comb to ensure that there are no nasty surprises when links disappear because they are very similar in color to the background and so on.

Page Modifications

It's entirely possible that the actual layout of the page is not to your liking. In this case, there are two options open to you when it comes to effecting change. The style sheet can be used for limited numbers of change. For example, if you found that the sidebars were too narrow for the site, they can be broadened (or narrowed if required) to a fixed width in pixels, by altering the following block:

```
td.sidebar {
    vertical-align: top;
    padding: 0;
    width: 200px;
}
```

But what if you needed some more drastic alterations to the site? Let's say, for example, that you wanted to add an extra column to each page in order to insert some advertising in the hope that you could generate some revenue from the site. In order to do this we need to look at the page.tpl.php file, since this is where the layout of each page is controlled. Depending on how adventurous you are, you could add some conditional PHP code in order to display the column with its advertising only at specific times. For our purposes, it is enough to simply add the new column.

Incidentally, the advertising we will use for the demonstration comes directly from the Amazon associates site, and if you are interested in using this type of advertising, make sure you check out the various Amazon-related contributions on the Drupal site. For the moment, the important bit is seeing how to add the column—you can take a look at the contributions or Amazon associates at your leisure.

Let's say we want the column to appear on the far right-hand side of the page, after the right sidebar, so that it doesn't really impinge on the use of the site in any appreciable way. If this is the case, we need to find the spot in the code where the right sidebar is added, and add the new column in there. Look for this snippet of code in the page.tpl.php file:

```
<td class="sidebar" id="sidebar-right">
    <?php print $sidebar_right ?>
</td>
```

As you can tell, this is responsible for adding a table cell that contains the right sidebar. Simply adding another cell after this should do the trick, so let's go ahead and try that. Make the following changes to the file:

```
<?php if ($sidebar_right != ""): ?>
<td class="sidebar" id="sidebar-right">
    <?php print $sidebar_right ?>
</td>
<?php endif; ?>
<td valign="top" width="120">
    <iframe src="http://rcm.amazon.com/e/cm?t=*************&o=1&
    p=11&l=ez&f=ifr&f=ifr" width="120" height="600" scrolling="no"
    border="0" frameborder="0" style="border:none;"></iframe>
</td>
    </tr>
</table>
```

There are several important points to note here. Firstly, the new cell, enclosed by <td> tags, was placed after the PHP if statement because we don't want it subjected to the same conditions as the right sidebar (it should simply display on every single page).

Secondly, as well as content being vertically aligned at the top of the cell, the width of the cell is given as 120 pixels because we know from the Amazon code that the width of the advertisement is always 120 pixels (this is because we have selected the ad to be of a specific dimension). Finally, the advertisement code that has been added is provided by Amazon, and if you wish to obtain ads like this, then at some stage you will need to register with Amazon to obtain your ID (blanked out in the previous code with * symbols).

Taking a look at the site now shows that the advertisement is displayed as expected:

Of course, there are plenty of different things you may want to achieve on your pages, so spending some time playing around with the code will help you out later on when you need to make more serious changes to the site. You might even want to add banner ads in the header section. Recall that we cheated slightly by turning the site's logo space into the whole header. Doing this means that there is still space allocated for other things within the header (even though this is not visible) and as an exercise you might want to see if you can make use of this space.

This reminds me to reiterate…

It is extremely important that you test out whatever changes you make to your site on more than one browser!

Testing your layout goes deeper than simply checking if everything is in the correct place. It is important that you ensure CSS and HTML is valid and correct, and resources to achieve this are available automatically in box_grey. Simply scroll down to the bottom of the page until you see this:

Validate XHTML or CSS.

Once your site is up and running on the Internet at a public domain, clicking on these links will help you ensure that your layout code is valid. If any problems are reported, then it is up to you to ensure that your site complies as closely as possible. Unfortunately, if you try this from your development machine you will more than likely receive an error message because these services will only work on public domains.

Summary

From learning about what considerations must be taken into account when planning your website's look and feel, to making changes to the code, this chapter has given you a firm grounding in the fundamentals of working with Drupal interfaces.

One of the most important aspects of customizing a site's look is understanding how Drupal is set up in order to leverage the power of themes. As we saw, themes provide a kind of template from which you can work to create your own unique site. This saves us a lot of time and effort because we no longer need to work from scratch. We also briefly touched on the possibility of generating themes from theme engines and hopefully you will feel confident enough to begin looking at this in more detail once you gain more experience.

With respect to building your site's interface, experience is very important. There are three main technologies that you need to spend some time working with: HTML, CSS, and PHP. In this chapter we looked at CSS in some detail before setting about modifying the style sheet supplied with our chosen base theme. Whatever theme you choose as your site's base, the tasks you face will be similar in nature to the ones discussed in this chapter and hopefully you will find that CSS is a most powerful and useful weapon in your armory.

The knowledge gained from working with images and HTML, as well as the application of the design considerations discussed will help not only with your Drupal site, but with any other web-based application that you end up working with. Gaining an appreciation for the various different types of design, as well as having to work with images and code, will allow you to create more ambitious graphical user interfaces in the future.

9
Advanced Features and Modifications

We are going to start out by looking at a grab-bag of modules that showcase some of the more advanced or interesting features in Drupal in order to give you the opportunity to add that *special something* to your site. Whether it is new type of content, an advertising policy to generate revenue from traffic, or even a way of providing nice, dynamic content, you should find something to add value to your site in here.

Remember though, that if what is required is not available in the default distribution or in any of the modules, you are not totally out of luck. The chances are someone else in the community has had to do something similar before, and you should get a few helpful responses on the forums explaining at least some of what you need. If at some point you do manage to create something utterly fantastic, please give back to the community by sharing your work with others.

With that said, it is often important to be able to make your own additions to a site in order to get it just right. Accordingly, we will look at some interesting embellishments using code that is freely available on the Internet. Incorporating JavaScript and other small, working units of code (commonly known as widgets) is the perfect way to enhance your site without having to learn everything about programming first.

So, as far as new modules go, we will take a look at the following:

- Flexinode
- AdSense

The first module deals specifically with content, whereas the other one enables you to integrate your website with another online business, namely Google—hopefully to earn a bit of cash. By the end of this chapter, you will be an ace at using slightly more complex contributions.

We will also talk about some more advanced modifications to the interface. It's always fun to be able to do something out of the ordinary with your site, and working with your theme files, using HTML, PHP, and CSS, is great training for the Web in general and not just Drupal. The *Advanced Site Modifications* section here will hopefully give you some ideas for your own site as well as give you an idea of what's involved in implementing them.

One final thing to remember before we begin is that you *must, must, must* make backups of the whole site, including the database, from time to time (preferably each time you successfully add a new feature). Further, you should also back up each of the pages you are working on before you begin working with them. The topic of making backups is discussed in the *Running your Website* chapter, which follows this one—I mention this just in case you feel it is time to make a backup of what you have now before you begin fiddling around.

Flexinode

At some point along the way you might find that none of the current content types really fit the type of content you want to be able to deliver. If this is the case, then the *Flexinode* contribution might be just what you are looking for. As the module's description says:

> *Flexinode is a module that allows non-programmers to create new node types (flexible content types) in Drupal when their needs are modest. Users can define the fields in the node edit form for their content type, and can either view the nodes as presented by the module or modify the presentation in their theme.*

In the case of the demo site, let's assume that we would like to build up a reservoir of vital statistics pages for endangered animals. In this case, we could go to the trouble of building a rough HTML template and use the page content type, inserting the relevant data into the various cells in our table. However, this would be a pain because if a variety of people were posting this type of information, then each of them would have to learn how to use this HTML template. Let's take a look how the *Flexinode* contribution can help out here.

Downloading and Installing Flexinode

This process should be quite familiar to you now; so we won't spend much time looking at it too closely.

> Flexinode at the time of writing is still being upgraded for version 4.7 compatibility—be careful and ensure that you obtain a suitable, stable version if you intend to use it on your live site.

Simply go to the Drupal website and download the correct version of the *Flexinode* module. Extract the files to the `modules` directory in your Drupal installation and then execute the `.mysql` script using something like the following command (remember to modify the file path to suit your individual system):

```
$ mysql -udrupal -p drupal <
C:\apache2triad\htdocs\drupal\modules\flexinode\flexinode.mysql
```

You will be prompted for a password and you can ensure that the relevant tables have been added by logging into the `mysql` command-line client and looking for the new *Flexinode* tables as shown in the following screenshot:

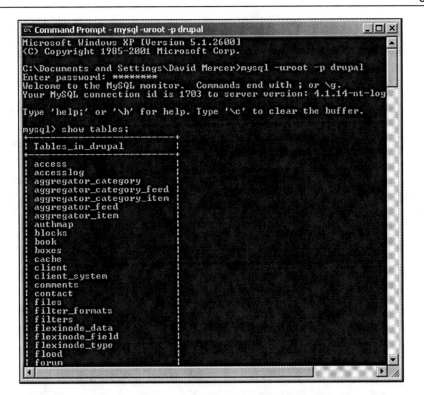

Notice that there are now three flexinode_ tables present in the drupal database. If you are not keen on using the command line, remember that you can use the visual interface provided by phpMyAdmin.

Funnily enough, this contribution comes with a bunch of contributions! What I mean is that there is extra functionality associated with *Flexinode* that is not enabled by default. Take a look at the extracted folder, flexinode, on your file system (under the modules directory). You will notice that there is a contrib folder present, and it contains a whole bunch of .inc files.

Each of these .inc files is responsible for providing the functionality associated with its namesake. For example, field_textarea.inc provides the code needed to include text areas into your content type, and so on. You'll also notice that there are a bunch of readme files available to help clarify what the corresponding .inc file does. For example, the README.colorpicker.txt file has this to say:

> *I am hoping that this will be useful in granting users control over the styles of their sites. I can imagine a flexinode with several color pickers, select boxes and check boxes that could be used to override the default styles of a theme for that particular user.*

Ensure that you read the readme file for each and every .inc file you intend to enable, as you might be required to move files or even install other modules first. When you are ready, head on over to the modules section under administer in your browser and enable the *Flexinode* module before clicking Save configuration.

Creating a Custom Content Type

Under the administer section, navigate to content and you will notice that there are a couple of extra content-related tabs shown on this page that allow us to specify and work with our new content types. Clicking on the add content type tab will bring up a page like this:

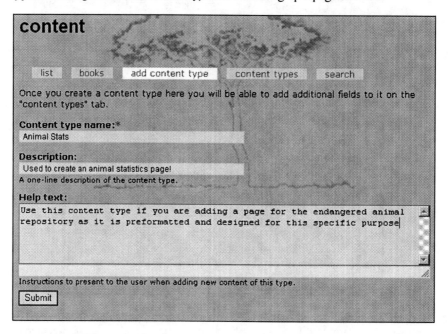

Once that is Submitted, you will be taken to the content types page automatically, where you can now begin working with the newly created type as shown here:

From this point you can click on either of the two links presented at the top right of the content type's section (in this case, the section is entitled Animal Stats). The first link, edit content type, allows you to change any of the information you supplied when you created the content type—for example, you might wish to modify the name, description, or help text. The second option allows you to add some submission guidelines and configure the standard Workflow options as shown here:

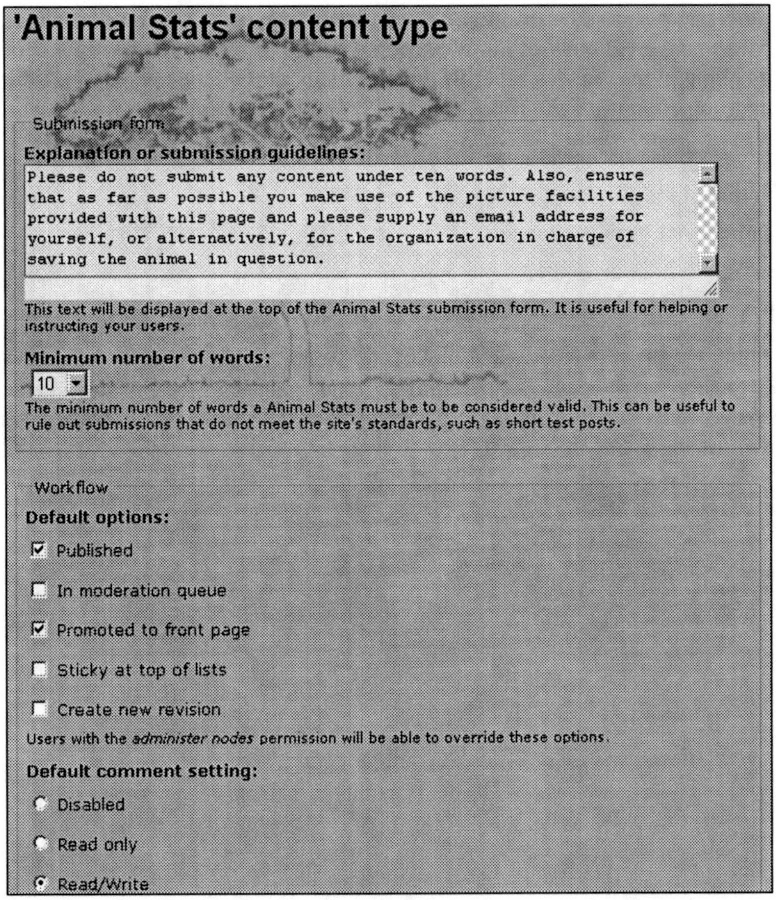

These standard options have already been discussed in earlier chapters at some length and you really need to make your decisions based on how you intend this content type to be used. For our purposes, file attachments have been enabled (even though this is not visible in the screenshot) to allow evidence for any assertions made to be supplied with the post. Comments are also allowed in order for people to be able to collaboratively ensure that facts are correct and up to date.

With those two options out of the way, the really interesting and powerful part of the *Flexinode* module comes into play. The Field list provides us with the option to specify a number of different types of input, which are then bundled into the overall content type. Now, this can be slightly confusing to begin with because you need to keep in mind that you are specifying *what is needed* in order to make content, and not the *actual content* itself.

So, before you begin adding different fields all over the show, think carefully about what you want your special content type to do and how it should look. Once you have a clear idea of what it is you are creating, it will be a lot easier to go ahead and build it.

Adding Structure

Our *Animal Stats* pages should be informative and interesting, providing interested parties with a comprehensive and coherent body of knowledge that serves to fix an image of the animal, its profile, and its plight in the reader's mind. If one thinks about the types of elements that a page like this would need, something like the following would probably be suitable:

- A paragraph or two introducing the animal
- A picture of the animal
- A summary of its current status
- A map of its habitat
- Contact information and/or links to more resources

With this in mind, we can turn to the field picker and see what it has to offer. Since the first thing we would like to show on the page is a paragraph, it makes sense to look for a text area to add to the top of the page. Selecting this option in the drop-down list shown on the content types page brings up the following form:

Here the text area is set as a Required field because any user who wants to add an Animal Stats page must have a bit to say about the animal in the first place—a reasonable assumption! Making this a required field has the advantage that it is now a good idea to select Show in teaser (because we know that there will always be a bit of introductory text). This means that whenever anyone happens to browse through the Animal Stats pages, they can read the introductory paragraph in the teaser.

Next, a weight of –9 is assigned to this field because we know that in all likelihood this field will always be displayed at the very top of the page. In the same way, you can simply pick and choose the rest of the fields according to how the page is to be formatted. Each field comes with its own set of considerations that you will need to set depending on how the content page is to be used. As always, it is easy to come back and modify things if they aren't working just right.

Once all the fields have been correctly chosen and set into the correct part of the page, content producers can then use the page as they would any other node. That's it! All that's left to do is to ensure that the content works as it is supposed to and that it fulfils its intended role correctly. Since we have already discussed how to use other content types, we will go no further here.

AdSense

Once you have your site up and running, with hopefully a fair amount of people visiting, it may be a good option to try earning a bit of extra revenue from advertising. Google provides the *AdSense* advertising scheme, which allows you to add customizable blocks of advertisements by simply cutting and pasting their code snippets into your pages. All that you need to do is to decide on the dimensions and colors that will best blend in with your site, and the rest is taken care of by Google.

Doing things this way, while certainly easy, might not be able to give you the control you want over your ads so Drupal provides an **AdSense** module to help out. This section will take a look at how the AdSense module works since it gives more control of what types of ads are displayed and when.

Before we begin, though, it is important that you register with Google in order to obtain an account and ID, which will be used in order to track the traffic that your site sends through the adverts. You can go directly to the AdSense site at: `https://www.google.com/adsense/`. Simply click on the prominently displayed Click Here to Apply button and follow the instructions. Alternatively, you can support the developer of the AdSense module by registering through their referral link displayed at this page: `http://baheyeldin.com/click/476/0`.

Installing and Configuring AdSense

The AdSense module installation is about as simple as they come and you won't need to modify your database or anything else for that matter, apart from copying the downloaded files into your `modules` folder. Once that is done, you can enable the module in the modules section under the administer link.

Once you have saved the new module's configuration, head over to settings and look for the new adsense link underneath the settings link:

Clicking on this brings up the new adsense configuration page, which also presents a link to tons of information on how to configure everything at admin/help/adsense. You must read through the notes associated with each option as they provide useful information on what ad types are available, their dimensions, as well as how the module actually works to display the ads.

We can go ahead and configure our ads now, but bear in mind that we will still need to manually add them to the site once this is done (discussed in the following section). The actual settings start off with the following:

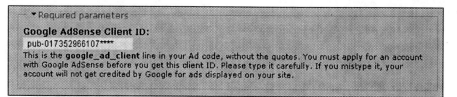

Once you have obtained your client ID you can simply enter it here, and any traffic that goes through the ads on your site will generate revenue for the owner of the supplied ID (in other words, you). The next section allows you to decide which pages should be able to show ads, and which should not:

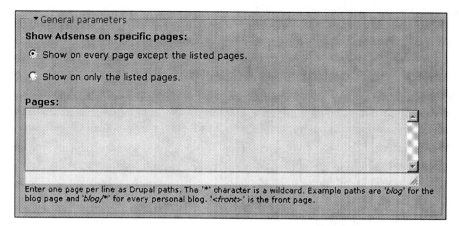

As you can see, you can decide whether or not you want to list all the pages you can display ads on, or all the pages you can't display ads on. Depending on what suits your site, you will need to make a choice of one or the other and then add the appropriate pages in the text area below your choice.

For the purposes of the demo site, we are happy to show the ads on all the pages, hence the text area is left blank, for two reasons. One, there is no section of the site where ads would be inappropriate, and two, ads are not shown to the administrator anyway, so we don't have to specify that we don't want to see them on the admin pages.

But what are the various types of ads that we can show? Well, the following table shows the various options you have available:

Ad Type	Dimensions
Ad Links 4-links 120x90	120x90
Vertical Banner	120x240
Skyscraper	120x600
Button	125x125
Half Banner	234x60
Ad Links 4-links 160x90	160x90
Wide Skyscraper	160x600
Ad Links 4-links 180x90	180x90
Large Rectangle	336x280
Banner Ad Links 4-links	468x15
Banner	468x60
Wide Banner Ad Links 4-links	728x15
Leaderboard	728x90

Why are there so many different types of ads? you may ask. The reason is that often there will be limited space that is suitable for advertising on the web page. For example, you might find that there is some space down the left-hand column of your site, in which case you need a long thin ad. Of course, you might also want to show ads running along the bottom of the page, in which case you want a long, horizontal ad.

It's equally likely that you need both types of ads at once, in which case it is important to make use of groups in order to distinguish one type of ad from another. Depending on where in a page an ad is placed, you might need to specify different colors or even a different type of ad entirely—all this can be handled by the use of groups.

An example of a group setting (under the Ad Type and Colors section) is as follows:

```
▼ Group 1 Attributes

Ad Type:

○ Text

○ Image

◉ Both

Ad Text Color:
AD857F

Ad Border Color:
E5E5E5

Ad Background Color:
E5E5E5

Ad Title Color:
AD857F

Ad URL Color:
AD857F

Alternate URL/Color:
None

Alternate info:

Enter either 6 letter alternate color code, or alternate URL to use
```

The colors chosen here cause the ads shown to be blended into the site so that they look like a natural part of the page's make-up. Depending on where you are placing your ads, you will need to fiddle around with the color settings to get everything looking neat and tidy.

You can set up to three groups at any one time, so don't feel limited to working with just one. You may decide that you would like an image-only advertisement to be shown in one area, but text ads in another—in which, case you have to make use of different groups.

The following option deals with Custom Channels, which you will need to read up in your *Google AdSense* account in order to get working. The website has this to say about them:

> *Custom channels allow you to track performance based on your specified criteria. By pasting channel-specific ad code into your pages, you can track a variety of metrics across a range of URLs. Use custom channels to track the performance of different ad formats, for example, or to compare different page topics to one another.*

This is left to you to study up on because it really is a Google-related issue and not a Drupal one. Once you have created a few channels, it is a simple matter of implementing them in the Custom Channels section of the adsense settings page.

Revenue sharing options is an exceptionally useful tool in that it allows you to allocate a percentage of the revenue generated from Google Ads to the author of the page that contained the ad. In other words, you can now use revenue from ads as a way to encourage blog writers to blog, story writers to write, and so on, because they now have a vested interest in making their content as popular as possible so that as much traffic as possible flows over their posts.

Unfortunately, if you decide to make use of revenue sharing, then you need to go back to the Drupal website and download an appropriate version of the **User Referral** module, because this is required in order to get this feature of the AdSense module working correctly. You should find it easy enough to install the module; there is a MySQL script that must be run, but recall that we have done this before in earlier chapters.

Once User Referral is installed and enabled, you will need to set the roles that are able to use referrals in the access control section under administer. You then have to create a new profile field on the profiles page under settings in the administration section so that users can enter their Google AdSense client ID into their my account section. In order to do this you will need to enable the profile module first (it is part of the core distribution, and so no download is required).

In this case, you should select a single-line textfield, and provide a few informative and sensible options as shown here:

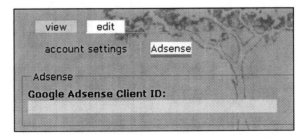

Now when users view their account information (or even upon registration, depending on whether this was enabled in the profiles section), they have a text area in which they can enter their Google AdSense ID:

With everything correctly set up, the following revenue-oriented settings were made for the demo site:

▾Revenue sharing options

☑ Enable Revenue Sharing
Note that enabling this will disable adsense code caching, which can cause more resource usage for busy sites. The referral feature requires the referral module to be installed.

Percentage of node views going to author:

[30 ▾]

Percentage of node views going to user who referred the author:

[70 ▾]

▾Content types
Content types that have revenue sharing enabled.

☑ blog entry

☐ book page

☑ page

☐ poll

☑ story

In this case, the author of the content will get 30% of the revenue generated from traffic at their content, but only blogs, pages, and stories qualify as potential revenue-sharing content—users who are working on polls and book pages, sadly, miss out. Remember:

> Any user who wishes to benefit from revenue sharing must have their own Google account and will need to supply their Google client ID in their profile before they can be credited for their share of the revenue.

Finally, Advanced options allows you to specify whether to disable ads, display a placeholder, limit the number of ads per page, or Enable AdSense Section targeting as follows:

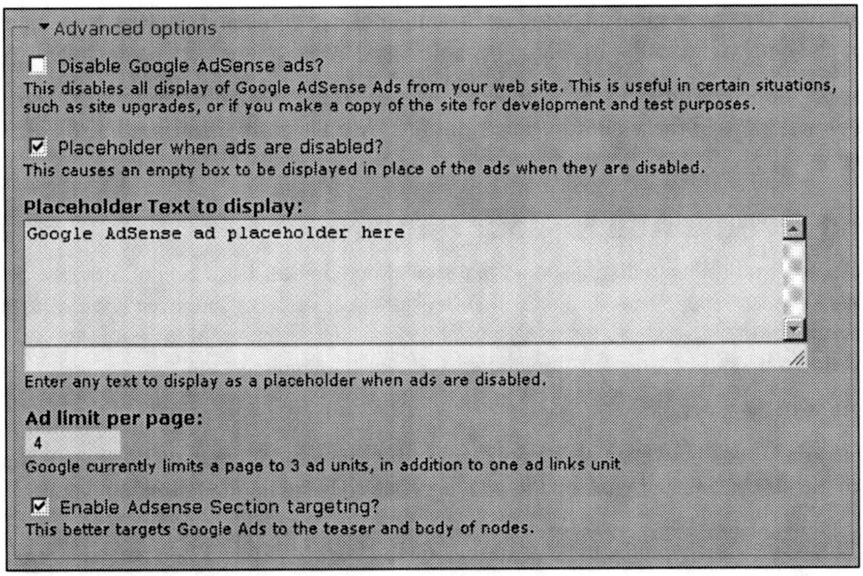

It's a good idea to always keep the placeholder enabled as this allows you to track where your ads are even when you are logged on as the administrator. It could be fairly time consuming to have to log in and log out every time you make a change to the whereabouts of your ads, but it is simple enough to know where they are by viewing the placeholder, as shown here:

The last item of interest, Section targeting, is a Google-related function as defined here:

Section targeting allows you to suggest sections of your text and HTML content that you'd like us to emphasize or downplay when matching ads to your site's content. By providing us with your suggestions, you can assist us in improving your ad targeting. We recommend that only those familiar with HTML attempt to implement section targeting.

In our case, we don't have to do anything because the module automatically targets Google Ads to the teaser and body of nodes for us. Simply enable it and away you go!

Once you are done configuring the groups and so on, click Save configuration. It is then time to actually make use of these configuration options by physically inserting the ads onto the site's pages.

Adding Google Ads to Your Pages

In our case, we would like to display an ad that runs down the left-hand side of the page below any and all other blocks. The reason for this is that the right-hand sidebar has already become quite full, while the left-hand sidebar is sparsely populated, so there is space here. While this ad will be housed within a block, we will also show how to add an ad directly to the site.

Let's begin with the block first...

You have already seen how to create a new block; so if you would like to do things this way, head on over to the blocks link and click on the add block tab to bring up the following page:

Block description:

Google Ads

A brief description of your block. Used on the block overview page.

Block title:

Advertisements

The title of the block as shown to the user.

Block body:

```php
<?php
if (module_exist("adsense"))
{
  print adsense_display("160x600", 1);
}
?>
```

The content of the block as shown to the user.

▾ Input format

○ Filtered HTML
- Allowed HTML tags: <a> <em> <strong> <cite> <code> <ul> <ol> <li> <dl> <dt> <dd>
- Lines and paragraphs break automatically.

◉ PHP code
- You may post PHP code. You should include <?php ?> tags.

Here we have given the block a new title, which unsurprisingly enough is Advertisements (the description as it will appear in the list of blocks is Google Ads). Next, we entered some PHP code to display the Google ads within the block. If you are wondering how I came up with this code, it is all discussed in the notes provided on the adsense configuration page. The important thing to note here is the adsense_display function, because it controls how your ads look via the settings you make in the adsense configuration page (discussed in the previous section).

The previous screenshot shows a fairly simple use of this function, but let's take a quick look at it in more detail so that you understand how it works in the event you need something slightly more complex. From the documentation, we can see that adsense_display takes the following three arguments:

- **Format**: This is a string of two numbers with an x in between. It can be any valid combination from the list provided. If this is not specified, then 160x600 is assumed.

- **Group**: This is the group that denotes the type (text or image) and color of the ad. This can be 1, 2, or 3. If this is not specified, then 1 is assumed.

- **Channel**: This is the custom channel for the ad, as configured in AdSense. This is an optional parameter, and if it is not specified, then 1 is assumed. If you did not configure any channels, then leave this parameter out.

Knowing this, you can see that in the previous screenshot, we have requested an ad of dimension 160x600 pixels, and that the ad should belong to group 1. The final argument is optional, and since we are not concerned with custom channels (as this is a more advanced option, which we leave for you to consider in the event your advertising policy becomes more complex in the future), we left it out entirely.

The final thing to make note of is that we set the Input format to PHP code in order to allow Drupal to implement the code we have entered for the block. Once this block has been successfully added to the system, we give it a high weight (so it displays after everything else) and enable it within the left-hand sidebar as shown here:

Displays Google Adsense ads	☑	10 ▾	left sidebar ▾	configure delete

That is all there is to it! The results can be viewed simply by logging out and taking a look at the page. In our case, due to the settings we made in the configuration section and the dimensions we specified, we get the following block displayed in the left sidebar:

That looks pretty good! *But how do we go about adding the ad to the page directly?* Simple! Open up the page.tpl.php file and insert the adsense_display function in the place you want it, as shown here:

```
<div id="footer">
  <?php if ($footer_message) : ?>
    <p><?php print $footer_message;?></p>
  <?php endif; ?>
<?php
if (module_exist("adsense"))
{
    print adsense_display("468x60", 2);
}
?>

Validate <a href="http://validator.w3.org/check/referer">XHTML</a> or <a
href="http://jigsaw.w3.org/css-validator/check/referer">CSS</a>.
</div><!-- footer -->
  <?php print $closure;?>
  </body>
</html>
```

This code snippet creates a long, flat banner that has its properties configured in the second attributes group (you will need to ensure you have made the appropriate settings, or change the group). When viewed on the site, we get the following ad (in this case, Group 2 was configured to show image ads):

It is important to remember that you don't actually need the AdSense contribution to display Google Ads on your website. In fact, you might even run into problems if you are not using a PHPTemplate theme, or trying to insert PHP code into an area of your template, and that area cannot make use of it. There are a couple of things you can look at if you run into problems:

- Ensure you are not logged in as the administrator because only the ad placeholders display for this user.

- Check your page's source code to see the result of the adsense_display function.

- Check that you have set valid dimensions for your ad—see the table presented earlier in the section entitled *Installing and Configuring AdSense*.

- Ensure that you are able to display the number of ads you require—it may be that you are limited in this respect.

The second point in this list is fairly important because viewing the page's source can tell you a lot about what might have gone wrong. In order to do this, click on View, and then Source in IE, or click *Ctrl+U* in Firefox and you should see something like this (assuming all has gone according to plan):

```
<div class="adsense">
<script type="text/javascript"><!--
google_ad_client = "ca-ref-pub-0173529661****";
google_ad_type = "image";
google_ad_channel = "";
google_ad_width = 468;
google_ad_height = 60;
google_ad_format = "468x60_as";
google_color_border = "E5E5E5";
google_color_bg = "E5E5E5";
google_color_link = "AD857F";
google_color_url = "AD857F";
google_color_text = "AD857F";
//--></script>
<script type="text/javascript"
 src="http://pagead2.googlesyndication.com/pagead/show_ads.js">
</script>
</div>
```

If something has gone awry, then it is likely you will be able to spot the problem from comments that are added to the Google ad code or from what is actually presented in the source code.

Problems with your ads on a development machine might not be the end of the world; by all means check the forums for answers. However, don't get too panicked until you have tried everything out on your live site and allowed sufficient time for Google to crawl your web pages. Until this is done, it is possible that Google is not displaying ads because it has no idea what your site is about.

Adding Google Ads to Your Content

There is also a method of inserting ads directly into your content. For example, if you wanted to show an ad within content, you would first need to enable the **Adsense filter**, by navigating to input formats under administer and modifying a current input format or creating a new one entirely. For example, the Adsense filter was enabled on the Full HTML input format as follows:

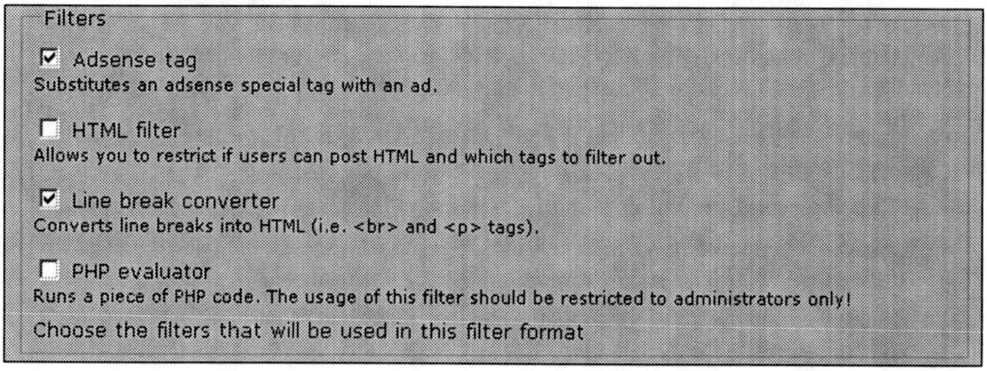

Now, when adding content that makes use of the Full HTML input format, it is possible to add an adsense tag, and the Full HTML option has an extra line of information outlining how to make use of it, as shown here:

Adding a page that incorporates Google ads is then a trivial task. Simply insert the correct format, group, and channel into your adsense tag and add it wherever you like in your post:

```
Title:*
Ads...

Body:*
Hi,

This is a page of Google Ads:

[adsense:336x280:2:1]

All the best...
```

The adsense tag has a special format as follows:

    [adsense:format:group:channel]

where:

- format is one of the supported ad formats (for example, 468x60)
- group is the Numeric ad group this ad belongs to; determines colors
- channel is the numeric ad channel

Viewing this page once you have logged off gives the following result (depending on the settings you made for the relevant group referenced from the tag):

There is also a special format to be used with `flexiblocks` in the format:

```
[adsense:flexiblock:location]
```

We don't discuss the use of **Flexiblock** here, and so we won't go into this now, but as an exercise you might find it worthwhile downloading and installing the Flexiblock contribution, and trying this out.

Advanced Site Modifications

One of the nice things about working with PHP-based applications like Drupal is that not only are they open source, but you can also combine them with pretty much any other technology you can get your hands on. There is a huge online programming community, and many people make their neat little scripts openly available for the likes of you and me to simply include into our own sites as we please. Not all are free, but many are, and many more are very cheap; so it is always worthwhile looking around at some of the scripting sites to see what you can pick up.

Here a few sites that you should consider looking over:

- `http://www.phpbuilder.com`
- `http://www.hotscripts.com`
- `http://www.php.resourceindex.com`
- `http://drupal.org/node/257`—*Customization and Theming*

In this section, we will take a look at what is available and what can easily be incorporated into a Drupal website. Many of you may be shying away at this point because you are not keen to get involved with hardcore PHP programming. Don't worry! The scripts are, by and large, autonomous and complete so that all that is required of us is a few cut and pastes in the right place, perhaps the odd tweak here and there, and away we go. Remember:

> Adding powerful and advanced features, like those seen on big sites, *is not that hard!*

It is important to be aware that you should always look at any and all licensing issues whenever you make use of other people's scripts. You will find that many are made available for free for non-commercial uses but you are required to purchase a license if you are using it for commercial purposes. As you get more confident with working with scripts, however, you should find that it is possible to build fairly powerful features by using your own code or tying together snippets of freely available code.

Since the modifications to come are based on JavaScript and AJAX, it is fair to warn you that Drupal 4.7 comes with built in support for AJAX via the `drupal.js` file. AJAX is a term used to describe JavaScript-based applications that are used to create responsive and dynamic web page elements. The goal of this chapter, however, is to show you how to incorporate really nice features *without having to learn any coding*. As a result, we won't discuss how to make use of the JavaScript functionality provided in `drupal.js` because this is really a task for developers, not site administrators.

If you are interested in creating your own AJAX widgets, take a look at the online tutorials provided on the Drupal site at http://drupal.org/node/42403. These will give you a good idea of where and how to start off in the event that you need to build a few widgets of your own. Any JavaScript-related development you undertake yourself should be done with Drupal's native JavaScript support.

> What we cover in the rest of this chapter is a bit like cheating—we are getting the advantage of some nice JavaScript effects without being subject to the burden of having to learn how to code them.

Many new or upgraded modules will (and do) make use of AJAX already. You might want to download and install a few of these to see what type of effects can be achieved using Drupal's native JavaScript support. Of course, the administration interface for Drupal 4.7 has already been AJAXified with the introduction of the collapsible page areas and so on (for example, on the settings page).

At any rate, let's take a look at the first new feature we are going to add.

Scrolling News Ticker

This is a nice feature of many sites that attempt to provide up-to-date information for their users. If you need to present several bits of information at once, then a dynamic news ticker could be just the thing. With a bit of work you can even integrate the news ticker with an RSS feed to present breaking news from other sites without having to do any work in creating content yourself.

We'll keep it simple and create a scrolling news ticker across the top of each page on the site. The ticker will show information stored in a .txt file on the site. While you can't tell that this information is scrolling across the screen from the screenshot, this is what the addition will ultimately look like:

You can hopefully tell from the various fonts displayed in the ticker above that it is possible to add HTML elements such as links to the individual items (shown in a bold font). This means you can use this ticker to add links to sponsors, or even add image links. There is quite a lot of scope for change; so we will look at how to get everything up and running—what you create with the ticker is then up to you and your imagination.

Obtaining the Ticker

The first task is of course to actually find a workable ticker script. In this case, a free ticker script was downloaded (after a brief search on Google) from **mioplanet** at `http://www.mioplanet.com/rsc/newsticker_javascript.htm`. The conditions of use presented on this page are fairly simple and you should make sure you understand the terms before you continue. Assuming you are happy to continue, download the JavaScript source-code file, entitled `webticker_lib.js`, and save it to the theme folder you are currently developing in—in the case of the demo site this is currently `box_grey_dev`.

> If you are going to use a few widgets like this, it may be better to create a `widgets` folder within your theme in order to keep everything neat and tidy and easy to locate.

Next, open up the `page.tpl.php` file and search for a suitable place to add the ticker. The actual code required to add the ticker to your web page is given on the mioplanet page, and you can simply copy and paste this directly into your site. Since I wanted the ticker to appear along the top of the screen, I added the code in here:

```php
<?php if (count($primary_links)) : ?>
  <ul id="primary">
  <?php foreach ($primary_links as $link): ?>
    <li><?php print $link?></li>
  <?php endforeach; ?>
  </ul>
<?php endif; ?>

<DIV ID="TICKER" STYLE="overflow:hidden; width:100%"
onmouseover="TICKER_PAUSED=true" onmouseout="TICKER_PAUSED=false">
<? include "ticker.txt"?>
</DIV>
<script src="webticker_lib.js" language="javascript"></script>

</div>
<table id="content">
  <tr>
    <?php if ($sidebar_left != ""): ?>
      <td class="sidebar" id="sidebar-left">
        <?php print $sidebar_left ?>
      </td>
```

As you can see, this places the script after the header information within the same `<div>` tag, but above the table that houses the main content and left and right sidebars.

The most important part of this script is the reference to the `webticker_lib.js` file. In this instance I have added the relative path to the file (`webticker_lib.js`) so that this will not have to change once the site is deployed to the host server.

If you find that your scrolling ticker is just not scrolling, try referencing it with the relative file path, for example: `/drupal/themes/box_grey_dev/webticker_lib.js`. In the unlikely event this doesn't work, try using the fully qualified path: `c:\\apache2triad\\htdocs\\drupal\\themes\\box_grey_dev\\webticker_lib.js`. If this works, remember to write a note somewhere that reminds you to change this path appropriately once you have deployed your site to the live host. It is generally *bad practice* to include absolute file paths like this in your scripts for precisely this reason.

In the event you have to enter a path and not just the filename, it is a good idea to escape backslashes with another backslash (\\) on Windows machines to prevent any confusion with special characters being misinterpreted—alternatively, use forward slashes.

Finally, notice that I have added a short PHP snippet to include a file called `ticker.txt` underneath the first added `<div>` tag. If you would rather test whether the ticker is working correctly before dealing with additional code, then replace:

```
<? include "ticker.txt"?>
```

with:

```
Hi! You should see me scrolling across your page.
```

and view your site in your browser. You should see the message scrolling across your page, like this:

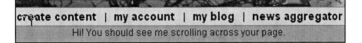

If that works, replace the text message with the PHP `include` statement, and let's move on.

Creating the Content

For our humble purposes, all we really need to do is feed the JavaScript file we have just installed on our site a list of lines to print out to the screen. Assuming that we are going to use a simple text file to hold our data, we need each individual item to appear in its complete form on one line. This is a bit of a limitation if you want to make complex scrolling items, but for the purposes of our demonstration, it is more than adequate. You can add in pretty much anything you want here; however, ensure that you test everything thoroughly before releasing it to the public.

Go ahead and create a `ticker.txt` file and add it to the same folder as the `webticker_lib.js` JavaScript file. Before you start adding lines of information to it, bear in mind that you should try to create a standard format for each news item, so that your work in creating new elements is minimized. In this case, each line is delimited by a single vertical bar, except the start and end of the first and last element, which have two in order to keep everything even.

The following snippet shows the current contents of the `ticker.txt` file on the demo site. These are the items that were used for the scrolling text in the first screenshot in the *Scrolling News Ticker* section:

```
|| <a href="http://www.mioplanet.com/rsc/newsticker_javascript.htm"
   target="_blank"><strong>Scrolling News Ticker</strong></a> by <a
   href="http://www.mioplanet.com"
   target="_blank"><strong>mioplanet</strong></a> |
| This book was brought to you by <a href="http://www.packtpub.com"
   target="_blank"><strong>Packt Publishing</strong></a> |
| It was written by <em>David Mercer</em> of <a
   href="http://www.contechst.com" target="_blank"><strong>Contechst Technical
   & Editorial Consultancy</strong></a> ||
```

Unfortunately, due to the limitations in page size of this book, what should appear as *single* lines have to be presented on *several*. You should, however, get the picture in that you can add some sort of delimiter to the start and end of the item, and within these you can add whatever HTML you like. You might even want to try experiment with adding images or even a special style to the style sheet and referencing it from here. In this way you could add a highlighted title icon or logo to each item, for example.

You will notice a bit further on in this chapter that the news ticker gets a nice, new background color. How you achieve this look is left as an exercise for you. (*Hint: follow the same method as the theme and declare a new* <div> *area with its own style.*)

The main problem with this script as it stands is that it requires you to manually enter each item, which will no doubt become a pain if you have to do it several times a day for the next ten years. There are several ways around this:

- Create a script to pull information from a database.
- Pull information from an RSS feed.
- Only enter content that changes infrequently—such as links to sponsors.
- Get someone else to do it for you.

While we won't continue on this topic here; it would be great experience for you to attempt any one or more of the previous list of options with the exception of the third, which is covered by default. Remember that you can use other scripts to help you out—whatever you can find out there on the Net is fair game to incorporate into your scripts. At any rate, let's get on with the next thing.

Dynamic Content Page

Assume that as the head honcho of your new site you want to add a page outlining all the latest and greatest posts, happenings, and goings on in your life and in your community. In the case of the demo site, we are going to add a quick pick page link to the main menu where people can quickly visit for a selection of the latest and most important happenings on the website—updated once a week, for example.

Now, there are plenty of modules that allow you to show a block of related posts and so forth, but this isn't quite what we want. Ideally, we want to present a list of selected items that allows users to select whatever topic is of interest. At the same time we don't want them to have to jump from node to node in order to view the content of each page.

What we need is some way of only reloading the new articles without actually changing the page we are on. Once again, this can be easily accomplished with the use of scripts that have already been developed. In this particular case, we are going to use a freely available **Dynamic Ajax Content** script, which is provided by the folks at DynamicDrive DHTML Scripts at http://www.dynamicdrive.com.

Incorporating the Application into the Theme

In this instance we are going to take the JavaScript file provided by DynamicDrive and paste it directly into the page.tpl.php file in between the <head> tags. You can get hold of the particular script at the following address:

`http://www.dynamicdrive.com/dynamicindex17/ajaxcontent.htm`. Now, it is not really important that you understand what is going on in the script; however, we will break up the code listing and take a quick look over what it is doing for clarity's sake.

Once you have copied the script, paste it into the PHP file, like so (I have chopped a bit of the actual code file out to save space):

```
<!DOCTYPE html PUBLIC "-//W3C//DTD XHTML 1.0 Transitional//EN"
        "http://www.w3.org/TR/xhtml1/DTD/xhtml1-transitional.dtd">
<html xmlns="http://www.w3.org/1999/xhtml" lang="<?php print $language ?>"
xml:lang="<?php print $language ?>">
<head>
  <title><?php print $head_title ?></title>

  <meta http-equiv="Content-Style-Type" content="text/css" />
<?php print $head ?>
<?php print $styles ?>

  <script type="text/javascript">

/*************************************************
* Dynamic Ajax Content- © Dynamic Drive DHTML code library
(www.dynamicdrive.com)
* This notice MUST stay intact for legal use
* Visit Dynamic Drive at http://www.dynamicdrive.com/ for full source code
*************************************************/

var bustcachevar=1 //bust potential caching of external pages after initial
request? (1=yes, 0=no)
var loadedobjects=""
var rootdomain="http://"+window.location.hostname

function ajaxpage(url, containerid){
var page_request = false
if (window.XMLHttpRequest) // if Mozilla, Safari etc
page_request = new XMLHttpRequest()
else if (window.ActiveXObject){ // if IE
try {
page_request = new ActiveXObject("Msxml2.XMLHTTP")
}
catch (e){
try{
page_request = new ActiveXObject("Microsoft.XMLHTTP")
}
catch (e){}
}
}
else
return false
page_request.onreadystatechange=function(){
loadpage(page_request, containerid)
}

...

function loadpage(page_request, containerid){
if (page_request.readyState == 4 && (page_request.status==200 ||
window.location.href.indexOf("http")==-1))
document.getElementById(containerid).innerHTML=page_request.responseText
}

...
```

```
if (fileref!=""){
document.getElementsByTagName("head").item(0).appendChild(fileref)
loadedobjects+=file+" " //Remember this object as being already added to page
}
}
}
```

```
</script>
```

```
</head>
<body <?php print theme("onload_attribute"); ?>>
<div id="header">
  <?php print $search_box ?>
  <?php if ($logo) : ?>
```

From this code you should be able to gather that once the script has been declared, we use a function, ajaxpage, to create a new page that can be loaded into a specific container on our parent web page. This checks to see which browser is being used, and attempts to ensure that the correct page_request object is created for the calling browser in order to implement some cross-browser compatibility.

Then, a new page is loaded using the loadpage function, which performs a few checks on the newly created page_request object before populating the document container (with the ID, containerid) with the page information. The containerid is specified in the page code to come, but is obviously very important in that it *determines where the new information will be loaded onto the parent page.*

Just to reiterate, it is not necessary for you to understand how these scripts work. They are a bit like the engine of a car—you can drive it without knowing exactly how it works. Having said this, JavaScript is a most valuable tool, and with the advent of AJAX to create responsive web pages, time spent studying these scripts would not be wasted.

> Remember, if you ever want to create your own widgets, learn how to make use of Drupal's built-in JavaScript support.

With those functions added to your page, the hard work is done! We now need to turn our attention to how we can make use of them when posting to the quick pick page.

Building the Content Page

Building a new dynamic page requires us to remember only a couple of important points. First, we need to actually attach the pages we are going to add to the post; otherwise we will not be able to add them to the page. The next is to actually tag a section of the page with the containerid tag.

Actually, we shouldn't start building the page until we have some content to go with it. So, for the purposes of this demo we will add a few pages of interesting content. The first page is a bit of news:

```
<table border="0" cellpadding="5">
  <tr>
    <td align="center" colspan="2">
      <strong>Latest News</strong>
    </td>
  </tr>
  <tr>
    <td colspan="2">
```

```
        The Contechst Wildlife Community was praised for its unswerving
        dedication to animal rights in a television interview last night.
        <br> The project founder said he thought we did a great job when
        asked by the reporter!
        </td>
    </tr>
    <tr>
        <td align="center" colspan="2">
        <em>Sponsored By</em>
        </td>
    </tr>
    <tr>
        <td align="center" colspan="2">
        <a href="http://www.packtpub.com" target="_blank">
        <img src="/drupal/files/PacktLogosmall.png" alt="Packt Publishers"></a>
        </td>
    </tr>
</table>
```

This page is prefixed with the date and the type of article—in this case it was saved as 09_02_news.txt on the file system. The reason for this is that when the file attachment is uploaded and attached to the post, you will still need to be able to clearly see which material is the most outdated when the time comes to remove it. The next file is just a bit of plain old content, which we won't bother to list here.

Now, let's head on over to the create content page and add a new page entitled quick pick. The first thing that we must do is attach the two content files to this post. Once that is done, ensure that you unselect the List options for both. Leaving these files listed would defeat the purpose of the page entirely. Next, the most important thing to do is take note of the names of the files that have been saved by Drupal. You can check these in the File attachments section as follows:

From the previous screenshot you can see that the two files have been saved as 09_02_news.txt and 09_02_notnews.txt in the files directory.

In the body of the page, we need to create a few links that will call on the ajaxpage script function we added to the page.tpl.php file earlier. The following HTML was added to the body text area of the quick pick page:

```
<table border="0">
  <tr>
    <td colspan="2" class="body" width="100%">
      <strong>Please select a link below to view that article:</strong>
      <hr>
    </td>
  </tr>
  <tr>
    <td class="body" valign="top">
      <br>
      <a  href="javascript:ajaxpage('/drupal/files/09_02_news.txt',
'contentarea');">Latest News</a>
      <a  href="javascript:ajaxpage('/drupal/files/09_02_notnews.txt',
'contentarea');">Plain Old Content</a>
    </td>

    <td id="contentarea" width="70%" align="center"></td>
  </tr>
</table>
```

As you can see, we have added two links, one entitled Latest News and the other entitled Plain Old Content. Within the links, the ajaxpage function is referenced and it is passed the names of the attached files as well as the id of the page element where the content of each page is to be displayed. A little further down you can see that we have declared a table cell with the id attribute set to contentarea, so this is where the dynamic content is going to be displayed.

Before we post this content, it is important to ensure that it is published properly. Make sure you set the input format to Full HTML otherwise there is a good chance that this will not display properly. Since this is going to be a main menu item, you also need to set the following:

▾ Menu settings

Title:

quick pick

The name to display for this link.

Description:

A selection of the most interesting articles and content posted over the last week.

The description displayed when hovering over a menu item.

Parent item:

Navigation

Weight:

3

Optional. In the menu, the heavier items will sink and the lighter items will be positioned nearer the top.

While you are at it, you should probably also consider disabling comments for this page unless you particularly want your main menu pages to be up for discussion. Posting this page to the site now gives the following initial page:

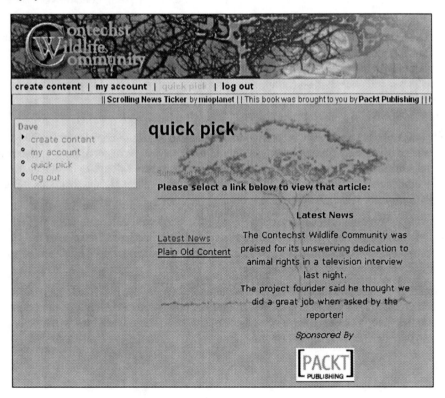

Now, the magic comes when the user actually clicks on one of the links. Instead of moving to a new node, we stay on precisely the same page, except that the content file you attached to this post is now displayed as shown here:

From the lighter color of the top link you can *hopefully* see it has been followed, and as promised, the Latest News article is now displayed in all its glory.

I'm sure you can come up with more novel uses for this type of page—remember to keep the attached files' sizes small so that users don't click on a link and then lose interest waiting for it to be displayed. If you want a bit of a challenge, write a PHP script that converts the <body> section of other posts into a file so that you can add interesting posts or articles without having to manually create the attached content files.

Hopefully, you will agree that we have created some very nice functionality for very little effort. That's all we have time for, but now that you know how it's done, I leave it in your capable hands to come up with novel ways of accomplishing whatever important tasks you might have.

Summary

This chapter focused on two quite different aspects of your website.

The first dealt with functionality and explored a couple of the more advanced modules available for us. Hopefully, you will find that you now know enough about the use of modules to feel confident in using any one you choose. Ultimately, you might end up creating and sharing your own modules for use by other members of the community, but for now, being able to generate a bit of cash on the side using AdSense as well as create your own custom content types should give you plenty to work with.

The second section of this chapter discussed how to use the resources available on the Internet in order to find complete solutions, or even partial code pieces that can be modified and/or incorporated into your site in order to give some great functionality. This has hopefully highlighted the fact that even if you aren't a programming expert, with a bit of searching and some basic knowledge of a few important web-based technologies, you can create some powerful features for your site.

All in all, you website should now be pretty much complete, or, if there is something you want to add that was not discussed directly here, you should find that you have enough general experience to go ahead and make whatever changes you want. Gaining the confidence to create an advanced website is simply about taking the time to learn your way around things, and this book has given you the platform from which to start.

The following chapter looks at administrative tasks associated with your new website, and doesn't relate to the development of your site as directly as these first nine have. Because of this, I would like to take the time to congratulate you on finishing your website now, as well as assure you that all the hard development work is done.

If you would like to get your site up and running as soon as possible, feel free to skip the next chapter and go directly to the Appendix, which outlines how to properly deploy your new site to its home on the Web. You can always come back to Chapter 10 and learn how to maintain and administer your site once it is up and running.

10
Running Your Website

By now, the vast majority of the development for the new site is complete! You should also feel confident that, from a development perspective, you can respond to whatever demands the site throws at you and work with Drupal with a high degree of proficiency. Like all things in the computing world, however, it is never sufficient to build something and then leave your creation to run by itself. There is always work to be done to ensure that everything runs smoothly.

Often, you will find that there are certain jobs that need to be performed every now and then that are not specifically related to Drupal, but are intrinsic to working with websites in general. These tasks can vary greatly in nature, but all those discussed here will be useful at some stage during the life of your website, even if you don't need them right now.

One of the problems with presenting a chapter like this is that we can't possibly hope to cover each and every nuance of the huge array of different platforms on which Drupal can be run. Internet Service Providers (ISPs) offer wildly varying packages, which can either be totally bereft of any type of helpful functionality, or packed full with all the latest gadgets—most ISPs offer a large variety of packages under one roof.

Because of this, we will look at functionality that is in common use and that, in the event you do not have access to the same software, will clearly demonstrate the tasks you need to perform so that you can still successfully operate with the software you *do have access to*. For example, by using the Apache2Triad package, we already have certain useful technologies that we can make use of on the development machine, such as phpMyAdmin.

> It may be helpful to read through this chapter before selecting a hosting package (assuming you haven't already) so that you can get a feel for the type of functionality that you will need in the future.

There are also a few other web-related activities inherent to Drupal that we should take the time to look over quickly. As a result, this chapter will talk about:

- Making backups
- Cron and scheduled tasks
- Throttling

- Patching
- Website activities—including search engine optimization and user maintenance

Armed with the information presented in this the final chapter, you will be a fully equipped Drupal-website administrator. However, the experience you gain from running a live website in itself should prove to be far more valuable than this humble book. Hopefully, you will find the entire experience richly rewarding and share your hard-won knowledge with the rest of the community in the future.

We're on the home straight, so let's get on with it.

Backups

There are plenty of reasons to make backups of both the file system and database. As mentioned several times throughout the course of the book, you should back up anything that is at risk of being damaged whenever you modify code, or add a new module, or even upgrade versions of Drupal. It sounds like a real pain to do this because the vast majority of the time, nothing goes wrong with the application. However, sooner or later, for some unfathomable reason, if you don't make backups, you *will* get stung in precisely the most painful spot.

Most especially, corrupting or breaking a database, which in turn leads to a loss of precious data, can be a real pain in the… back end of your application! So, while it is fairly easy to back up the files on the file system by simply making copies of the directories in question, or indeed copying the entire drupal folder (whatever you have named it), it is of paramount importance that you learn how to back up the database too, because this is not as trivial—it will become easy with practice, though.

Before continuing, it is important to have a *strategy* for backing up files, folders, and data. It is good idea to back up the entire site at regular intervals, as well as backing up the database even more frequently. These backups should be clearly marked so that you know when they were made, making it easy to determine which one to use in the event of some sort of disaster. You might also consider holding these backups away from the main file system, perhaps on a CD, so that if something really bad happens, you don't have to rely on your host's disaster-recovery policy; you have your own.

There are two ways of backing up your database (or any part of it) that we will consider here. One way is to make use of phpMyAdmin, which comes as part of the Apache2Triad package. Let's start with that.

phpMyAdmin

phpMyAdmin is an exceptionally popular and commonplace tool for interacting with MySQL via the Web. Instead of having to learn how to use the MySQL command-line client, phpMyAdmin provides us with a graphical interface, which makes it a lot easier to view and maintain databases tables and content. Issuing commands is also made easier with the interface for many of the most commonplace data-related tasks.

The following steps can be followed in order to create a backup with phpMyAdmin:

1. Log into phpMyAdmin and select the relevant Drupal database.
2. Click on the Export tab along the top of the page, and set up the options as shown here:

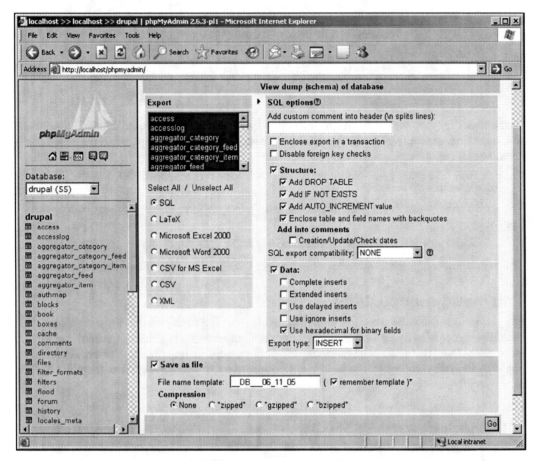

In the screenshot, all the tables were selected for backup, all the Structure checkboxes were selected in order to prevent us having to manually drop a corrupted database, and a useful name (which automatically contains the database name once the backup file is generated) was provided—appending the date as shown is a good idea as it will help you to keep track of which backup is which.

3. Click Go once you are satisfied with your options, and this will then create a SQL file (although there are other formats to choose from such as LaTeX or XML) from which you can recreate the database if needed.

Once you have a backup file, it is a simply matter of causing MySQL to run its contents in order to recreate the database. In order to do this, click on the SQL tab at the top of the page, and enter the name of the .sql file you would like to run against the database, as shown here:

That makes life fairly simple, but it isn't the only way. If you have gotten used to using the command line, or simply prefer it, then we have already seen how it is done, when we issued the command to load the original database:

```
C:\ mysql -udrupal -p drupal < C:/apache2triad/htdocs/drupal-4.6.4/
database/database.mysql
```

You would simply modify the path and filename to reflect the specifics of your new backup file, like so:

```
C:\ mysql -uroot -p drupal < C:/backups/drupal_13_04_06.sql
```

Another way of creating backups is by using the mysqldump utility from the command line.

The mysqldump Utility

It is probably worthwhile spending some time using this because it provides greater flexibility should you ever need to perform anything out of the ordinary. I will confess, though, that for most database-related tasks phpMyAdmin will perform admirably. If you don't have access to phpMyAdmin on your hosted site, or if you are keen to get to know mysqldump, then by all means continue…

To create a backup, simply type in something like the following at the command line:

```
C:\ mysqldump drupal > drupal_13_04_06.sql
```

This will create a backup file called drupal_06_11_05.sql in the current directory. You can then ensure that this has worked by viewing the contents of the file, which will contain reams and reams of SQL statements. There are plenty of different options that you can use to get a variety of different types of backup file; you can simply type in:

```
C:\ mysqldump -help
```

in order to obtain a list of what's available. mysqldump is a powerful and flexible tool, and knowing how it works will benefit you in the long run if you are going to attempt some more advanced backup options.

To reiterate, it is good practice to back up your database on a regular basis, regardless of whether your need to do so for upgrading purposes as doing this will protect you from a total loss of data in the event that some sort of disaster destroys the database or loses its information.

Cron and Scheduled Tasks

In order to keep the site running smoothly and keep it up to date, there are a variety of chores that need to be performed on a regular basis. For example, we saw earlier in the book that the aggregator module needed to be run on a regular basis so that it could update all its feeds and so forth. The Drupal developers are well aware of all the tasks that need to be handled; so they bundled everything up into one handy script—cron.php.

You need to set the **crontab** or **scheduled task** to execute the cron.php script, which is housed in the main folder of your Drupal installation, so that it can perform all the necessary tasks. The cron script basically searches through the site and executes any tasks that apply to modules or other things (like log handling) so that they all stay updated.

Let's take a look at how to control the crontab, followed by setting up a scheduled task for the Windows users among us.

The Crontab

If you are not particularly keen to learn how to make use of the crontab on your hosted site, then feel free to skip to the section entitled *Poormanscron* a little later on in this chapter. It is recommended that you do learn how to make use of the crontab regardless, because it will no doubt come in handy someday when your Drupal site is not immediately available.

All the variables set in the crontab are numerical constants, with the exception of the asterisk character, which is a wildcard that allows any value. The ranges permitted for each field are as follows:

- Minutes: 0-59
- Hours: 0-23
- Day of month: 1-31
- Month: 1-12
- Weekday: 0-7 (Sunday is either 0 or 7)

You can include multiple values for each entry, simply by separating each value with a comma. The command you wish to issue can be any shell command, and can be used to execute web pages, like the cronfeed.php file. Many hosting companies will have an interface such as the following one, which allows you to work with the crontab easily:

This is a web interface to the crontab program. For example, * * * * * would mean every min and 0 0 * * * would mean at midnight

Please enter an email address where output from commands run via crontab will be sent: | davidm@contechst.com |

Minute	Hour	Day	Month	Weekday	Command	
0	*	*	*	*	php /home/contechj/public_html/rank.php	Delete
0	0	*	*	1,2,3,4	php /home/contechj/public_html/catalog/cronfeed	Delete
0	0	*	*	*	/usr/bin/lynx -source http://www.cwc.com/cron.php	

[Commit Changes] [Reset Changes]

In the final entry you can see (hopefully) that the cron.php script is set to run at midnight every day using the command:

```
/usr/bin/lynx -source http://www.cwc.com/cron.php
```

whereas, for example, the first task is set to run every hour (remember to substitute your own site's URL in place of the highlighted code in the previous snippet). Notice too that the php command was not used to execute the cron script as it was for the other two scripts—this is because the cron.php file needs to be accessed as a web page so that certain environment variables are properly set.

Set your cron job to run at regular intervals to ensure that your site is kept as up to date as possible! It is recommended that cron.php is run several times a day.

Windows Scheduled Tasks

On the off chance you are using a Windows-based server, or simply wish to enable scheduled tasks on your Windows PC while you are developing, you can make use of the Scheduled Task wizard. The following instructions, taken from the Drupal site, explain exactly how this is done:

1. Go to Start | Programs | Accessories | System Tools | Scheduled Tasks.

2. Double-click Add Scheduled Task.

3. The Scheduled Task wizard will appear. Click Next.

4. Select the program to run. Choose your browser from the list (for example, Internet Explorer or Firefox). Click Next.

5. Give the task a Name, such as Drupal Cron Job, and choose the Frequency with which to perform the task (for example, Daily). Click Next.

6. Choose specific date and time options (this step will vary, depending on the option selected in the previous step). When finished, click Next.

7. Enter your password if prompted. Change the username if required (for example, if you'd like the task to run under a user with few privileges for security reasons). Click Next.

8. On the final page, select the checkbox Open advanced properties for this task when I click Finish and click Finish.

9. Go to the task's setting page either by checking the checkbox at the end of the last step, or by double-clicking on the task.

10. In the Run box, after the text that is there now (for example, C:\PROGRA~1\MOZILL~1\firefox.exe), enter a space and then type the address of your website's cron.php page in double quotation marks (for example, C:\PROGRA~1\MOZILL~1\firefox.exe **"http://localhost/drupal/cron.php"**)

11. To set a frequency higher than Daily (for example, Hourly), click the Schedule tab, and then click Advanced. Here you can set options such as Repeat task, every 1 hour for 23 hours. Click OK when finished.

12. Change the start time on the task to one minute from the current time. This will allow you to test the task and make sure that it is working.

13. When all settings have been configured to your liking, click Apply and OK (note that you may be prompted for your password).

If you find that you are unable to set a cron job to run on your host site once it is live, then you can use a neat trick and set your Windows scheduled task to access the cron.php script directly from your home PC instead using the instructions just listed. This means that the cron script is executed, depending on your settings, as often as your PC is online and able to access web pages.

This last point highlights how easy Drupal has made things when it comes to performing necessary tasks on a regular basis. All that's required is a browser application of some sort to access the cron.php script, and any tasks that need to be run by the Drupal site will be run. You could access this script from your own browser, or set your own PC to do it whenever you start it up, or any other number of things.

Poormanscron

It should come as no surprise that there is a contribution that can make life even easier. **Poormanscron** is a contributed module that does away with the need to set the crontab or a scheduled task entirely.

It works by checking whether the cron script has been run in the last unit of time (whatever you have set this to be; by default it is every hour) each time a web page is browsed. If it finds that there is a cron run due, it will cause this to happen after the page has been served (so that the user does not have to wait for the tasks to complete before viewing the page).

Basically, *Poormanscron* means that you are freed from having to learn anything about cron jobs. This is convenient, but is also a double edged sword! It is quite likely that you will need to make use of cron jobs for other tasks, and if you use Poormanscron for Drupal, then all you are doing is postponing the time when you have to sit down and learn how to use the crontab or scheduled tasks. At any rate, you have seen examples of how to use all the options; so all that remains is for us to take a look at how to work with Poormanscron:

1. Download the Poormanscron module from the Drupal website.
2. Extract the files to your modules folder.
3. Enable the module in the modules section under administer.

That's all there is to it—provided your site has regular use, your cron tasks will run smoothly and you need not worry about accessing the cron.php script manually or setting the crontab.

After some time, however, you might get a bit sick of seeing logged cron messages all the time. If you want to administer the Poormanscron module, then head on over to poormanscron under settings in the administration area, to bring up the following page:

Home » administer » settings

poormanscron
Runs Drupal cron jobs without the cron application.

Time intervals

Cron runs interval:

`60`

Minimum number of minutes between cron runs. Cron will actually execute during the first page request after the interval has elapsed.

Retry interval:

`10`

The number of minutes to wait after a cron run error before retrying.

Logging

Log successful cron runs:

`No`

If you want to log successful cron runs to the Drupal watchdog, say Yes here. If those messages annoy you, disable them by selecting No.

Log poormanscron progress:

`No`

If you want to log the progress of a poormanscron run to the Drupal watchdog, say Yes here. If those messages annoy you, disable them by selecting No.

[Save configuration] [Reset to defaults]

As you can see from this, there are a number of options available to control how often cron jobs should be run, how long to wait before retrying after an error, and what your logging policy should be. In this instance logging is disabled because there is nothing that urgently requires manual verification on the demo site (for the moment). If you added new software and had to confirm that it was being properly executed by the cron.php script, then you might consider switching logging back on.

Throttling

Every once in a while someone makes a site that becomes wildly popular. Having loads of people visiting a site can put some serious strain on the server's resources and cause all sorts of problems as the congestion builds. Even if a site is not exceedingly popular, it is possible that it may come under a **denial of service** attack from somewhere.

Before even thinking about setting up the throttling mechanism on a site, it is important that you know what resources are at your disposal:

> If you have already ensured that there are facilities in place to handle a *large amount of traffic*, then you have made the throttle module redundant in effect.

If you are unsure about what resources are available on your site, check with the hosting service and find out what they are giving you.

Assuming you anticipate there will be a need for some sort of congestion control, a good way to deal with surges in traffic or bandwidth usage is to enable the throttling mechanism that comes with Drupal, in the form of the aforementioned throttle module. This is easy enough to accomplish by enabling it in the modules section of the administration tool. Once that is done, you can configure how the module acts on the site in general by navigating to the throttle page under settings in the administration area. This will bring up the following page:

---

throttle

If your site gets linked to by a popular website, or otherwise comes under a "Denial of Service" (DoS) attack, your webserver might become overwhelmed. This module provides a congestion control throttling mechanism for automatically detecting a surge in incoming traffic. This mechanism is utilized by other Drupal modules to automatically optimize their performance by temporarily disabling CPU-intensive functionality.

Auto-throttle on anonymous users:

`300`

The congestion control throttle can be automatically enabled when the number of anonymous users currently visiting your site exceeds the specified threshold. For example, to start the throttle when your site has 250 anonymous users online at once, enter '250' in this field. Leave this value blank or set to "0" if you do not wish to auto-throttle on anonymous users. You can inspect the current number of anonymous users using the "Who's online" block.

Auto-throttle on authenticated users:

`100`

The congestion control throttle can be automatically enabled when the number of authenticated users currently visiting your site exceeds the specified threshold. For example, to start the throttle when your site has 50 registered users online at once, enter '50' in this field. Leave this value blank or set to "0" if you do not wish to auto-throttle on authenticated users. You can inspect the current number of authenticated users using the "Who's online" block.

Auto-throttle probability limiter:

`10%` ▼

The auto-throttle probability limiter is an efficiency mechanism to statistically reduce the overhead of the auto-throttle. The limiter is expressed as a percentage of page views, so for example if set to the default of 10% we only perform the extra database queries to update the throttle status 1 out of every 10 page views. The busier your site, the lower you should set the limiter value.

[Save configuration]   [Reset to defaults]

This page deals with congestion from the point of view of how many people are using the site. In this case, Drupal is instructed to engage the auto-throttle on anonymous users provided there are 300 or more online, and the same for authenticated users provided there are more than 100 of them online. The final option deals with actually limiting the amount of work the throttle mechanism has to do so that it itself does not become a resource hog.

But what if you know that it is a specific module that is consuming more than its fair share of resources? In this case, you would simply enable the auto-throttle for that specific module in the modules section of the administration tool, as shown here:

Name	Description	Enabled	Throttle
adsense	Display Google AdSense ads on your site to earn revenue.	☑	☐
aggregator	Aggregates syndicated content (RSS and RDF feeds).	☑	☑
archive	Displays a calendar for navigating older content.	☑	☐

This can be done on a block-by-block basis as well, by navigating over to the blocks section and doing the same thing. *But what does throttling blocks ultimately mean?* Basically, if your server is under strain and you have set a block to be automatically throttled, it will be disabled and not contribute to the load on the server.

You can take a look at your log message to determine what the throttle module is up to at any given time. For example, I set the throttle mechanism to engage after only one user visited the site. The following log message was then created:

details	
Type	throttle
Date	Thursday, April 13, 2006 - 14:21
User	David Mercer
Location	/drupal/node?destination=node
Referrer	http://localhost/drupal/
Message	Throttle: 2 guests accessing site; throttle enabled.
Severity	notice
Hostname	127.0.0.1

It's not much, but at least it makes it clear when the throttle is on. Once the load has dropped sufficiently, a corresponding message will be sent stating that the throttle can be disengaged and things can return to normal.

While this next point is not directly related to throttling, it is important that you gain some idea about the performance of your site and what you can do to ensure it is good. Take a look at http://drupal.org/node/2601 to learn about how to:

- Analyze your site's performance
- Reduce the load on your servers by preventing access to certain parts of your site for web crawlers of various kinds, using the robot.txt file
- Learn about Apache performance and PHP and MySQL tuning

Any knowledge you gain now can be put to good use preemptively to guard against poor performance which may discourage users in the future—even though it is unlikely that you will notice any performance-related issues early on.

Patching

From time to time, it becomes clear that there is a bug in a module or some other aspect of Drupal. This is especially a concern whenever there is a major overhaul of the software and everyone is working frantically to keep up—since Drupal is only just moving to the new 4.7 version at the time of writing, this is more pertinent now than at any other time. When this happens, invariably people head to the forums to find out if anyone else has had the same problem. Often, as is the case with a bug, other people have also been stricken with the same problem and it may be that someone has been able to fix the problem.

If some kind soul has sorted out the problem on their machine, then it is most likely that they will submit a **patch** file to the forum so that it can be used by everyone else in order to fix their code. At this point it is important to realize several things:

- If you don't want to have any problems, ensure you only download well-tested and stable software for use on your site. Often CVS versions of a module still contain bugs or errors, and so it may be better to wait until a module is *released and tested for your specific version of Drupal.*
- Patch files are not specific to Drupal. They are simply files that explain a list of lines of code that should be added or removed in such a way that it is possible for a **patch utility** to implement those changes without the need for human intervention.
- Patch utilities are not native to Windows machines—they come with Unix-based operating systems such as Linux.

Linux users will need to take some time to learn how to make use of the patch utility if they find they need to implement it. Windows users need to go a step further and download a patch utility first. Luckily there is a download of common Unix utilities available at http://unxutils.sourceforge.net/. This contains the patch utility among other things, and you will need to extract the content to a folder—the patch.exe file will be within the usr\local\wbin folder in whichever directory you extracted the files to.

The patch.exe file can now be used just like any other command-line utility. We have already used the mysql command utility several times, so you have some experience with this. The general syntax when using patch is as follows:

```
c:\ patch [options] [originalfile [patchfile]]
```

In this case the `originalfile` is the file to which the changes should be applied, and `patchfile` is clearly the patch file that contains the changes to be implemented. There are a host of options that you can look through, so check out the man page for the patch before working with it. You can find one at `http://www.hmug.org/man/1/patch.php`. A typical command might look something like this (of course, you need to ensure that you enter the correct file paths to your files if you are not working in one directory):

```
C:\patch buggy_code.php buggy_code.patch
```

Now there is an important path-related issue that needs to be resolved here. If you would like to use `patch` from anywhere on the command line, you need to add its file path to your Path system variable—otherwise, you would have to navigate to the `usr\local\wbin` folder on the command line before using `patch` each time (you could alternatively add `patch.exe` to a folder already in your Path, but it is probably better to keep everything separate).

To do this:

1. Open up the Control Panel and click on System.
2. Click on the Advanced tab and click on Environment Variables
3. Add the path to the `patch.exe` file into the Path environment variable in the System variables section as shown here:

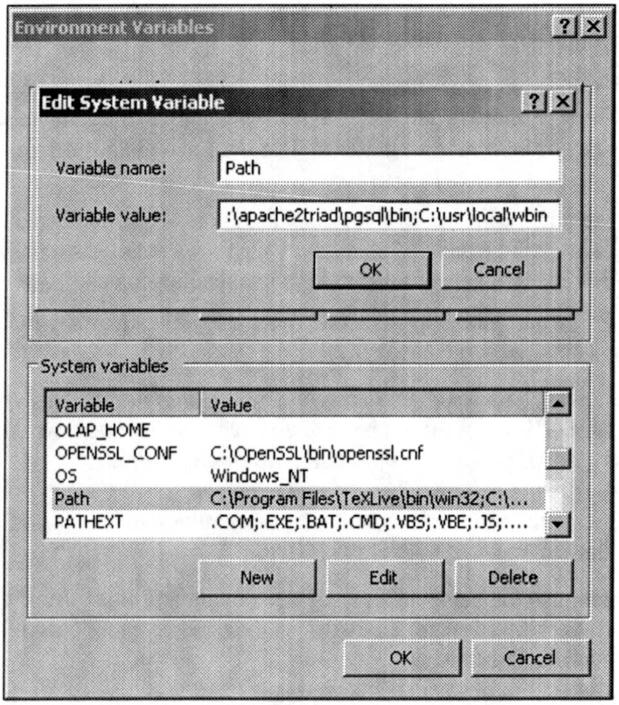

4. Once you are done, click OK.

Note that each path set in the Path environment variable is separated by a semi-colon. You must ensure that you do not change anything other than adding the single path; otherwise you may well break other important applications.

With that done, you now have access to the patch utility from anywhere on the command line. The important question now becomes whether or not to use a patch file. *How do you know whether you need a patch?* The answer to this really lies in searching Drupal for an answer to any given problem you might have—often there are patches submitted on the module's download page, so make sure you search through this as well as look through the forums for more info.

Finally, just because a patch has been made available does not necessarily mean that it will fix the problem. Often, you will find that patches themselves create other problems. For example, viewing the issues page for the Flexinode module shows the following:

Project:	Status:	Category:	Priority:		
Flexinode	active,fixed,patch	\<all\>	\<all\>	Search	advanced search

Summary	Status	Pri	Category	Version	Last updated	Assigned to
Multiple Checkboxes – foreach() error solution	patch (code needs review)	critical	bug	4.6.0	7 hours 18 min	
Teaser does not work correctly with flexinode node	active	normal	bug	cvs	12 hours 4 min	
Textarea teaser not using node_teaser (was: doesn'	patch (code needs review)	normal	bug	cvs	12 hours 16 min	
Required file field breaks submission	active	normal	bug	cvs	15 hours 2 min	
Fine grained, per-field, permissions.	patch (code needs work)	normal	feature	cvs	18 hours 15 min	Bèr Kessels

At the time of writing, there were several patches available for several different things. Depending on what you needed done, you would:

1. Find the relevant patch file.
2. Download it to your machine.
3. Use the patch utility to implement the patch.
4. Attempt to use the updated code.

Make sure that it is in fact a patch file you are downloading and not an entire file that is intended as a replacement. Patch files will more often that not end with a `.patch` extension. As mentioned, the best way to avoid problems is to only use code that has been proven to be reliable, failing which, it is more than likely you will need to practice implementing patches—enjoy!

Website Activities

Once you have developed your site and have it up and running on the live servers, you will find that your ISP probably offers a fair amount of toys for you to play around with. Some of these can be very useful for the budding website administrator. *But what could we possibly need, now that the entire site has been built?*

There are plenty of different tasks that still lie ahead of you. For example, are you sure that malicious people out there can't hotlink to your site and reduce your bandwidth? *What is hotlinking? What is bandwidth?* These questions constitute only a very small part of the types of concerns that must take focus once development is completed. I have to admit, that while the subject of the book was to *build a site*, that task is only one side of the coin!

In the case of the demo site, the following administration panel is provided by the hosting service provider:

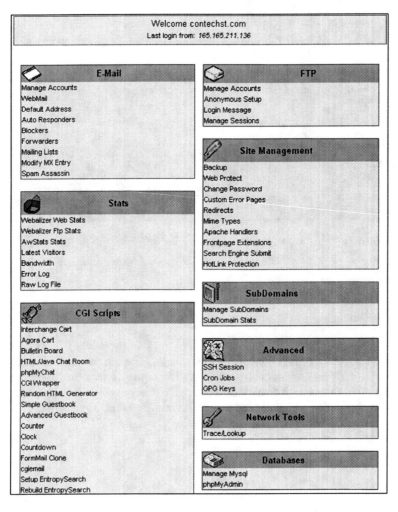

Obviously, there are a lot of toys to play with here and it is recommended that you spend some time finding out what is available for you to use and how to use it. Knowing what you have available is very important because it means you are better able to plan *how you work*. For example, the demo site's hosts offer an automated Search Engine submit facility that allows the new website to be submitted for indexing to *all the major search engines*—much better than simply waiting around for the site to begin appearing on them.

Another important thing to note here is that most hosting services will offer a full array of statistics for your website. Things like where people have come from, how many accessed the site, which pages are being accessed, and so on. Drupal comes with modules that do pretty much the same thing, so check to see whether the site's native statistics are sufficient or whether you need to consider installing a new module—something like the **GraphStat**, **Tracker**, **Watchdog**, or **Recorder** modules may be more what you have in mind.

Since it is possible you have an entirely different set of options available on your hosted site, we won't discuss this any further here, but there are still a couple of other matters that warrant attention. Let's begin with one of the most commonly requested: **Search Engine Optimization**, or **SEO**.

Search Engine Optimization

One of the most common goals for a website is to appear high up on the big search engine rankings. As you should know, having a good ranking increases the chances of potential users finding your site among the mass of other sites. *So what is it that you can do to make your site rank as highly as possible without actually having to pay anyone to do it for you?*

There is no straight answer to this, unfortunately, and many people will give you just as many different answers. However, there is a core set of tasks you can take up that are known to help—they might vary in importance, but it is probably worth performing all of them. The following table highlights the most important optimizations or tasks, which you should consider performing (where possible):

Optimization	Explanation
Write web-enhanced copy	IMPORTANT: Think about how your target users would find your site. *What type of words would they use to find a site like yours?* Once you have come up with a list of key words and phrases, ensure that the writing on your site makes use of these phrases whenever possible.
	If you are using Google AdWords, then you can check the popularity of various search terms yourself—simply put them forward as potential target keywords and check on their stats, which Google provides before they are added.
	For example, if you had a site that deals with mobile gadgets, and you wanted to make the phrase cellular phone a term that you rank highly on, then instead of writing something like:
	This device can be used to call other people, you should write:
	This G1 super cellular phone, can call any other cellular phone from wherever you are.
	Admittedly, you cannot control the content of other people's comments and pages, but this would still apply to any and all standard pages you write—such as the *introduction* page, *about us*, or *FAQ*, or even your own personal blog.

Optimization	Explanation
Use meaningful file names	While this is not as important as the first point, it certainly will help to have everything named meaningfully, because search engines do look at file names. Instead of naming a page 19, you should name it something like `awesome_webpage.html`. Don't go overboard on this because it is not too important.
	Look through the modules available with help for renaming files if this appeals to you—something like Node (key)words should do the trick.
Use meaningful anchor text	IMPORTANT: Search engines, in particular Google, place a large amount of emphasis on the anchor text used in links. As a result, make sure all your links have meaningful text associated with them. For example, you would rewrite the following sentence:
	`Donate to the wildlife community <a href ="<yourlink>">here</a>.`
	to:
	`Donate to the <a href ="<yourlink>">wildlife community</a> here.`
	The reason for this is that the word here is not particularly meaningful to a search engine, even though humans can easily make the connection. For the sake of your rankings, simply move the link to the key phrase Wildlife community to place more emphasis on it for the search engine.
Write meaningful metatags	As many people will tell you, metatags have become less and less important as time goes by. However, they are still useful, and you should at least go to the effort of filling them out properly. The two metatags that you should consider making use of are the `keyword` and `description` tags. For example, the following shows a possible tag:
	`<meta name="keywords" content="CWC wildlife conservation biosphere">`
	Metatags have been the subject of some abuse, and you should view the W3C consortium's guidelines for their usage: `http://www.w3.org`.
	In order to make these changes, you would have to work with your theme—most likely the `page.tpl` file, or whatever is its equivalent!
Manage your links	IMPORTANT: A high level of importance is placed on the perceived popularity of a website. Search engines can judge the popularity of a website by looking at how many links there are to the site, and how popular the sites that link to it themselves are. For this reason, you should ensure that you link to and link from only sites that you feel are suitable partners.
	Effectively, you should search for as many relevant link pages as possible, or actually speak to the relevant sites to determine whether you can provide mutual links. The more links you have from popular sites, the better your ranking will be. You can also try to get one-way links to your site—these are also rated highly by search engines.
Write meaningful `alt` tags for images	Search engines don't see pictures like humans do, so there is nothing you can do about images... *or is there*? Instead of naming your images `02_03.jpg`, you might consider giving them names like `cruel_hunter.jpg`. Don't stop there either. Instead of adding an image like this:
	`<img src="cruel_hunter.jpg">`
	write it like this:
	`<img src="cruel_hunter.jpg" alt="Hunter making his kill ">`
Submit your site to search engines and online directories	Make sure your site is listed wherever possible. Most hosting packages provide an automated SE-submission facility, which will automatically forward your site to search engines for indexing. Otherwise, look for other SE web page submission tools, or search out your own lists and directories to become part of.
Read up on lists, forums, and online tutorials	There is a lot of helpful information out there. Make sure you do your own research and come up with an SEO policy that is right for you.

You will find that if you are prepared to put in the time to develop your links and constantly upgrade your site, you will eventually recoup the benefits that accrue over time. However, don't expect everything to happen overnight—gaining popularity can be a tedious process!

Maintaining Users

It is quite likely that while some people register with the full intention of making regular use of your site, they will move on and their account remains hanging around without actually doing anything. It might be prudent to add the **User Maintenance** module early on to keep track of how and whether your users are active, so that you can remove those who don't meet certain criteria.

Go ahead and download the module off the site. It requires a bit of work to get ready:

1. Extract the files to your `modules` folder.

2. Run the `.sql` script against the database (remember to have a backup available) with the following command:

   `C:\ mysql -udrupal -p drupal <`

   `C:\apache2triad\htdocs\drupal\modules\user_maintenance\user_maintenance.sql`

   Ensure that you replace the highlighted file path with the one that reflects your setup if need be.

3. Enable the module in the modules section under administer.

To use the module, head on over to the settings section under administer once the module is enabled. In the drop-down list in the menu you will notice that there is now a new user_maintenance menu item available. Click on that to bring up the following page:

As you can see, it is now quite easy to select how long you are prepared to keep an active account on your site despite the fact that the user has not logged on after registering. The reason it is wise to get this contribution up and running as soon as possible is that it cannot work retrospectively. In other words, if you run into this problem after three years of collecting wasted accounts, this contribution cannot tell which accounts it should delete; it only works for those accounts that were created while it is enabled.

Summary

This chapter has rounded off the picture painted by the previous chapters by taking a look at some of the most important website-related chores that you will have to undertake. Knowing how to make backups at the click of a button, or being able to tell who is using your site for what purposes and when, gives you the power to maintain and manage your site efficiently and with a minimum of fuss.

With the end of this chapter, we come to the end of the book. For those of you who now need to upload your new site your live domain, the appendix contains further instructions on deployment.

Congratulations on finishing the book, and I wish you all the best in your future endeavors on the Web. Please remember to take the time to give back to the Drupal community so that it can continue to flourish and help others.

A
Deployment

The big day has finally arrived! By the end of this appendix your site will be live, and only a few minor deployment issues now stand in between you and your online aspirations. *Actually that's not quite true!* I should make it clear that there's nothing particularly complex about deployment; it's just that you need to keep on top of a lot of different issues. Making silly errors at this stage can have dramatic effects on the final product because we are dealing mainly with configuration issues when we deploy a fully developed application. Of course, making errors is not the end of the world, because we are going to test everything very thoroughly.

At first glance, deploying a site like Drupal has got to be pretty easy—it's just a case of copying the drupal folder over to the new server! *Or is it?* There are a number of concerns that go hand in hand with ensuring everything goes smoothly during the transfer. For example, the database will also have to be rebuilt exactly as it is on the development machine—I'm sure that since most of you have spent some time configuring everything and populating tables, you'll be anxious to not have to do everything all over again. Apart from this, there are the connection parameters and some security issues to think about.

Specifically, the appendix looks at how to:

- Get everything ready for deployment
- Transfer the files to their new home
- Set up the site, including the database
- Test everything thoroughly

Chins up, we're nearly at the end; and it hasn't been all that bad, has it? I for one will no doubt start my very own blog—it's really tempting!

Getting Ready to Deploy

First thing's first; *are you sure you are completely happy with the site as it is?* While it is not a huge problem to make modifications to your site after deployment, there is no point in making things hard for yourself by having to recode some pages or make design changes then, when you can get them done now. If everything is in order, then we can begin with the preparation process.

Preparation comes in three stages. In no particular order, we need to ensure that we have a nice, clean, working version of the site, a nice, clean, working copy of the database, and finally, a nice, clean file system ready for the files on the host site. Let's take a look at how this is done.

Make Sure the Host Is Ready

Intuitively enough, you have to make sure you have an adequate host. By this I mean you have a host on which you can *create a MySQL database*, and that allows *access to a file system*, and whatever other goodies you think you may need. To make your life easy, it is also nice to have an FTP account available so that you can transfer files across to the host file system. More often than not, you should be able to log on to your FTP account with your administrator's username and password automatically. If you're not sure what all this is about, then try the following URL in your browser (assuming your browser supports FTP):

```
ftp://ftp.your_domain_name.com
```

If you are prompted for a password or are shown the contents of your home directory, then congratulations, you have an FTP account. If you don't have one, then you should consider getting your host to give you one, or finding out from them how they upload files. Incidentally, instead of being prompted for your username and password every time you use your FTP account, you might want to send them in the URL, like so:

```
ftp://username:password@hostname/
```

If you're worried about security (by this I mean: you *are* worried about security), then it's best to leave out the password and simply pass the username, because otherwise this can cause security problems if URLs are logged in a non-secure place. Remember that this information is already being passed in an unencrypted format. If you wish to do everything securely, you should speak to your host about how to secure file transfers.

If you don't have access to an FTP account, then don't panic! Read the section entitled *Transfer the Files* a little later on in this appendix—it will still be easy to move your files to the host site.

Once you have made sure that there is somewhere to upload the Drupal files to, and something to do it with, you need to create a database. Goodness only knows how many different ways this can be done in; so we won't go into each and every one here.

Take a look at your site's administrative interface and see if there is a section that allows you to create and control your MySQL database (you might find that your host provides our good friend phpMyAdmin). For example, the demo site's host has the following Manage Mysql link in the Databases section that provides an interface used to create databases. It also provides phpMyAdmin in order to administer those databases:

Clicking on the Manage MySQL link brings up the following page. Once you have the database, ensure that you have made note of its name—often hosts will append something to the name you choose as shown here in the demo site's database creation interface:

Sql Account Maintenance

Databases

contechj_contechst Delete

User: [▾] Db: [contechj_contechst ▾] [Add User to Db]

Db: [   ] [Add Db]

As you can see, the database has been called contechj_contechst, where contechst is the name I chose for the live database, and contechj_ is the part that was added. Before we continue, it is important to note that this database needs a user, so ensure that it has one, as shown here:

In this case, the contechst database now has the user contechj_david, and with that, the host site is pretty much ready to receive the new Drupal website. Remember, these usernames, passwords, and database names are all important for the configuration of the site, so ensure that you don't forget any of them. If you get stuck, get help from your host's support team; that's what they are there for.

Get the Files Ready

Before you do anything, you will need to make a master copy of the site before deployment. Make sure you zip up and store the exact version of the drupal directory that you send across.

> At the moment the target URL for the Drupal index page will be something like
> http://www.domain_name.com/drupal/. If you want it to be
> http://www.domain_name.com/, then you will need to zip the files without the parent
> directory so that files are extracted directly to the public_html folder on the live site.

While we are on the subject, you may as well clean up the Drupal file system properly so that you don't end up saving erroneous files.

If you're like me, then you probably create backups of all the files you modify as you work. As far as Windows machines go, these are denoted by .bak, and placed in the same folder as the original file. Make a backup of your drupal folder before deleting anything, just to be safe. Then remove all backup files from the drupal folders.

While it might seem a bit excessive to do this at the moment, there are a couple of good reasons for it. First, having any sort of unused files lying around on your host file system is poor security practice. Second, *why clutter up your brand-new installation with files you don't need?* You will find that it is a constant battle to keep everything neat and tidy as you go anyway—so start as you mean to go on. Finally, if you have worked on a lot of files over the course of the development phase, you are adding a lot of unnecessary size to the upload.

> For security reasons, you should probably move your CHANGELOG.txt file and update.php files to a different location—take them out of the website and hold them elsewhere, where hackers can't get hold of them. If you need to make use of the update.php script, then you can add it back to the site then.

Next, open up the configuration file, settings.php, and remove the username and password. As you can probably deduce, the current database name and password will change to the ones you set when you created a new database on your host (if they're not the same), but there is no point in transferring any type of sensitive information like this—especially since people often prefer to use the same username and password for a variety of things.

Once this is done, you have to wait until the next section to add one more file and you can then make a master, zipped copy of your Drupal site—call it RTP (Release to Public) or something similar to distinguish it from other versions.

If you are working on a Linux box, you can **tar** and **gzip** your files if you wish—it will obviously help with the upload time. If you are developing on Windows, then you might want to make sure that your host can unzip .zip files since they will more than likely be using a Linux server—there shouldn't be a problem, however. In the unlikely event that there is, the best thing to do is download and install a gzip utility for Windows at http://www.gzip.org/, which you can then use to zip up your files in the .gz format.

Get the Database Ready

As it stands, the database might hold plenty of silly posts which you used for testing, or it may hold a few important pages. There's no hard and fast rule here; just try not to transfer over a whole lot of stuff that you will end up deleting straight away anyway.

Talking of backups, that is really the main point of this section. In order to deploy the database, you will need to make a backup of it. It is this backup file that is then transferred across to the host site and used to create a new database there. Since you already have all the information you need regarding backups, we need look at them no further here.

Once you have created your backup file of the entire Drupal database and added the resulting .sql file somewhere to the drupal folder (anywhere will do so long as you can find it again), you are now ready to begin transferring files across to your host. Note that you should remove the .sql file from your site as soon as you have made use of it—hold it somewhere out of the document root in case you need to use it again.

Transfer the Files

You should now have a final, clean version of your online store, with a copy of the database, all zipped up and ready to go. Assuming there are images and a fair bit of data held within the site, you can be sure that the size of the upload is quite substantial. For this reason, you need a reasonably high speed connection—dial-up connections can be slightly erratic over long periods of time, so it may even be worth using a friend's computer or your office connection to send the files to the host site.

By far the easiest method would be to use a native upload feature from the host's file manager over a quick connection. If this is available to you, simply use it to upload the archive file across to the host server. The demo site has this facility as shown here:

Please select files to upload to /home/contechj/public_html

docs\contechst_RTP.zip	Browse...		Browse...
	Browse...		Browse...
	Browse...		Browse...
	Browse...		Browse...
	Browse...		Browse...
	Browse...		Browse...

Overwrite existing files: ☐

Upload

Notice that the ZIP file is being uploaded to the `public_html` folder, since this is the document root from which all web pages on this server are served.

Alternatively, assuming your site has an FTP account enabled, you can either attempt to use FTP drag and drop, which is exactly the same as moving files around on your PC in Windows, or you can use an FTP utility.

When in doubt, simply get in touch with your host service and ask them for information about how to transfer files. The administrative interface and file manager for the vast majority of sites are easy to use, and you will have no problems uploading files. Because of this, we won't waste time discussing FTP utilities in detail. Simply ensure that, ultimately, the ZIP file ends up in the document root of your host's server. Remember not to leave the zip folder lying around in the document root once it has been used.

Setting Up the Site

At this stage, you should have a working database and be aware of what the username and password are for that database on your live site. You also have your archive file uploaded to the host site. At last, we finally move from working on the development machine to working on the live site. First thing's first though; we need to…

Set Up the Files

You will need to extract the archive file to your `public_html` folder—most likely your hosts will provide you with this functionality. Take note of the second option in the list shown here:

With these files extracted, you should now have a replica of the files from the development machine on your host's site. Check this by browsing through the live site. You should also find that if you attempt to browse one of the pages from a web browser, you no longer get a page-not-found error, but some other type of error—most likely a MySQL error because we don't have a database connection yet:

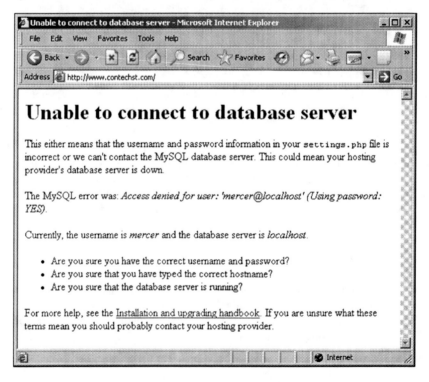

This is great news because it means that we are able to browse the files that are now on the live site with no problem. The fact that there is a Drupal error message here confirms that we are in fact browsing Drupal pages—note that the error message shown in the previous screenshot mentions a username and server that are not correct. This is here to demonstrate more clearly that we are browsing Drupal but we have not yet entered the correct database or configuration settings.

Set Up the Database

If you have access to phpMyAdmin on your host site, then open it up and follow along:

1. In the left-hand panel on the phpMyAdmin home page, click on the name of the database you installed earlier. (Recall that for the demo site, this was entitled contechj_contechst.)

2. In the new page that opens up, click on the SQL tab along the top of the page.

3. Click Browse under the Location of Textfile option.

4. Locate the file you would like to run against the database, and click Go.

If all goes according to plan, you will get a message informing you of the successful modifications to the database. You can then take a look through phpMyAdmin to ensure that the database has got whatever tables are needed.

It is possible that there may be issues between your host's system and the one you used to create the backup. For example, I initially received the following error:

```
Server: localhost ▶ Database: contechj_contechst
X Error

SQL query:

CREATE TABLE IF NOT EXISTS `access` (
  `aid` TINYINT( 10 ) NOT NULL AUTO_INCREMENT ,
  `mask` VARCHAR( 255 ) NOT NULL DEFAULT '',
  `type` VARCHAR( 255 ) NOT NULL DEFAULT '',
  `status` TINYINT( 2 ) NOT NULL DEFAULT '0',
  PRIMARY KEY ( `aid` )
) ENGINE = INNODB DEFAULT CHARSET = utf8 AUTO_INCREMENT =1

MySQL said:

#1064 - You have an error in your SQL syntax.  Check the manual that corresponds to your
MySQL server version for the right syntax to use near 'DEFAULT CHARSET=utf8
AUTO_INCREMENT=1' at line 7
```

This is because differing versions of MySQL sometimes use slightly differing syntax and it was necessary to remove all the DEFAULT CHARSET=utf8 statements from the .sql file before everything ran smoothly.

If you do not have access to phpMyAdmin, then you will simply need to install the database using the `.sql` file in whatever manner is appropriate for your particular site. Recall that you are able to run the `.sql` file from the command line if you have access to that—if not, it's time to get in touch with the support team and find out how they recommend you run the contents of your `.sql` file.

Configure the Site

With the database in place, go back to your `settings.php` file in the `sites/default/` folder on your live site and alter it according to your system's setup—take care to ensure that you add precisely the names and passwords required by your *live database* to `$db_url` as well as the correct URL for the live site in `$base_url` if that is required.

Once you have set the configuration settings appropriately save the file and then try browsing some pages. With a bit of luck you will see everything more or less as it was on the development machine.

Access Problem?

Try to log in to the administrator's account. I suspect that more than a few of you will come across a somewhat nasty surprise in that the browser will no doubt tell you that it cannot find the page you are looking for. If this is the case, it is more than likely because the `.htaccess` file was not successfully ported to the live site:

> *You must ensure that Drupal's* `.htaccess` *file is present on the live site!* `.htaccess` in the Drupal parent folder contains instructions and information vital to the healthy operation of the site. Ensure that you transfer it directly, or cut and paste its contents into the live site's `.htaccess` file.

When viewing the contents of the `.htaccess` file on the live site (in Drupal's parent folder, most likely in the document root depending on how you have things set up), you should see something like this:

```
<IfModule mod_php5.c>
  php_value magic_quotes_gpc          0
  php_value register_globals          0
  php_value session.auto_start        0
</IfModule>

# Reduce the time dynamically generated pages are cache-able.
<IfModule mod_expires.c>
  ExpiresByType text/html A1
</IfModule>

# Various rewrite rules.
<IfModule mod_rewrite.c>
  RewriteEngine on

  # Modify the RewriteBase if you are using Drupal in a subdirectory and
  # the rewrite rules are not working properly.
  #RewriteBase /drupal

  # Rewrite old-style URLs of the form 'node.php?id=x'.
  #RewriteCond %{REQUEST_FILENAME} !-f
  #RewriteCond %{REQUEST_FILENAME} !-d
  #RewriteCond %{QUERY_STRING} ^id=([^&]+)$
  #RewriteRule node.php index.php?q=node/view/%1 [L]
  ...
```

If that is the case, then you should find that it is possible to browse the live site as normal. Take heart, we are nearly done! The only thing left on the list of things to do for the moment is…

Testing

What is the goal of testing in this instance? Well, between now and the end of the chapter, we want to go from where we are to a fully functional, and most importantly, live and operational site. In order to get there, we need to ensure not only that everything works as expected from the customer's point of view, but also that the site is properly implemented and that we can administer it with no problems.

To give you an example of the type of thing that might rear its ugly head, take a look at the following error message I received the first time I tried to do a bit of administration on the live site:

> - The directory *files* is not writable
> - warning: mkdir(C:\apache2triad\temp): Permission denied in /home/contechj/public_html/includes/file.inc on line 91.
> - The directory *C:\apache2triad\temp* does not exist.

Can you spot the problem straight away? Drupal is complaining that it cannot write to a `files` directory that should be contained within `c:\apache2triad\temp`. It's not surprising that this should be the case, because on the live site, there is *no* `c:\apache2triad\temp` directory. In fact, the only reason this fully qualified path is here is because I initially wanted to demonstrate the private download method despite the fact that public access to files is suitable here.

This means that we need to re-enter the settings that were made with the development machine in mind to reflect the specifics of the live system:

> **File system path:**
>
> `files`
>
> A file system path where the files will be stored. This directory has to exist and be writable by Drupal. If the download method is set to public this directory has to be relative to Drupal installation directory, and be accessible over the web. When download method is set to private this directory should not be accessible over the web. Changing this location after the site has been in use will cause problems so only change this setting on an existing site if you know what you are doing.
>
> **Temporary directory:**
>
> `temp`
>
> Location where uploaded files will be kept during previews. Relative paths will be resolved relative to the Drupal installation directory.

Assuming you have the requisite permissions set so that Drupal can write and read in these folders, this particular problem is solved. (If you already have files on the site then you might need to move them to the directory you specify here.) Now, all that's left is to test out everything else in the administration tool to ensure it works correctly!

Here is a checklist for you to use in order to ensure that, from a user's point of view, the site works nicely:

Site Checklist

Use at least two different browsers.	One browser may implement some features that others do not—you might find that something you rely on heavily works on your browser of choice but not on others.	[ ]
Resize your browsers for a variety of pages.	This helps to determine whether you have HTML elements that have not been set correctly. For example, some section may use the full page width, while others expand only to a certain limit.	[ ]
Access pages from slow as well as fast connections.	You might find that certain pages load very slowly over a dial-up connection. This might mean you need to rethink image and page sizes.	[ ]
Check all links—Text and Image.	Often, links break during deployment because of differing file paths and so forth. You should: • Check all links and buttons on each page • Check all links in blocks • Check that large as well as small images display appropriately • Check that any ads link correctly	[ ]
Check each page's look.	Important, because not all browsers can render certain style sheet settings.	[ ]
Use each page.	This is vital for ensuring that users can: • Register accounts • Manage their accounts • Add content depending on permissions • Correctly access content depending on their roles • Make use of all the site's facilities Ensure that: • The search engine works correctly • Contact emails can be sent properly • Privacy and conditions of use are shown along with any important copyright information.	[ ]
Try to break the site (as a restricted user of course).	Just as important as ensuring everything works properly (if not more important), is ensuring that nothing can be broken at will.	[ ]

If you can perform everything listed in this checklist with several browsers, with no problems, then you can be reasonably certain that the site will hold up when it goes live. Of course, you will need to monitor it very closely for the first few months of its operation to make sure that nothing drastic goes wrong. Providing a webmaster's email address is a good way to let users complain if they run into problems. Open lines of communication between you and your users will help foster strong ties and improve the quality of your site.

Summary

For a task as important as building a full-featured community-driven website, it is necessary that you spend a lot of time considering your options, and developing and testing your site. Since it is not really feasible to do this sort of work on the live site, you need to employ a development machine to aid you. Because of this, the topic of deployment is an important one in the overall scheme of things because it is deployment that actually links your finished development to the live site.

This chapter outlined a solid process for preparing for deployment. It was also necessary to set up a new database on the host site, but this proved to be relatively easy because any good host makes the task fairly simple by providing a tool like phpMyAdmin to work with the database.

Hopefully you came to realize that the deployment process itself is not particularly complex for a Drupal site, since the only real configuration work that needs to be done is modifying the settings.php file to reflect your new system's configuration. Having the complexity of the site's deployment reduced to configuring a single file is a real advantage for Drupal users.

While the actual deployment of the site is fairly simple, it was shown that there were quite a few issues to deal with, and not the least of them is testing. It is critical that a full suite of tests is carried out on any site before it goes live—losing valuable users to silly errors is the last thing that any competitive site needs.

Index

[PACKT] PUBLISHING

Thank you for buying Drupal: Creating Blogs, Forums, Portals, and Community Websites

Packt Open Source Project Royalties

When we sell a book written on an Open Source project, we pay a royalty directly to that project. Therefore by purchasing *Drupal: Blogs, Forums, Portals, and Community Websites*, Packt will have given some of the money received to the Drupal project.

In the long term, we see ourselves and you—customers and readers of our books—as part of the Open Source ecosystem, providing sustainable revenue for the projects we publish on. Our aim at Packt is to establish publishing royalties as an essential part of the service and support a business model that sustains Open Source.

If you're working with an Open Source project that you would like us to publish on, and subsequently pay royalties to, please get in touch with us.

Writing for Packt

We welcome all inquiries from people who are interested in authoring. Book proposals should be sent to authors@packtpub.com. If your book idea is still at an early stage and you would like to discuss it first before writing a formal book proposal, contact us; one of our commissioning editors will get in touch with you.

We're not just looking for published authors; if you have strong technical skills but no writing experience, our experienced editors can help you develop a writing career, or simply get some additional reward for your expertise.

About Packt Publishing

Packt, pronounced 'packed', published its first book "*Mastering phpMyAdmin for Effective MySQL Management*" in April 2004 and subsequently continued to specialize in publishing highly focused books on specific technologies and solutions.

Our books and publications share the experiences of your fellow IT professionals in adapting and customizing today's systems, applications, and frameworks. Our solution-based books give you the knowledge and power to customize the software and technologies you're using to get the job done. Packt books are more specific and less general than the IT books you have seen in the past. Our unique business model allows us to bring you more focused information, giving you more of what you need to know, and less of what you don't.

Packt is a modern, yet unique publishing company, which focuses on producing quality, cutting-edge books for communities of developers, administrators, and newbies alike. For more information, please visit our website: www.PacktPub.com.

Building Websites with Joomla!

ISBN: 1904811949   Paperback: 340 pages

A step-by-step tutorial to getting your Joomla! CMS website up fast

1. Walk through each step in a friendly and accessible way

2. Customize and extend your Joomla! site

3. Get your Joomla! website up fast

Building Online Stores with osCommerce: Professional Edition

ISBN: 1904811140   Paperback: 380 pages

Learn how to design, build, and profit from a sophisticated online business.

1. Install, configure, and customize osCommerce

2. Enhance and modify osCommerce

3. Learn from a sample, fully functional site packed with useful   features such as gift certificates and discounts, cross- and up-selling, RSS feed aggregation, enhanced product image   handling, and bug fixes.

Please check **www.PacktPub.com** for information on our titles

Printed in the United States
93489LV00004B/387-394/A